Last Chance
By
Edward Aronoff

Three Came Home Publishing

Printed in the United States of America

Three Came Home Publishing Co.
P.O. Box 1253
Banner Elk, NC 28604

This work is based on true events. Only the names of some people, and places have been changed to protect their privacy.

DEDICATION

To my wife, Reka
who has helped me time and time again.

ACKNOWLEDGMENTS

To all the people in my life that made this a story
based on true events

Table of Contents

It's hard to die, especially when you are twenty-one

Chapter 1: Sydney

A single tear made its way down her cheek. The now familiar wrench of her stomach began and she steeled herself for the anguish that she knew would follow. She sobbed once, twice, and slowly lay her head on the pillow. She lay there numb, and so completely absorbed, she was not aware of when the daylight became dark. After a long period of twisting and turning, thankfully she fell asleep.

Sydney woke with a start. At first she could not focus on where she was. Gradually it became familiar again. The wispy ghosts became curtains and the chains of purgatory turned into the familiar chime of the grandfather clock.

She stared at the clock on the night stand. The red numbers stood out starkly, like bloodshot eyes staring back at her. Two-fifteen A.M. The crimson glow lit up the three new pill bottles that stood as glaring reminders. *What was it Dr. Slater had said?* "Take the clodronate two times a day, the pamidronate four times a day, and the Percocet only as needed. Then he said as an afterthought, "Yes, when the pain gets too strong."

Sydney pushed herself up and sat on the edge of the bed. "I feel so weak," she mumbled. The death sentence weighed heavily on her.

Suddenly she felt a jolt of anguish. "Paul... My God, Paul! In all the excitement, I forgot about him. Damn, he'll be here this Saturday. I can't let him see me like this..." Then it came to her suddenly, *"No, I can't let him see me at all."* Sydney hung her head and her tears came freely.

It was four weeks ago when Sydney had walked into her sister's office upset and agitated. The two women had an easy relationship and genuinely enjoyed each other's company. But it had not always been that way. There was a time, when they were young, and again, when Woman's Home Magazine was first starting up, that the sisters would argue passionately. At first, when they were children, it was over whose doll was lying broken on the floor; then, after the magazine was born, over a layout or a model's placement. Then, as now it would lead to some bad feelings. But somehow they had worked it out and now that their magazine was a huge success, Sydney and Theresa, had found positions that suited their talents, and they supported each other nicely. Theresa still held feelings about their childhood problems, along with severe complications with her father, but with therapy, she managed to keep them in check.

Theresa's MBA from Harvard had prepared her for the leadership role and she ran the magazine firmly and efficiently. Sydney, a Yale graduate and Ecole de Paris student, was head of the art department and used her imagination and painting skills to make Woman's Home a leader in advertisement. She specialized in the women's fashion and bridal departments. In the lean years, Sydney had done both advertising and art, but since the magazine had grown so large the two departments had separated and an outside firm now was in charge of the advertising campaigns.

As soon as Theresa looked up from her work and saw her sister's face she knew something was very wrong. She got up quickly, walked around the desk and took both of Sydney's hands. Sydney looked away.

"Syd, what's the matter?" Theresa's brow was wrinkled with concern.

Sydney looked at her older sister, her own anxiety clouding her features. Trying to keep a brave face, she failed and her eyes moistened. She broke eye contact and sat down on the overstuffed executive couch next to the window and stared out at the New York skyline. Theresa quickly walked over to her, sat down on the arm of the couch, and put her hand on her sister's shoulder. She waited expectantly.

Theresa glanced down at her sister's platinum hair and felt a twinge of envy. The sisters contrasted widely in both looks and manner. Theresa favored her father. She was a tall woman hovering near five feet ten inches. Her hair was jet black and when combed straight down reached shoulder length. She had wide shoulders and an ample bust that boxed down to her generous hips. The austere, Saint John's business suits she wore did nothing to flatter her figure. She also wore no-nonsense, sensible shoes.

Sydney was more like her mother. She was a petite five feet four inches tall, with natural platinum blond hair that she wore pulled back in a pony tail. This highlighted the classic, angular lines of her face. She was quick to smile and even quicker to laugh at the comedy of life around her. Her bust, that always seemed to be straining at the silk shirts she wore, slimmed down to a smallish waist and blossomed out again to feminine hips. She favored Christian Dior skirts and blouses, and the penny loafers that she wore made her look younger than her twenty one years. Both women were unmarried.

Sydney had dated some of the eligible bachelors around New York until she met Paul Grant, the scion of a French-American family. They were engaged and planned to marry in the spring. Theresa had chosen another lifestyle.

Sydney tried to speak but couldn't. She got up and walked to the full length window and looked down. From the thirtieth floor the people scurrying around the New York streets looked like the ants in the glass ant farms Sydney was fascinated by when she was a little girl.

Slowly she turned and looked at her older sister. "Theresa," she began, with a voice so soft that Theresa had to strain to hear her. "I... I... have a problem..." Her voice trailed off and she looked back down at the street.

Theresa was silent but inside her stomach churned.

The heavy oak door opened noiselessly and Theresa's secretary walked in with a notebook in her hand. "Miss Bannon, the Japanese representative is here for his ten o'clock appointment. Shall I tell him to wait?"

Sydney walked back to the couch, sat down and looked at the gloomy skyline again. She was glad for the interruption.

"Yes, Susan, take him to the boardroom and give him some coffee... No, I guess you better make it tea." The secretary smiled at the subtle humor.

"Yes Ma'am," she said, still smiling as she began to close the large door. "I'll tell him you'll be with him shortly." Susan's eyes stayed on Theresa just a few seconds longer than was polite, giving Theresa an oddly familiar sensation.

Theresa dwelled on the look for just a moment and then forced her mind back to Sydney. There was a slight impatience in her movements as she addressed her sister. "Syd, I'm going to burst, please tell me what's going on?"

Sydney brushed away a tear from the corner of her eye with a delicate movement and began to get up. "You're busy now sister, I'll come back later."

Theresa stood up as if to block her way. "No you don't," she said with a wry smile, "You're not leaving me hanging like that all afternoon. Is it Paul?" she said suddenly, as if she just happened on the truth.

"No," Sydney answered in a small voice, "it's me."

Theresa sat back down slowly. Her face was deadly serious. She cleared her throat as she always did when she was nervous and waited impatiently for Sydney to begin.

Sydney turned and faced the window. Suddenly her shoulders squared with resolve. She turned back to her sister again, hesitated for a moment, then began to speak. "About a month ago I was showering when I began to wash under my arm and I felt..."

Theresa's face turned ashen. With a leap of understanding she knew what Sydney was going to say next. "But you're so young," she blurted, "that doesn't happen to young people."

Sydney's head dropped. "Oh, God, sister, I only pray you're right."

"Have you seen a doctor? ...We'll get you the best specialist!"

"No, Theresa, let me go to Dr. McCann first. If I need a specialist, he will send me to one."

For a few moments Theresa was speechless, then she found her voice.

"Sydney," she said gravely, using her sister's unfamiliar whole name, "lots of people beat this and you will too." She searched her mind to say something more comforting. As soon as she spoke again, she knew she had said the wrong thing, but it was too late. "They take the breast off now only as a last resort..."

Her voice trailed off and Sydney began to cry softly.

Theresa watched with her feelings in turmoil as Sydney left, absently closing the large oak door behind her. She stared into space for a few moments and then swiveled her chair and faced the New York skyline. The dark rain clouds were finally giving up their moisture and rain drops began to litter the window panes.

Chapter 2: Theresa

Theresa tipped her chair back and thoughtfully stared at the darkening sky. In the distance it was still clear and splashes of purple, pink and red followed the orange sun over the horizon to New Jersey. Lone birds, their bounty clamped firmly in their beaks and claws, winged their way home to their nests. Theresa always envied their freedom. Even as a child she was a workaholic and now she was rarely free of some kind of work and responsibility.

Why should I care what happens to Sydney, she thought, *he always loved her more than me anyway.* Suddenly Theresa felt ashamed. A tear formed in the corner of her eye. "It wasn't Syd's fault," she murmured. She wiped the tear with an abrupt movement of her hand and let the chair come upright. She swiveled back to the desk and angrily picked up the Japanese report she had been working on. She tried to get back into the work she had been doing when Sydney told her the tragic news, but she couldn't concentrate and finally gave up.

Theresa pressed the intercom. "Susan?... Never mind... Just tell the Japanese representative I will be there in five minutes."

Theresa got up and paced. She looked at her hand and realized it was trembling. Quickly she went to her purse and pulled out her cigarettes. "I'll call Roz!" She reached for the phone and stopped. *No, I can't call her every time some little thing happens. I'm a big girl now and I'll deal with this myself.* She put the cigarette to her lips, flicked the lighter lit it, took a deep breath and let the smoke move out of her lungs. Crushing the cigarette in the ashtray, she stood up and walked to the full length mirror next to the door. She looked at her image, first turning right and then left. She patted her ample hip and silently swore she would get back on her diet, tomorrow. She studied her face and tried to relax the frown wrinkles on her brow. Then she looked past her image, trying to locate the pain she felt. Her therapist had told her whenever the past came up don't push it down, bring it up and look at it. As she looked at the stranger in the mirror, her mind went tumbling back to her fourteenth birthday. That day was never far from her. She could see the solid oak door to her father's study now. It was always vividly clear.

****

Theresa rushed down the hall, her face flushed and her eyes aglow. "Daddy, daddy, where are you?"

"Here, in the library, Theresa."

She opened the oak door, smiled and curtsied. "Mr. Bannon, you shouldn't have."

The man that looked back at her had love in his eyes but his heart was troubled. He smiled back at her and bowed his head politely. "Miss Bannon, it was my pleasure."

Thomas Bannon was a self made man. He was only five foot seven, but backed down to no man. He was muscular, which came naturally, from the manual labor he had done all his life. He had a full head of shock white hair that gave him a look of solid maturity, which was a fair measure of the man. He had an affable way with other men and, when he worked for the Mitchell and Cohen Brother's Road Company, had risen to supervising the labor gangs that actually laid the roads. He was known among them to be strict but fair. His manner was such that he could mix with the working men and the executives with equal ease.

Chapter 3: Bannon

Thomas Bannon had come over from Ireland in the third class section of an immigrant boat, many years ago. All he had known in his previous life was poverty. He had tilled the Irish soil, trying to scratch out a living for his family.

His wife was horrified when Thomas used protection to prevent more children. He told her they could not afford another mouth to feed. She told him it was against the Church's teachings and they would all go to Hell. Thomas prevailed and even when she called him a "Heathen Protestant," he would not relent. Secretly she was glad. *Life was so hard...*

Thomas was devastated when their farm failed. Kate was sure God was punishing them for their great transgression.

Thomas called her a fool and set out for the United States alone where he believed a man could be free of the priests, and the streets were paved with gold. Sadly, he found out that the streets of the new world were not paved with anything but macadam.

Thomas worked for two years at any job he could find. In six months, he had saved enough to send for his family. When they arrived, he moved them into a one bedroom flat on Houston street, in New York City. Thomas worked on the streets in many jobs while his beloved wife, Kate, took care of the girls and cleaned the houses of people more fortunate than she.

They were about as happy as hard working, lower class people could be, until Kate Bannon got sick. Her health quickly spiraled downward and Thomas was devastated. He called the doctors in and begged them to save her. Finally, money and hope gone, he called a priest. After the priest left, Thomas sat by his wife's bedside crying softly. All the lights were out and only a lonely candle flickered, casting dancing shadows on the wall. The little boy in Thomas thought the shadows might be spirits waiting to take Kate to her grave.

Kate's eyes flickered open.

"Kate, me darlin' gurl." He held her frozen hands to his chest in a futile effort to warm them.

"T-Thomas," she said so softly he had to bend close to her to hear her. P-p-promise me this..." Her eyes closed and her voice faded into nothingness.

"Kate... Kate!" Thomas raised his voice in fear.

Kate opened her eyes and smiled weakly. "I am still with you Thomas." A tear escaped from the corner of her eye and rolled down her cheek. Thomas reached down and caught it on his finger. He then put the wet finger to his lips, and began to cry again.

Her small face became earnest and she looked at Thomas with intensity. He feared for the effort she was making. Finally she spoke.

"Thomas, I want you to promise me something."

"Yes, me darlin', anythin'."

"First, take care of my girls, my sweet darlins."

"Of course, me darlin' I will love them as I do you."

"And Thomas, you're a man of the church, as I am, and I want you to promise me something else."

Thomas nodded, deep in abject misery.

I want you to promise me to be faithful to me forever, and not to marry again so we may meet in heaven and be together, forever, as one."

"Always, me darlin' Kate, always."

With a fervent burst of energy she grabbed his shirt and raised herself close to him. "Promise me, promise me... forever."

Thomas held her close. "I promise."

Suddenly he felt her go limp and he gently placed her back on the bed. Her body was cold and tinged with blue. Gently he reached down and closed her staring eyes, folded her hands and wept. "Forever, me darlin', forever."

On a cold, wet night in New York City, a land as different from the green, rolling hills of her beautiful, County Cork, as night is to day, Kate Bannon had breathed her last. The poor woman had died of what the doctor had called heart trouble, but Thomas knew its name was overwork.

Thomas had little time to mourn. Now, he had to be father and mother. He made arrangements for an immigrant Irish woman to come in and stay with the children while he worked.

In a few months after his wife died Thomas thought about marrying again, but his promise loomed strong. Besides, what sane lass would want to raise two children not her own, and me with nothing else to offer, but hard work? And, of course, she would probably want a family of her own. And me having the devil of a time feeding three mouths, how would I do with five or six? *Better to be alone,* Thomas thought. *Besides, I promised. And a deathbed promise, too.*

Luckily, his eldest was a girl and she was soon playing mother to her younger sister.

To complicate his life, because of a shortage of men, in January 1944 Thomas Bannon was inducted into the United States Army. For the next six months he trained to be a soldier. He was soon once more back in Europe, but not in Ireland, rather he was facing a landing on the shores of France. He was now a rifleman in Dog Company, third battalion, First Division approaching Omaha Beach, Normandy, France.

For the next eleven months Thomas fought his way across France and Germany until the surrender came in May 1945. Thomas finally told his chaplain about his home status of having two children and no wife. After a scathing chewing out by the chaplain for not telling him about the children, Thomas was given an abundance of points and was soon on a ship going back to his girls.

On the ship back, he had the great fortune to meet up with Elliot Cohen, the son of the road building magnate. They became great friends and Elliot assured Thomas that when they got back home, there would be a job for him at the Mitchell and Cohen Brothers, Road building firm. Life was beginning to take a rosy glow for Thomas.

Thomas was hard working and meticulous in his work, and before long was made a foreman by the owners.

Thomas was a banty-rooster sort of man who would fight at the drop of a hat or at an insult, real or imagined. He was a short man, but heavily muscled with a head of black hair that had turned steel gray by the time he was twenty-five and stayed that way from then on. After his discharge he joined Elliot and they began to work for Elliot's grateful father. Thomas worked hard on the New York streets, laying the macadam for the automobiles now pouring out of the post-war factories. Usually when he finished work he was so tired from the long day, he would fortify himself a bit before he faced the problems he knew he would have at home.

It was just such a night as this when he stopped at Pat Mulroon's Touch of Erin saloon.

Chapter 4: Bannon

As soon Bannon as he got seated at his favorite table and raised a glass of whiskey to his lips, his eyes fell upon the great mirror behind Pat Mulroon's bar.

What he saw in that glass was the image of a young man, who was a stranger to him, rapidly approaching his table. The lad was dressed in a cheap business suit and tie with a white shirt that was frayed at the cuffs.

He had come in the bar earlier and asked for Thomas by name. When he was told Thomas would probably be in soon, he sat down at the bar and nursed a beer while he patiently waited.

The lad approached the table in a retiring manner, but Thomas instinctively tensed. His mind raced for recognition of this lad and any wrong he may have done him. As the young man reached the table, he politely took off his derby hat, which was the fashion, revealing a shock of flaming red hair. Thomas relaxed. The lad's freckled face and bright red hair was the map of old Ireland itself and despite his usual caution, Thomas immediately liked the boy. He nodded a greeting and sociably asked the youngster to sit down, glad for the company. But in his gut Thomas knew it was not to pass the time of day that this lad wanted.

The boy sat quietly nursing his beer, while Thomas talked of football, rugby and politics. Then he started to complain about his job. As soon as he spoke of the laying of the blacktop on the cursed hot streets, the boy's face lit up.

"Excuse me soir, but that's just what oi cume to talk to yer about."

Thomas' face wrinkled in puzzlement. "Ye got business with the roads, lad?" He looked at the boy's clean hands and clothes. "Ye don't look like ye have."

"Ye might say I do, soir. Ye see, I'm an engineer fer the people what makes the stuff ye lay in the streets."

"Oh, ye works fer the big boys." Suddenly Thomas got annoyed and looked impatiently down at the beer he was nursing. "What's all this got to do with me, boy?"

"Well, soir, as I said, I'm with them... in their research department... an' we bin workin' on a new macadam that will not melt in sommer nor crack in winter. And it will stand up to any of the heavy-weight cars they are puttin' out terday. But with all the research we done there is something missin' in the mix and so far the company' nere bin able ter find it."

Thomas' eyes narrowed and his face reddened. "So... what yer tellin' me is them big shots an' you is gonna put my job outta business." Suddenly a wave of fear came over Thomas. "Damn, boy, I got three mouths ter feed. Why are ye tellin' me this stuff."

The young man spoke soothingly. "Well, soir, I bin told yer a good man and one who would not turn his back on a dollar, soir."

Bannon's eyes narrowed and he slapped the table making the beers bottles jump. "Not if it's an honest dollar!"

The young man's face turned serious. "Oh, yes, soir, only honest business, soir." The boy's face was guileless, and now he was smiling with a wry grin.

Thomas had an overwhelming feeling this boy could be trusted.

"Ye see, soir, oi got some of the stuff an' got ter playin' with the road pitch at home, soir, an' wouldn't ye know it oi found the missing link they wuz lookin' fer. But oi found it at home...," he said it again, to make sure it sunk in.

Thomas looked puzzled so the boy repeated the idea. "What the company has bin lookin' for in the lab, oi found at me own home. My macadam is so tough and durable a million cars a day wouldn't make a dent in it for ten lifetimes."

Thomas chugged the rest of his drink and leaned back, pushing against the booth to ease his tired back. He tipped his hat back and sighed. "That's interestin', boy, but oi gotta be gitten home." Bannon slid to the edge of the booth and stood up with an annoyed look on his face and started to put on his coat.

The young man reached across the table and put his hand on Thomas' arm.

Bannon glared down at him.

"But, Mr. Bannon, ye don't understan'. Oi heered ye are a reasonable man with lots of experience and contacts in the state road department. If oi'm ta be in the road building business with my new road-pitch, oi'll need sich a man."

Thomas shook the boys hand off and slipped his coat onto his shoulders. He stopped and stared at the boy his coat half on, half off. "Ye need yer head examined, lad." He slipped his arm in the sleeve and then muttered, "Who do ye think ye are, ter think ye can go up agin' the big boys."

"No, soir, oi agree," the young man said firmly and persistently, "that's what oi need you fer. Oi need a partner with the right contacts, fer my new road building firm."

Partner, did he say partner? Suddenly what the lad was saying hit Thomas like a ton of pitch. All at once he realized that the lad had discovered the holy grail of roads.

Wonder of wonders, if he iz right... He sez he has a new macadam that can stand up to the heaviest cars on the road and not break down or wear out. But the whole thing is nary good to him, no damn good at all, without knowing the right people to market it. God in Heaven I know them all. I have all the contacts a man would ever need.

Thomas understood now what the boy had been saying. His half-on coat forgotten, he slowly sat down again with his eyes glowing with future glory.

****

The fledgling company prospered. Thomas was as popular with the state road officials in a business suit as he had been in coveralls. In fact, he was so well liked and trusted, that the product was immediately tried, tested, and accepted on every level of the state road department. No contest. The other firms had nothing like it. Bannon's macadam was so superior it would have been foolhardy for the state not to use the new company's product.

The new company was sued by the young man's employers but it was too late. Thomas had filed with the patent office for the new road material and the patents were clearly original. Although the judge suspected something underhanded, he had to rule in Thomas Bannon's favor.

The money began to roll in and soon the two men were rich. The young man married and wanted to travel, so Thomas marshaled his new resources and bought him out. Being no fool the young man wisely retained a small interest in the firm that would last him the rest of his life.

Working now only for himself, Thomas really began to push. Before long, the name Bannon was on every road contract in a three state area, with ambitious plans to do business in many, if not all, the other states.

As soon as he could, Thomas let the immigrant woman go, and got his children a live-in maid. Theresa was finally free.

****

It was on her fourteenth birthday that the problem with Theresa had started.

Her birthday party was over and the children were preparing to go home. Theresa rushed about the house looking for her father to share the best present a girl could ever have. The smiling housekeeper pointed to the library and Theresa hugged her and then ran for the door.

Earlier, when Theresa was seeing the other children out the front door, one of the boys ran back in breathlessly shouting at her to come outside and tugged at her relentlessly until she came. When she stepped out she saw him. A beautiful white and brown, paint pony with a new saddle, trimmed in silver. Theresa ran up to the horse and, with her eyes shining, ran her hands all over his flanks. She went up to the front of him and hugged him while he nuzzled her ear. She giggled and kissed him while the other children danced around and begged her for a ride. She promised them all they would ride, but on another day. Today the horse was hers and her daddy's.

Her heart beat faster as she looked at the hand written sign that hung from the saddle.

To Miss Theresa Bannon
from Mr. Thomas Bannon.

She flung open the door and rushed in. "Oh, Daddy, he's beautiful," she cried, and rushed to her father. Just as she reached him he went rigid and turned away, cold and unresponsive. Theresa stopped abruptly. She stared at him in disbelief, uncomprehending, her teenage feelings desperately hurt. "Daddy, what's wrong? I just want to hug you for the most wonderful present in the world."

Thomas Bannon cleared his throat, got up and paced the floor while Theresa, now sullen, watched him. Since they had moved into this grand house, with the new maid to take care of them, Theresa had gotten very close to her father. Every night when he came home she would rush to him with his pipe, slippers and a cold beer. She would then sit in his lap her head on his chest, and luxuriate in the warmth of their new found closeness. Before he had made his new fortune her life was drudgery. Now it was a delight. She felt just like the girl in the story her mother had once read her, a girl named Cinderella. Why does he push me away? Teresa just knew there was something wrong with her.

But the real trouble was locked inside Thomas Bannon.

After her thirteenth birthday, Thomas began to notice his daughter beginning to change. It seemed that, overnight, her breasts swelled, her hips broadened and suddenly before him was a fully developed woman with a child's mind. Try as he might to avoid them, when Theresa now sat on his lap, carnal feelings flooded his body and his mind and he became plagued with guilt. Unlike before, he would abruptly terminate their time and brusquely leave or rudely eject her from the room. Damn that promise!

Thomas was desperate. Now that Theresa had free time, and no mother, she yearned for contact with her father. At the same time when she came close, his mind and body churned with shame. Like a kite in a storm he twisted this way and that. But no matter who he turned to he could not share the thoughts buried deep within him. For a while he began to drink heavily but that solved nothing. In desperation and in fear for himself, he turned to his wife's church.

Thomas had not been there since his wife died, but now he was desperate. Not knowing what to expect, he went to St. Barnabas where he and his beloved wife had often attended, and kneeled before the candles at the side alter to beg forgiveness from the Blessed Mother. Kneeling in abject misery, he stayed in the that position, his mind troubled, his heart full of woe. The vigil lights flickered casting shadows on him and the image of Mary with babe, her face serene and her left arm extended delicately to the penitent.

Suddenly there was a hand on his shoulder. He looked up and saw the black hassock, and kindly face, and his heart opened. Here was help at last.

"Have you some difficulty my son?"

A sign from God, Thomas thought. "Father would you hear me confession?"

"Of course, my son."

Thomas entered the confessional and kneeled. The screen opened and he could make the outline of the kindly priest. Relief covered him like a warm blanket on a cold day.

"Bless me Father, for oi have sinned. It has been, er, many, many months since me last confession... Father, oi have a turrible fear oi will do sumethin' very wrong... please help me Father, please."

Thomas began slowly but soon his feelings began to spill over and he rapidly poured out his heart in confession. With shame, he told the priest of his sexual feelings when his daughter was close to him and how he had to push her away. "...So you see, Father, oi am full of self loathing for these turrible thoughts that oi confess to you...

Suddenly there was an explosion of anger from the other side of the screen. Thomas recoiled at the words.

"These thoughts are blasphemous!" the priest shouted.

Thomas could not see him clearly but he could tell the cleric was red faced, eyes popping in anger.

"You are unclean and cannot enter the Lord's presence in this state. There is a Demon is inside you and just confession will not help you," he said his words spilling over each other angrily. "Even an exorcist is not enough! You must be cleansed by God himself. Get out, get out of my church! Get out, GET OUT!"

Thomas was shaking and began to sweat. "But Father..."

"Get out! Get OUT!" The priest's voice boomed again.

The cleric sounded like the voice of doom and Thomas quickly left the booth. The priest followed him, his voice reverberated through the empty church, "get out, get OOOOOOUT" The last bellow urged Thomas stumbling out the church door.

After Thomas left, the priest sat down in a pew, trembling and sweating profusely. He stared into his own past. Tears trickled down his cheeks and splashed down on his hassock. His mind lurched one way and then another.

My two sisters, they were the ones. They were in league with the Devil. Always parading around in their underwear, always showing their bodies off... just to tempt me. He put his head in his hands and swayed from side to side, squeezing his eyes shut to block the vision. *Oh, God, the temptation, the forbidden fruit.* He tried to get up but weakly sat down again. His mind raced dizzily. It was bad enough before ordination, but after...

The priest hung his head. "Incest! God forgive me for I cannot forgive myself." As he made the sign of the cross his head dropped and he prayed fervently. While he prayed, a suffocating miasmic cloak that was his private Hell closed about him, chasing away all reason.

****

Soon, Thomas began to dread the visits from his daughter and Theresa became more and more confused. She began to retreat into herself and this

25

added to the growing gulf between them. Angering her even more was the way she saw him welcome Sydney. The younger daughter was still very innocent and sweet, and posed no sexual threat to Thomas. He welcomed her with open arms and she snuggled to him, loving the smell of his pipe about him.

The heat of shame, anger and even hate crept over Theresa as she watched her younger sister rush over and take her place on his lap and in his heart.

The day the breech between father and daughter became complete was on Theresa's very next birthday, her fifteenth. The day had been so wonderful and the companion horse, to her pony, so beautiful that she thought she might try to thank her father properly. The similar sign hung from the pony's side and encouraged her.

To Miss Theresa Bannon
from Mr. Thomas Bannon.

After her party she searched her father out and finally found him sitting on a couch in the living room. Her heart leaped as he greeted her with a smile and held his arms out to her. She ran to him with abandon and snuggled up to him as before. For a moment he returned her warmth. Then, as if his heart went cold, he began to squirm and push her away. Theresa desperately needing his love, resisted him and held on, pressing herself even closer.

Thomas was getting upset. His face began to color red and he felt the heat of shame over his body. He tried to get away from his daughter and began to sweat profusely. Over all the objections of his mind, his carnal nature won and he felt himself begin to stir. In a panic he began to push Theresa off him. She hung on for dear life using all the strength she had developed when taking care of the house. Finally realizing he could not get her off him without hurting her, he fell back with her still clinging on to him.

Suddenly he went cold. "Theresa, you smell," he said with feigned malevolence, "go get a bath and then you might hug me again."

Theresa went limp with shame and quickly got off his lap. Like many teenagers, she was overly concerned with cleanliness and took long showers, two, sometimes, three times a day. For the next month every time Theresa tried to get close to her father he would drive her away with a simple twitch of his nose and a, "Go bathe, please."

Thomas had certainly found something that worked and Theresa began to studiously avoid him. She noted that her younger sister Sydney did not and thus began a circle of anger and depression in her that would require countless hours of therapy and persist for the rest of her life.

Unfortunately, without her ever knowing it, Theresa's relationships with boys changed forever at the same time. By her junior year of high school, all of her friends began to date. She had, by this time, left the awkward stage and like the proverbial swan, turned into a beautiful young woman.

She received many calls, returned few and accepted none. At the infrequent dances she attended, she remained aloof, dancing only with the other girls who were not asked. When she was home, she bathed four or five times a day.

Chapter 5: Sydney

Dr. McCann walked to the sink and began to wash his hands slowly and carefully. When he finished the nurse handed him a towel. He accepted it absently and nodded his head to her. The nurse looked at Sydney, smiled briefly and quietly left. Sydney slipped her arm back through her gown and waited expectantly.

The doctor walked back to Sydney as he wiped his hands. He was thoughtful as he balled up the towel and tossed it into a clothes basket. He leaned his hip against the exam table and folded his arms. He waited a few moments as he gathered his thoughts.

He was used to bad news but he knew his patients were not. Finally he spoke. "Sydney, you have a swollen lymph gland under the left axilla and a small mass in the left breast."

Sydney's face fell. The doctor's eyes narrowed as he saw the young woman suddenly turn old.

"You mean... you mean, I have breast cancer?" Sydney's stomach wrenched and she felt the first wave of anguish she would feel countless times again.

"No," he said patiently, "I mean you have a swollen lymph gland and a small mass in the breast.

We will have to do several other tests to be certain about anything."

After a little more explanation that Sydney did not hear or comprehend, Dr. McCann called the nurse back in, gave her some instructions and abruptly left the room. The nurse told Sydney what to do next then she also left.

Suddenly Sydney felt trapped in the sterile room alone with only her thoughts. Somehow, it now seemed like an effort just to put on her clothes. Suddenly the enormity of what the doctor had just told her fell on her and she put her clothes in her lap, sat down on the cold metal chair, and cried fiercely.

The rest of the day was a blur. Sydney remembered making an appointment with a Dr. Slater, an oncologist that Dr. McCann had recommended, and picking up her medications, but she could remember little else.

One paramount thought kept cycling through her distraught mind. *Paul! What would he say? What would he do? Was his love strong enough? Would he stay with her through this? What kind of way was this to start a marriage.*

Although she hardly remembered getting there, Sydney was finally home. Somehow she felt safer in her own sanctuary. She lived on the top floor of a high rise in the East River section of New York and when it was a clear day she could see all the way to the New Jersey shore. When it turned dark at night, Sydney would look at the blinking lights of a million homes, and if she lifted her eyes just a little she could see a vast blanket of stars stretching to the end of time.

When Sydney's salary had finally reached her worth, she had searched for and had finally found this apartment. It was expensive, but it was everything she always wanted. Her eye for graphics gave her a talent for decorating and she surrounded herself with muted, earth tone colors and the objects she loved.

Sydney felt anxious. Time was now precious. Each second now became a loss when before they were stepping stones to a happy future. She wandered through the apartment, lovingly touching the things she had put together to make a home. She fingered the frame of the Gauguin painting and stared at the almost child-like figures on the canvas. The painting was way too expensive, but she had to have it. It stood out starkly against the eggshell white of the living room wall. The painting hung over a white couch, while the easy chair that she sat in to read or look at the painting was a Confederate gray. The pure white rugs hanging on the walls were filled with pictures of elephants and Balinese dancers. They were placed strategically about the room, as were modern pieces of iron serving as holders for the large pieces of glass that were coffee and end tables.

The liquor cabinet beckoned her. She walked over to it and poured a double scotch. She put it down and ran a finger down the neck of a modern, twisted lamp. She turned one on to dispel the gloom, but when it hurt her eyes, she quickly turned it off. She reached down and picked up a match and struck it.

Shadows danced on the wall as she lit the candle on the coffee table. Sydney sat down and stared at the many shadows and their macabre dance.

Sydney sipped the scotch then stood up and wandered into the bedroom. It was spacious and functional. The walls were colored a soft blue. With her king sized bed facing the floor to ceiling window, she was able to see out over the city. That way, if she were late to bed or early to rise, she could see the evening stars or the rays of the morning sun.

Sydney turned the light on and then, nervously, off again. She walked out of the bedroom, through the living room into the small kitchen. It was painted a bright yellow bordered by a pale red wallpaper finished off with black tile. It was designed to be cheery. Just now it did not cheer her up. She fingered the tile and absently placed a dried dish back in its place.

Sydney could not stop moving. Nervously she went back through the apartment to the bathroom. She began to take off her clothes. Maybe a hot bath might help. Usually her bathroom was a delight to her. The tub was a pale green and large and deep enough to accommodate two people. The handles and spout were gold. The sink matched the tub and all the towels were the same pale green color. The tile above the tub was a western brown with splashes of blood red. A dressing table surrounded by mirrors and hidden lighting finished the room. Today the bath-room did not delight her. Sydney took off her silk shirt and bra and looked at her breasts in the mirror.

Sydney shook her head, took a towel and dabbed her eyes. *The breasts looked normal,* she thought, *but what lay underneath?* The thought frightened her.

Sydney bent over to turn on the hot water. Suddenly she straightened. She slipped into her robe, walked back to the living room and stared down at the East River. *It would be so easy to jump,* she thought. She shook her head, dismissing the thought. "I must contact Paul," she blurted aloud, "I must tell him." Abruptly, she picked up the phone, then hesitated and stopped. Slowly she put the phone back in its cradle. Her hand was shaking as she reached for the scotch. She pensively wrinkled her brow and sat down. *No,* she thought, *I will not tell him. I will beat this or I won't. If I beat it and he is still free, I will go back to him. If I lose...,* she shrugged unconsciously, *he will not be burdened by... whatever comes after.*

Sydney downed the rest of her drink in one gulp attempting to drown the gnawing pain gathering in her stomach. She sat numbly on the overstuffed couch, her stocking feet curled beneath her as the day turned into night. The setting sun cast longer and longer shadows into the room until, finally, the only light left was the glow of the cigarette in her hand.

Chapter 6: Paris

Paul Grant weaved through the Paris traffic with the skill of a seasoned veteran. *It's a war on these streets,* he thought, *and either I am quick or I am dead.* He put his fingers through his long hair nervously and worried about being late. The usually wild Paris traffic seemed to move particularly slow today and Paul fumed as his late model Eurocar convertible lurched forward in short starts and stops. Another car suddenly cut in line in front of him and Paul leaned on his horn. Beeeeeeep, "You crazy bitch!" To stop in time, Paul had to stand on his brake. When he finally stopped without hitting her he cursed at her over his windshield. The young woman gave him a finger and continued edging in.

"Why don't they stay home and have babies?" he muttered to himself as he gave in and let her in line. Ordinarily Paul was a civilized man but when he was in the wild traffic of Paris he turned into a Neanderthal, and became just like the millions of other Parisians.

After fifteen more minutes of stopping and starting, Paul angrily pulled into the parking garage of the Eurocars Limited building. He slammed into his parking place, his tires protesting the last turn by squealing loudly and echoing in the concrete jungle of cars. He grabbed his briefcase, and jumped out of the convertible. Even in his rush to get to his meeting he got a flush of pride when he saw his name written in bold print above the parking space. He ran to the elevator and waited impatiently for it to arrive.

The time in the elevator was well spent. As Paul stepped out on the floor for the executive suites, his hair was brushed back and he seemed calm and controlled.

Paul was an up-and-coming executive of Eurocars limited. This company was a creature created by the governments of Great Britain and France, along with private capital, to rival the great motor car firms of Japan and the United states. They had done very well on the open market, using German and Hungarian engineering along with Japanese production methods.

"Good morning Mister Grant."

In the two years he had been there, Paul had risen in the company quickly. He was trim and fit, and the Armani suits he always wore enhanced his image. His prematurely gray hair at his temples made him look settled and solid, and most business people trusted him immediately.

"Good morning, Collette." Paul nodded his head and smiled at the secretary as he strode purposefully towards the meeting room.

As Paul passed by the young girl he did not see her sigh visibly, nor could he see the steamy thoughts she had of him. Dreamily she turned back to her work as he disappeared from view.

Paul opened the door to the conference room and quietly stepped in. Marion Dupré, his supervisor, was seated in the middle of the long conference table.

As Paul closed the door she immediately stood up, crushed out the cigarette she had been smoking, and with a broad smile walked towards him with her hand extended. They shook hands warmly and Marion motioned Paul to a seat next to her. After they were seated she slowly and carefully took another cigarette out of a pack lying in front of her and put it between her lips. She took a lighter out of her purse, but before she could light it, Paul reached over and gestured for her to give him the lighter. Marion handed it to him with a smile. He pressed down the starter mechanism and the flame jumped up from the wick and burned brightly. Paul put the light under her cigarette and Marion puffed several times. The end of the cigarette glowed and Paul took the lighter away and put it down on the table in front of her. She dragged hard on the cigarette, pulled the smoke into her lungs and expelled it with satisfaction. As an afterthought, Marion held the pack towards Paul and offered him a cigarette. He smiled and shook his head no.

Marion Dupré was a woman near age fifty. She had a cold and austere business-like manner and seldom smiled. Her hair was midnight black with streaks of gray. She wore it pulled back tightly on her head and tied in a bun. Her large, thickly rimmed glasses made her dark, brown eyes appear larger than they were. Her head was full of figures and she was seldom wrong in business.

Her poor husband had tried to keep up with her, but he was hopelessly lost in her backwash as she rose rapidly in the turbulent, post war European business wars. Before she emasculated him, he had given her two children. He now spent his time drinking and expounding on politics to anyone who would listen. Marion certainly would not. She took on a series of younger men, most of them lasting just a month or two. At the present time she was alone, content to pick up a stray male at the occasional bar she frequented.

Marion had two daughters who were younger images of herself. She had hoped, it now appeared vainly, to pair one of them with Paul. Marion was uneducated, but well versed in the making and shipping of automobiles. She had started in the accounting department, and with skill and determination, had risen to head of sales. With a little luck, a lot of skill, and Marion in charge, production and sales had skyrocketed. Now, Eurocars was number three in the world in auto production and rapidly gaining on number two.

Paul looked around the empty room. "Where is everyone, Madam? I thought I would be late and now it looks like I am here before anyone else."

Marion smiled in a motherly way, her usual cold manner melting before Paul's boyish charm. "No, Paul, you are not late. This meeting is for you *seulement*. That means it's for you *alone*." Marion quickly turned away so Paul could not see her almost burst out laughing at the look on his face.

Instinctively Paul's stomach tightened. His mind raced. Sales had been good, his reports were on time, what could be wrong? *Why did she send for me?*

Still smiling, Marion walked to a covered easel. She lifted the cover and Paul saw a large red business graph with the sales graph leveled in a plateau. Paul was puzzled. *This could not be my division*, he thought, *our sales are going through the roof.* He leaned forward in his chair and waited for Marion to speak.

Marion tapped the pointer in the palm of her free hand and searched for the proper words. Of all the people in the company, she would hate to lose Paul the most. Not only was he her top salesman, but if he took the company's offer he would be a thousand miles further from her daughters. *Oh well, business comes first.* She looked directly at Paul. Even with the worried look on his face he was appealing. He had a boyish quality that came through his manhood. A woman could mother a man like that, she thought with a silent sigh.

Paul was twenty-nine years old with coal black hair that grayed at the temples. Even with his Armani suit, one could note his broad shoulders and lithe body that narrowed down to a size thirty two waist. He was fit and tanned and walked with purpose and determination. He exuded a combination of sexuality and competence that had driven him to the top of Eurocar sales in Europe.

Marion shook her head slightly and forced herself back to the present business. "Paul, this is a graph of our business in Europe."

Paul sighed and relaxed, his body almost slumping.

"We are not losing ground there, but we are not gaining either. Just when we think we will gain the number one slot, Volkswagen comes out with a new line, or Toyota starts a new ad campaign and we are number three again."

Paul looked puzzled and cocked his head and screwed up his face. Marion was amused by the look of him. *It is not often his brow is so wrinkled,* she thought.

Now for the coup de grâce. Marion sat down opposite Paul, laid the pointer down, smiled and folded her hands. She hesitated, looking at him serenely. "Paul, the company wants you to become the head of sales in Europe and make us number one in the world."

Paul was stunned. His mind flashed to Sydney. He heard Marion's voice but he could not completely understand her words. He forced himself back to Marion.

"... Of course you will get a larger salary..."

His mind raced. Sydney! We could be married right away. I would base my sales in Switzerland or Germany....

"...And you would report directly to me... What do you think? Of course, you can have a few days to mull it over..."

Paul was nodding his head but his mind was far away in another time at another place, trying to remember the first time he saw Sydney. *Where was it? Oh yes, the Louvre. What was I doing there? The Mona Lisa, yes, my weekly meeting with that Italian lady. I was so lost in her beauty. The mother of all paintings, the mother of all women...*

****

The half-smile captivated Paul. He stared at the DaVinci masterpiece and like the millions of people before him, was totally captured by her enigmatic smile. He looked back at her with his own boyish smile and thought, *Your secret Madame, whatever it is, is safe with me.*

Paul had been to the museum many times before with his parents when he was a child. He thought it foolish that he was here by himself today when he should be studying for his university exams, but his weekly meeting with the painting was drawing him there. Anyway he was tired of the study and it was either here or the latest Bogart movie. For some strange reason fate had chosen the museum.

Paul sensed her before he saw her. When he turned to look he was dazzled. In front of him was a beguiling young girl dressed in a tan silk blouse and jeans that fit her as if she were poured into them. Her platinum blond hair was pulled back in a pony tail accenting the angular features of her face. She had long athletic legs and a waist you could span with your fingers. She walked with an animal grace that stirred, Paul's heart and mind. She had on no makeup and didn't need any.

Paul searched his mind for some opening words that would not scare her away when to his amazement she smiled and came right to him. Up close he could see she had clear, blue, intelligent eyes and a captivating smile. She held up her guide book and spoke in broken French with an American accent. "Monsieur, Could you tell me how to get to the Paris Opera, *si vous plait?*"

Paul smiled inwardly at her struggling French but waited patiently until she finished the question.

"Mademoiselle," he said slowly, and then in perfect English, "if you would walk out the main entrance, you will be on the Rue De Rivoli. Then if you look straight ahead you will see a large street going off at an angle. That is the Avenue De Opera. If you then go straight ahead, you will pass two main streets, first the Rue De Etienne, and then the Boulevard De Italiens. Finally when you reach the confluence of Gluck, Halevy and Myerbeer streets, you will be there." Paul was sure the look on her lovely face was worth the small deception. They both laughed.

"You're an American?" she asked.

"Yes and no. My father is from Texas but my mother is French. I was raised here in Paris but lived the summers with relatives in Houston."

The young woman's laugh lit up the room. In the relaxed manner of the Americans, she stuck out her hand. "My name is Sydney Bannon."

Paul took her hand and felt the electricity between them. "I am Paul Grant. If you like I can show you the way to the Opera house. It's only a few minutes from here and I was just about to leave anyway," he lied.

From that day on they were inseparable. They went to other museums and frequented the opera. Sydney adored opera and seemed to know everything about them. And Paul was a willing and apt pupil. After the music, they tried every Italian restaurant on the West Bank and in the evening they would walk arm in arm along the Seine. On Sunday they drove aimlessly around the French countryside, tasting wine from the vineyards and gathering vegetables from the farms they visited. Their first love making was long and sensuous. Paul fell deeply in love with Sydney and she returned his feelings.

Paul begged Sydney to move in with him so he could concentrate on his studies. She made arrangements to finish her own schooling, and without telling her father, moved into Paul's flat. They lived happily together for their last two years of school.

It was only when Sydney's sister, Theresa, asked her to come back to New York to help her with the new magazine she had started, that they considered parting. Paul would have gone back to the States with her but after finishing school he had begun to work for the Eurocars Company and had quickly become a top salesman. When he thought about speaking to his supervisor about leaving for New

York, she beat him to the punch by making him an offer he couldn't refuse. He was to be head of sales in the future European common market, with a fat salary increase. Now, Paul would have to discuss the situation with Sydney but was sure she would agree to his accepting the position.

I will buy Sydney an engagement ring and we will pledge our fidelity. And we will marry in one year. In the meantime, we will see each other every month, me flying to New York one month and she to Paris the next. I am sure Sydney will agree to that.

****

Paul forced himself back to the present. "No need to think it over. Yes, Madame, I will take the position."

Marion smiled, but in her heart she felt the twin stakes of pleasure and pain.

Chapter 7: New York

Sydney sat down at her desk and reached for her stationary. She stopped and lit a cigarette then quickly ground it out. She had not smoked since she had experimented with tobacco in high school but had started again when she was told about the cancer. *Hah!* she thought, *just when most people are told to quit, I begin.*

When she found out about her smoking, the oncologist insisted that Sydney stop immediately and for the most part she had. But, when life became unbearable, she would light up again. *Stupid habit, stupid girl,* she thought.

Sydney picked up the scotch she had poured and noticed her hand was trembling. She hadn't even thought about giving up the drinking. A little whiskey seemed to help her over the rough spots. Lately though, it was more than a little. She had started today at noon but vowed to discipline herself and not take a drink until after five in the afternoon, starting tomorrow.

Sydney sipped the drink then carefully put down the glass. She straightened the paper and picked up the pen. She tapped her pursed lips with the blunt end of the pen and stared into space. She turned to the mirror on the right of the desk, and it became a corridor of time. She saw herself and just in back of her was Paul, young, virile and handsome. She smiled as she remembered the boat on the Seine. It was just a small skiff that they took out regularly. Paul was teasing her about lazing back while he did all the rowing. He asked her to change places with him and do a little work. Indignantly she got up. The boat rocked wildly and she tried to sit back down again. Too late. "No, no, you'll tip us over," Paul yelled and tried to steady them. He was not quick enough. Over they went, both of them laughing as they hit the cold water.

She thought of the long, gentle talks they had while walking in the countryside. The excitement of skiing and hiking the Swiss mountains and after that, the intimate times, the warmth of the fire in the lodge... It was too much. Sydney dropped the pen and hung her head. Tears rolled down her cheeks and she began to sob. "Oh Paul, Paul, if only you could be with me," she murmured softly through her tears.

Sydney sat at the desk for a long while. The day turned into night and long shadows loomed as the room became dark. For a long time she continued to sit in the dark, as if it were too painful to move. Finally she dried her eyes and turned on a light. Her mouth compressed and she got a determined look on her face. With deliberation she picked up her pen and began to write.

Dearest Paul:

It is with a heavy heart that I write to you...

Sydney stopped and stared at the paper. Suddenly she picked it up and angrily tore it into a hundred pieces. She threw the pen as hard as she could against the wall and screamed. She went to her bed and curled tightly into a fetal ball. A few minutes later she sat up, tears streaming down both of her cheeks. After a moment of hesitation she reached for the phone and dialed Theresa.

****

The next morning Sydney rose to the clatter of the alarm. She quickly performed her usual morning toilet, including carefully filling the test tube she had been given. She did not feel like make-up and used only a light shade of lipstick. When she was done she looked at the clock and realized it was still too early to go to the clinic. She tried to sit in her easy chair and read. No good. She got up and paced. *It's too early for a drink. Lord I sure could use one, but I will stick to my new rule, no drinking until five in the afternoon. How about a cigarette? No, I don't dare. Dr. McCann would have a fit if I smoked just before my tests.* She looked out the window at the dreary New York morning. *If only Paul could be here,* she thought. *No! I must find out where I stand before I involve him in this problem.*

In an obtuse way she was glad this day had come. Dr. McCann had recommended Dr. Martha Slater as her oncologist. He had told her that Dr. Slater was a tireless worker for her patients and would leave no stone unturned, and no treatment untried, for their well-being. In Dr. McCann's opinion, she was the best woman's cancer specialist the profession had to offer.

Finally it was time. Shakily she went down to the garage the tenants called the Dungeon. It was dreary down there but Sydney loved the rest of the building. They had security and the people were quiet and very pleasant. But the crowning glory was the view. When she looked one way she saw the East River and when she looked the other, there was the bustling skyline of New York. And at night, yes at night, she could almost reach out and touch the stars that covered the city in a celestial blanket.

Sydney was one of those people that loved New York. She reveled in the beat and throb of the city and went to every show and act that came to town. She was a calm person, but fed on the frenetic pace of the Big Apple.

She was trembling when she put the key in the door of her Mercedes Convertible. It was a cold, gray winter morning, and when she thought about it later, she had no recollection of driving through the streets to the Cancer Clinic.

She parked her car and walked to the elevator, pushed the button for the tenth floor and noticed her hand was shaking. She quickly put the offending hand in her coat pocket as if putting it out of sight would calm her.

The clinic was a huge concrete and steel monster that housed the latest and best in the never-ending fight against cancer. Even with that belief, Sydney did not feel assured as she entered the steel cage that would take her up to Dr. Slater.

The elevator door opened into another world. Here it was quiet and white and orderly. The click of her leather heels on the polished tile floor was the only sound she heard. Sydney walked to the receptionist desk and was given her entrance forms by a disinterested, gum-chewing girl, who smiled perfunctorily, then returned to her reading. Sydney sat down in one of the chairs in the waiting room and began to fill out the forms. When she got to her paternal history it was easy, her father was indestructible. She never remembered him having a sick day, ever. As for her mother, Sydney remembered being alone a lot as a child, when her mother was confined to her bed. She was never really certain exactly what her problems were. *Ah, Kate, dear Kate how I need you now.* Sydney made a mental note to speak to her dad and find out just what her illness was. She did not want to invade the secrecy her father put around her mother's death, but now that information could be important.

Sydney finished the forms and handed them back to the receptionist. The girl flashed the same smile through her official mask, asked Sydney to be seated again and stated that someone would come for her soon. Sydney sat back down in the chair and nervously drummed her fingers on the wooden arm. She looked around at the other patients. There were three other women. No men. Little wonder. They have their own problems, but none that could be solved in this place. She noticed that the women were all considerably older than she was. Suddenly her brown study was interrupted by the sound of her name.

"Miss Bannon?" A pleasant, smiling woman in a starched nurses' uniform stood before her. "Would you come with me, please."

Sydney smiled wanly and stood up. Her knees buckled but she caught herself quickly. A flash of concern showed on the nurse's face but returned to the bland smile she wore after Sydney caught herself. Sydney dutifully followed the nurse down the absolutely white corridor. The nurse's rubber heeled shoes were silent but Sydney's leather heels clicked loudly on the polished tile floor and she self consciously minced her steps to quiet the sound.

The nurse stopped at a door marked exam, opened it and motioned Sydney in. She quickly walked by the nurse into the sterile room. The glare of the enameled white walls almost hurt her eyes. They seemed to be even brighter in this small space. *They sure could use some color in here*, Sydney thought. The nurse handed Sydney a patient gown that seemed to appear magically in her hand.

"Please take everything off and put the gown on with the opening in the front. Dr. Slater will be with you in a few minutes."

Sydney nodded and took the gown. The nurse left and suddenly she felt very alone. She undressed quickly and placed her clothes on a rack provided for the purpose.

Sydney looked around the small room. *Purpose,* she thought, *that's why this room is so sterile, it's designed only for one purpose. No warmth, no feeling, only purpose. Like the kill floor of a slaughter house or a Nazi death camp. No feeling, only purpose.* Sydney shuddered and felt a deep empathy for the animals and the death camp victims.

Sydney sat on the examination table. It had stirrups that looked ominous. Suddenly she had a childish impulse to grab her clothes and run from this place. She fought the desire. She sat on the edge of the exam table with her head down. She got anxious and again the desire to run came over her. She gripped the edge of the vinyl table, clinging hard to reality. Suddenly she realized how much she missed Paul and the physical and emotional strength he would have given her. She let go of her grip, brushed away the tear that had formed at the corner of her eye and then quickly grabbed the table again with both hands. *If only I still had my mother...*

The door opened and Dr. Slater stepped in. She is a tall woman, probably forty-five years old, Sydney estimated, with olive skin, graying hair and serious brown eyes. She wore a lab coat with a stethoscope hanging out of the large right pocket. She nodded to Sydney and then almost like an afterthought, added a fleeting smile to her greeting. Sydney said, "Hello," and her voice cracked. She cleared her throat. *Now I sound just like Theresa,* she thought.

The doctor opened the file in her hand and quietly read Sydney's history.

Sydney stared at her expectantly.

The doctor looked up and asked Sydney to slide back to the center of the table. With a look of annoyance the doctor removed the metal stirrups.

Slowly and carefully, the doctor examined both of Sydney's breasts and armpits, then she felt her neck, mumbling something about "Super clavicular nodes." Then she asked Sydney to lie down and probed her abdomen and listened to her heart and lungs. After she finished the exam Dr. Slater sat down on the lone chair in the room and began to write. Sydney sat up.

When Dr. Slater finished writing her notes she looked up at Sydney and for a few moments did not speak. Sydney could not tell if the doctor was trying to find a way to tell her something or just collecting her thoughts. Sydney continued to sit on the exam table and nervously waited for Dr. Slater to speak. She began to tremble. A small bead of sweat trickled over her lip and she tasted the salt in her mouth.

"Miss Bannon," Dr. Slater began carefully, "the blood tests show that you have a raised alkaline phosphatase. This means your liver function is slightly off. It also appears to me you have a swollen lymph gland under the left axilla and the exam shows a mass of some sort in the left breast. Of course we will have to do a fine needle aspiration, a biopsy, and a hormonal assay, but this suggests to me that you do have some kind of tumor. If you would make an appointment next week we can begin the tests."

Sydney felt as if a giant clenched his fist in her stomach. Her mouth was dry and it was hard to speak. "Dr. Slater..." she croaked. She cleared her throat, swallowed and then spoke more clearly. ...right now my life is on hold. I must find out what I am facing so I can make some serious decisions concerning other people, including a fiancé. Can we do the tests right away?"

Dr. Slater nodded her head in understanding, impressed at the young woman's maturity. She walked to the intercom and pressed a button. "Nurse, would you come in here please." A few long moments passed as the doctor re-read the chart and the patient waited nervously for the nurse to appear. Finally the door opened and the nurse entered. Dr. Slater handed her a pad. "Nurse, I want the following tests done on Miss Bannon, *today*. Ultrasonography, chest x-ray and a scan. Also get me a hormonal receptor assay."

"Did you say today, Dr. Slater?"

"Yes, today."

The nurse shrugged her shoulders then nodded and turned to leave.

"...And I want a biopsy ordered for tomorrow morning."

The nurse again looked surprised for just a moment and then jotted some notes on the pad. She smiled fleetingly at Sydney and then quickly left.

Dr. Slater took Sydney's hand and smiled at her warmly. *Had her own daughter lived she would have been just about this girl's age.* Her heart went out to Sydney.

"My dear girl," she said reassuringly, "even if the biopsy is positive we do not necessarily take off the breast. That is what used to be done. We are more civilized now."

Suddenly Dr. Slater seemed almost motherly. Sydney was relieved a little, but only a little.

"Let me tell you a little about breast cancer. If you are aware, it will seem less scary to you." The Dr. paused and took a breath as if what she was about to say was difficult. "Breast cancer is the leading killer of women between the ages of thirty five and fifty...."

Chapter 8: Paris

"That's strange, a letter from Sydney's sister," Paul muttered. He nodded and thanked the mail boy. He started to open it and stopped. For some reason his hand was trembling. Suddenly the letter seemed ominous. All at once his office seemed to be closing in on him. He panicked and began to breathe hard. He stuffed the letter in his jacket pocket and quickly left the room.

"Collette, hold all my calls, I'll be back in a few minutes."

"Ouí, Monsieur Grant." Collette stared at Paul's back as he moved quickly away from her. Her brow was creased in concern of his behavior.

Paul half walked, half ran to the elevator. The 13th floor below had a quiet place away from the business activity. He got off the elevator and his leather heels clicked rhythmically as he made his way down the austere hallway. The further he got the more quickly he walked. When he reached the end of the hallway, he stopped. He sat down on a leather bench near a large window overlooking the city. His eye caught the Arc de Triomphe and he felt a momentary surge of pride in his fellow Parisians. In his mind, he gave a brief tribute to the Free French Army and to the

Americans that ran the Germans out of this lovely city. In a few seconds his mind turned back to the letter.

Taking the crumpled letter out of his pocket he stared at it. *A letter from Theresa,* he thought, *that's strange. I hope nothing's wrong. Why would she write me? Only one way to find out.* Anxiously he tore opened the envelope.

Dear Paul:

It pains me to write this to you but circumstances dictate that I must. Enclosed find the engagement ring you gave to Sydney.

Paul's heart stopped and his face turned ashen.

Due to recent developments Sydney has decided that she cannot marry you at this time. She has asked that I return the engagement ring to you, and requests that you not contact her further. She will not be available to receive your calls nor will her family be allowed to forward them.

Sydney sends her best to you and begs your understanding. She says she will contact you and explain all this at a later time. In the meantime she urges you to go on with your life. Most sincerely,

Theresa Bannon

Paul sat down on the bench, devastated. He stared at the letter in his hand disbelieving what he had just read. "Just last week everything was perfect," he said aloud, "She told me she loved me and could not wait to see me." Paul felt a spurt of anger and then he was furious. "Another man!" he hissed through clenched teeth. "Goddamn her. She doesn't have the guts to tell me to my face. What's gotten into her! I was sure she loved me..."

Paul got up and grabbed the bottom of the window and opened it. He stared at the Paris street below. For a split second he thought of jumping. Even up this high he could hear the furious honking of horns. The wind howled and he felt its strength, its force making his sleeves and pant legs flap. He turned the envelope over and the ring fell out into his free hand. He slipped it in his finger and angrily drew his arm back to chuck it out the window. As his arm came forward the sun glinted off the ring and caught his eye. He shook his head and stopped. He stared at the ring for a few moments and his eyes glistened over. Slowly he lowered his arm and gently placed the ring in his pocket. He backed up a step, closed the window and sat down again. Suddenly he felt weak and disconsolate. He thought of long walks, and love and laughter, of warm nights, silken hair and moist kisses. He put his elbows on his knees and his head in his hands, the terrible letter sticking out of his fingers at an odd angle, and he cried.

Chapter 9: Europe

Sally Baldwin was thin and energetic. She was also Sydney's best friend. She had been with the magazine since the first edition of Woman's Home, and had risen to second in command of the art department. Sydney knew Sally could run the department as well as she could and that was precisely what she had asked her to do.

Sally sat crosswise on the armchair, her stocking feet hanging over one overstuffed arm, while her elbow rested on the other, her hand propping up her head. She was pouting and her brow was creased with concern.

She shook her head and spoke in the sharp nasal accent peculiar to New Yorkers. "But, I can't do the whole job, Syd."

Sydney stopped packing, looked over at her friend and smiled knowingly. "Are you looking for a compliment, Sally? You know you can do this job as well as I can."

Sally took her hand from her head and sat up. "Even if I could, Syd, why do you want to run away from this problem. Why don't you stay and fight."

Sydney did not answer. She carefully folded her cashmere sweater, laid it on top of the other clothes and closed the lid, but the lid would not close completely. Sally smiled and got up, walked over to the suitcase and promptly sat down on it. Sydney awkwardly pushed down on the bulging case then added her knee and the lid snapped shut. Sally got up and Sydney grunted as she put the heavy suitcase on the floor. "Man, that'll give you a hernia." Both women laughed.

Sydney reached to the top of the dresser and her hand curled around the scotch she had been drinking. She picked it up and walked to the picture window, tinkling the ice in the glass. The window went from floor to ceiling and Sydney loved to lie in bed at night and look out at the New York City lights blinking back at her.

It was now grey and dreary outside and the rain pelted the window panes. Sydney stood at the window quietly sipping the scotch and looked out over her city. I will miss all this. Sally was talking but Sydney could not quite understand her. She sounded like she was far away.

Sydney fixed her attention on one rivulet and watched it race the others to the bottom of the pane. It lost. She shook her head sadly and turned her attention back to Sally.

"...If you won't stay then at least you must cawl me every day," she said in her New York twang.

Sydney smiled. "I won't promise a daily call, Sally but I will keep in touch with you." Sydney took a last look around the room. "Well, I'm ready to go."

Sally stood up. She looked as if she were going to cry. "We'll miss you, Syd."

Suddenly the intercom came on and a strange New York voice filled the room. "Apahtment fifteen fawteen you cawled a cab?"

Sydney raised her voice. "Be right down." She put the scotch down and silently vowed not to drink again until after five P.M. She laughed to herself. Maybe it's five o'clock in Europe. Sydney slipped on her deerskin gloves and took one more look around the apartment. She felt a pang of nostalgia and shook her head. I'm doing the right thing. I have to go.

Sally lifted the smaller bag and walked to the door. Sydney was right in back of her, rolling the larger suitcase behind her.

The ride down the elevator was a silent one. *Isn't it strange,* Sydney thought, *people are always quiet in an elevator. It can even silence Sally, and that is almost impossible.* She laughed to herself.

When they got to the ground floor the burly cab driver was waiting at the elevator and took the bags.

When they reached the taxi both women stopped and faced each other.

"Theresa felt terrible not being able to be here, but Amsterdam flooring is one of our biggest clients and their president himself was coming with his advertising people. I just barely got away myself."

"Tell Theresa not to worry about it. I love her just the same. Anyway, she has to keep my checks coming, so tell her to keep her nose to the grindstone. You too!"

Tears welled up in Sally's eyes and rolled down her cheeks. "I just hate it that you're going and I hate what's happened." Sally broke down completely and began to cry and sob. Sydney hugged her and patted her back.

"Wait a minute here," Sydney said, laughing, "just which one of us has the problem?"

Sally laughed through her tears. Brusquely she wiped her eyes with the back of her hand. "This is so silly of me. I just wish there was something I could do for you."

Sydney stepped back and took Sally's hands. "There is. You can keep my department going strong and maybe I can come back hale and hearty and we can be partners."

For a brief moment Sally's eyes glittered. "You mean it?"

"Of course I do."

"I love you Sydney." They hugged again.

The cab driver shook his head, and said "Jeeze," under his breath, then slid into the driver's seat.

"I love you too, Sally. You know what? No wonder the cabbie hasn't beeped, he has the meter on. I have to go."

"Bye, Syd."

The two women hugged a third time, fiercely. Finally, Sydney broke away. She opened the door to the cab and got in, rolled down the window and blew a kiss. "Tell Theresa that I love her." They were still waving goodbye as the taxi turned the corner.

Sydney sat back relieved to be alone with her thoughts. She loved Sally but she was always drained when she left her.

"Where to lady?"

"New York International Airport" Sydney answered absently.

"Where ya off to, lady?" the cabbie said, not really caring, just making conversation.

"Maybe to a funeral."

"Oh?" the cabbie said, puzzled.

"New York International," Sydney repeated abruptly, not wanting to talk.

"Yes'm."

She caught his leer in the rear view mirror and all of a sudden Sydney became aware of the cab driver. He was burly, hairy and had a sullen look on his face. Sydney felt a tinge of fear and shifted her feet to be ready for anything.

She was tense for a while and of course nothing happened. She laughed at herself, relaxed and watched the familiar city speed by. She tried to read the magazine she had brought. When she looked up, on occasion, she marveled that she could not tell if they were speeding through the streets to the airport or were just standing still with the city rushing by them.

She looked at her watch anxiously. *No need to be in a hurry,* she thought, *and yet time was now so valuable a commodity it was never to be wasted. Not an hour, not a minute, not a second. Every moment was precious.* A tear rolled down Sydney's stoic face. She quickly dabbed her eye.

Finally they were there. As the taxi slowed for the airport traffic Sydney watched the planes leaving the runway, lumbering upward into the sky. She envied their power and direction.

The taxi drove up to the terminal and the driver stepped hard on the brake. The tires squealed and Sydney braced herself. Even then she almost slid off the seat.

Leaving the motor running, the driver jumped out and opened the door for Sydney. Then he quickly went to the trunk got her luggage and deposited the bags on the sidewalk, his mind and eyes were already looking for a fare back to the city. Sydney paid him, tipped the redcap who appeared magically, and was free of her luggage. The redcap tagged her bags gave her a receipt and politely told her to go on to the counter inside.

When Sydney got to the counter she wondered how the large crowd waiting to check in were all going to fit on one plane. The line of people wound around like a large, unruly snake, impatiently waiting their turn at the counter. Small children clung close to their parents while older ones took advantage of the chaos and explored. Wily, veteran travelers sat on their luggage, husbanding their strength for the ordeal they knew lay ahead. Sydney noted where the redcap put her bags and got on line. Several children darted in and out of the line and Sydney wistfully watched them. There was one particular boy about two years old that captured her attention. He was platinum blonde, much like her own color hair, with a cherubic face and a permanent, mischievous smile fixed on his face. He would wander a little ways from his mother but always managed to keep within sight of her indulgent face. Sydney caught his eye and they smiled broadly at each other.

Was Sydney too late? Was she never to feel life within her? Would she never hold a babe to her breast? *I hope I have a breast to give him,* she thought, ruefully. A tear formed in the corner of her eye again and she brusquely wiped it away, the moisture staining her glove.

The travelers chatted gaily with each other, but Sydney felt alone and depressed. Finally it was her turn at the counter and in a few moments she was done, bags away, ticket and seat assignment in her hand and an hour to spare.

Sydney went to a row of chairs, sat down and tried to read. She glanced at the clock on the wall. Still fifty minutes before takeoff. She loved airports and began to wander around, taking it all in. She stopped at the magazine counter where Woman's Home was prominently displayed. She looked critically at her latest cover. A young, innocent face looked back at her. Sydney smiled, remembering the photo shoot at the beach.

Much to Theresa's fiscal dismay, Sydney always wanted realism on her Magazine covers. She and her sister always argued about the expense but Sydney usually won out. This summer's issue would be shot in Miami.

Unfortunately for Sydney, the three young models she brought with her discovered South Beach, and from then on it was difficult to keep the girls' minds on their work. Finally after imposing strict curfews and a promise to let the girls stay an extra two days, they wrapped up the shoot. Sydney rested while the young girls followed their hormones. Sydney remembered vividly the grateful feeling when the plane touched down at the New York Airport and she delivered the models to their boyfriends and families.

Suddenly through the buzzing sound of the busy airport Sydney honed in on an announcement.

"TWA flight one oh six, bound for Frankfurt, and Budapest, now boarding at the overseas gate."

Sydney quickly paid for the magazine and left to look for her gate.

She weaved her way through the throngs of people heading towards their flights and finally reached her gate. Sydney felt strange as she handed the smiling attendant her ticket. She felt out of body, as if she were looking at herself about to board the plane instead of her actually getting on. She shook her head to bring herself back and with the other passengers walked down the walkway to the tarmac. She climbed the steel ladder and stepped aboard the plane. Sydney showed her boarding pass and the stewardess smiled and pointed to her seat. Sydney sat down in the first class assigned seat, leaned back and closed her eyes. She had an overwhelming feeling that everything was unreal. She felt light, as if she didn't really need the great bird to fly.

Suddenly she felt panic, a great urge to run out the plane door gripped her and she had to grab both armrests to force herself to stay in her seat. A thin line of moisture appeared on her upper lip.

"Ma'am?"

Sydney opened her eyes. The stewardess was looking at her oddly.

"We're going to take off in a few minutes, can I get you something?" The stewardess had a pillow in her hand and offered it to Sydney.

She shook her head no.

"Just as soon as we're airborne, we'll be serving drinks."

Sydney nodded, grateful that she would soon have a scotch. The young stewardess also nodded and left to attend to other passengers.

I wonder how she knew I needed a drink, Sydney thought.

As if it was all in a dream Sydney stared out the window at the maintenance crew getting the great bird ready for its flight. She had risen depressed and had stayed that way until Sally's visit. Now she had fallen back into that damned mood again. It was a state she felt frequently. Suddenly the plane lurched. Sydney's gloom was invaded by the stewardess going through her monotonous instructions. Sydney heard it only in snatches.

"...Fasten the seat belt... exits there and there... pillows available in the overhead compartment... serving lunch and drinks just a few minutes after takeoff."

Sydney stared absently out the window as the Boeing Stratocruiser rolled and undulated awkwardly towards the runway. Suddenly Sydney felt a small jolt in her ribs. She turned and in complete surprise noticed that someone else was sitting beside her. *My God,* she thought, *I need to become aware of my surroundings again.*

"Excuse me, my dear." Sydney heard the lady next to her speak in a cultured European accent. As the woman bustled about in her seat, getting comfortable, she had accidentally elbowed Sydney.

Sydney nodded her head to forgive the minor intrusion. She noted, in the brief encounter, that her seat mate had the same color gray hair as Dr. Slater. Sydney's tears now came freely as she remembered Dr. Slater's pronouncement. The message was not good.

****

Sydney sat anxiously at the edge of her chair waiting for Dr. Slater. Despite her desire to stay calm, she trembled.

Wait, wait, wait, she thought. *This damnable waiting is the worst thing of all.* Her eyes wandered. Dr. Slater's office was muted, the walls covered with mahogany paneling. One entire wall was covered with built in bookcases filled with medical books. The wall next to it was filled with diplomas. Sydney got up and began to read the first diploma hanging prominently on the wall.

Elizabeth Slater
Bachelor of Science
Columbia University
College of Science

Her eyes dropped to the second diploma.

Elizabeth Slater
Doctor of Medicine
University of Georgia

Sydney stopped reading as the door opened abruptly and Dr. Slater walked in. Adrenalin spurted through her and her heart began to pound. She looked for some sign on the doctor's face. It was blank. Fear clutched at her. In her heart she knew the message would not be good.

Dr. Slater smiled fleetingly at Sydney and put the papers she held down on the desk. She looked at Sydney's face for a few moments as if she were searching for something and then sat down resignedly. A small, sad smile remained on her face. Sydney remained standing, but her heart stopped.

"My dear girl, the biopsy has come back positive. You have a cancer in the left breast. It is an intraductal carcinoma. Unfortunately, the bone scan shows there has been some metastatic invasion..." Dr. Slater stopped, afraid she had gone too far, too fast. She shook her head and continued. "I will not tell you any stories, it is very serious. But, it is not totally hopeless. We need to immediately begin a regimen..."

Sydney did not hear the rest of what Dr. Slater was saying as she went into a kind of shock. She was too stunned to cry. She just stared at the doctor, slack-jawed. Her beautiful life, destroyed in an instant. In very slow motion, unconsciously, Sydney sat down.

"You are young and strong, and that is on our side..."

Sydney put her hands on the sides of the chair and began to rock back and forth. Suddenly she stopped and looked ruefully at the doctor and interrupted her. Her heart constricted and she choked as she said the words. "Dr. Slater, how long do I have to live...?"

For some strange reason the doctor was stung. She hadn't thought about the death of this beautiful young girl. All she thought of was gathering her considerable abilities to prolong her life. The doctor braced herself but could not help but look away as she spoke. Her voice was clinical and cold. "Under ordinary circumstances, statistics tell us, you have between six months and two years."

Sydney's mind and body seemed to separate and she almost collapsed. She began to tremble and cry in earnest.

It is very hard to die when you are twenty-one.

****

Sydney remembered little of how she got home. She unlocked the door and stepped in, stumbling over the shoes she had left there earlier that day. She tried to catch herself but struck her shoulder against the sharp edge of the foyer wall and went down to the floor. She lay there too hurt to cry or move. After a few minutes she pushed herself up to a sitting position, put her back against the wall and cried from depths she did not know she had. This last silly accident had now put her at the bottom of whatever Hell she had fallen into.

When the pain finally slowed, she dragged herself to the couch and slowly and painfully pulled herself up. She sat there staring into space. After a few minutes she fumbled with her purse and found the pack of cigarettes and her lighter. She threw the purse randomly on the floor, lit the cigarette and dragged deeply. The room was dark and still. A momentary glow lit up her face from the end of her cigarette. Her face was lined and her brow furrowed.

After a few puffs, Sydney nervously ground out the cigarette and lit another. She looked at the glowing end objectively. "Cancer huh," she said aloud, "well I didn't smoke before and I got cancer, so what difference does it make now?" Despite the logic she ground the cigarette out after taking one drag.

Sydney rapidly became a recluse. She would speak to no one. She would not return calls from Paul, Theresa, or her father. Her wire recorder said she was away and would contact the caller when she returned. She even had the valet put her car in another location. She would not answer the door. She did not eat or sleep, but sat or paced in the darkened room all day and all night. Cigarettes and scotch were her constant companions. She began to look emaciated and the few clothes she wore hung in an ungainly fashion from her once curvaceous body. The anguish that constricted her heart came with regularity now and depression hung over her like a black, macabre shroud.

Sydney got up and looked out the window. The day matched her mood. It was overcast and gray. She stumbled to the couch in the living room and sprawled out and stared into the gloom. Tears ran down her cheeks. After a few minutes she got up and paced. Was she rash to dismiss the treatment Dr. Slater recommended? So what if she lost her hair, it would give her more time.

Time. Time. That's what I need, more time. Time to be with Paul. Time to love and be loved. Time to find a house, make a home, time to have a baby... to live, time to live... I have run out of time.

After a while she dried her eyes and sat back down. She had to decide what to do with the time she had left. The constant depression and alcohol had made her mind muddled. If she were careful she knew she could live off her savings, and Theresa said she would help, so she would have an income from the magazine. She also knew Sally could do her job almost as well as she could, so that was not a problem. And, if worse came to worse, she knew her father would help her.

In the very back of her mind was a thought that was trying to surface past the depression. She almost had it! *What was it that Frank Sinatra had said on that radio program? "Live every day just as if it's your last." Why not,* she thought, *what is it that I haven't done that I would dearly love to do?* A vision of Paul came to her mind and she pushed it down. Then it hit her. "The opera!" she said aloud, "The opera season is just beginning. It starts in Vienna and works its way through Salzburg, Milan, and finishes in Budapest."

"Mozart, Donizetti, and Puccini. Italy, Hungary, Vienna. What a way to go!" She even forgave herself the pun. She quickly picked up the phone, stopped and then stared at it. She laughed. *It was two o'clock in the morning. Maybe she could get a travel agent out of bed for an emergency trip to Europe.* She laughed again.

It was the first time since Dr. Slater told her the bad news, that she had not thought about death. In fact, since the idea about going to Europe came to her she now felt more alive than she had in what seemed like forever.

She would start right now and make an itinerary. She would go to each city, first class. *"No! not first class, but by bicycle." She would cycle her way across Europe and live in student hostels. "Yes, yes, I will go city by city and see every opera."* She laughed aloud, *"I will be an operatic Deadhead. And play tennis. Yes, I will bring my rackets and play with anyone, no everyone."* She would see the real Europe, live among the people and listen to all the music she never had time for.

"Well damn, it may be two in the morning here but it is eight in the morning in Europe. I will call there right now." There was no time to lose. Sydney turned on the light and fumbled with the phone. She stopped suddenly and put it back. *"Paul,"* she said aloud, *"I must tell Paul. He will be there. He could meet me. We could be together."*

She stood up and walked to the mirror. For a moment she was afraid to look at the image. Mustering her courage she stared at the stranger looking back at her. She was aghast. *Who is this?* she thought. Her usual sleek platinum hair hung in tangles. Her stained robe covered the sagging skin and the slumping shoulders. She fingered her hair and smoothed it out. She put her fists in her eyes and rubbed them as if to erase the sight. She opened them again and stared at herself but this time more critically. She fingered the tangles again. "I will see Maurice the first thing tomorrow morning," she muttered, "he'll fix this." She let her hair fall back. "I'll have a massage and I'll stop this maudlin sentiment."

She put the scotch down on an end table. "I'm going to start eating and in a few days I'll be myself." She walked back to the couch and slowly picked up the phone. *"I will call Paul."* She hesitated. *"No! I must let him go,"* she said with anguish, *"he deserves better than to watch me die."* Sydney put the phone down and began to cry freely. She cried until she had no more tears and then she cried some more. When she finally stopped, she just stared into space for a few minutes and then, hesitantly, she picked up the phone and asked the operator to dial Paul's number in Paris. When he said hello, she felt as if her heart would break. Her face contorted in anguish and she reached down and broke the connection. *"I can't, I can't,"* she sobbed, *"Theresa will have to help me."* Then from a never-ending well she began to cry again as she dialed her sister. The clock on the wall said two forty-five A.M.

****

The great plane shuddered and jolted Sydney awake.

"Jaj Istenem!" (Oh, my God) she heard the gray-haired lady exclaim.

The intercom crackled and the captain came on. Sydney heard his calm voice speaking in French. She was puzzled until the stewardess repeated it in English. "The captain says we are entering an area of turbulence. Please fasten your seat belts, secure any loose items around you and raise your seat to the upright position."

The gray haired lady repeated, "Istenem," and began to raise her seat. She put her pillow in her lap and bent her head in prayer. Magically, a rosary appeared suddenly in her hand and she began to mumble.

Sydney watched her numbly. *If we go down,* she thought, *it would be over for me in a hurry.* She caught herself. *Christ, you are really something,*

Sydney! You'd take a hundred people with you just so you can have a quick death? Good going, Sydney!

The turbulence stopped and the plane quieted again to its normal drone. The woman wiped her moist brow, smiled weakly at Sydney and the rosary disappeared.

The stewardess appeared again and this time she spoke in English. "The captain says we are through the turbulence now and it's safe to move about the cabin, if necessary. If you do not need to move about please stay in your seat with the seat belt fastened." She repeated the admonition in French.

The gray-haired lady sighed. "I am glad dat is over vit. It's not dat I am afraid to die, but I have several grandchildren...," she shrugged her shoulders, "...and who vood raise dem?"

The word 'children' triggered Sydney and her eyes teared.

"Istenem, have I said someting to make you cry? Vat is it, my dear, can I help?"

Sydney smiled weakly and dabbed her eyes. "No, it's just..." Sydney began to cry again, this time in earnest.

"Oh, my poor dear," the woman said in her thick accent, and began to gently pat Sydney's back.

Maybe it was because she was a stranger, or because she was so kind and she looked like a mother should, and maybe some of both, but whatever the reason, Sydney began to pour out her painful account.

The woman nodded her head gravely as Sydney told her the whole story, from the time she found the lump in the shower to the death sentence she received from Dr. Slater.

"So you see," Sydney continued, "I decided to come to Europe, see my favorite operas and travel the countryside. Kind of a 'see Naples and die'." Sydney smiled ruefully at her own joke.

Her new friend did not smile. She continued to nod gravely as Sydney finished. She was thoughtful for a while and then spoke. "My dear girl, my name is Maria Cukor. Vat is yours?"

"Sydney, Sydney Bannon."

"I vant to know your name because vat I vill tell you now I vood tell you as a friend."

Sydney dried her eyes. She had to lean forward and concentrate. Although Maria's English was good, her accent was thick and she sometimes garbled the words.

She took Sydney's hand in hers, leaned forward and put Sydney's hand to her cheek. The pudgy warmth of the woman's hand felt good to Sydney.

"I live in Budapest, in Hungary." She leaned towards Sydney and lowered her voice as if she were in a conspiracy. "On the left bank of the Danube in Pest, dere is clinic managed by a man named Laszlo Kodaly. He is a doctor of the first rank. But not only that, he has combined along with conventional treatment, alternative treatment from all over the vorld."

Sydney's smile was fixed on her face but she could not help but think, *Oh God, a kook, a cultist.*

"As you can imagine, other, more conventional doctors frown on this kind of medical heresy. Although I have not personally been treated dere, I have two friends who have. And they svear by dis doctor. They told me he changed their diet and their outlook on life. Since they have told me of their results I have heard of others who have also done wery vell vit his treatment..."

Sydney listened skeptically. She smiled and nodded but deep inside she rejected the notion. She thought silently, *Someone as dedicated as Dr. Slater would certainly have heard of these new advances and utilized them.*

Sydney thanked Maria for her advice and lied when she promised she would call the clinic when she got to Budapest. Both women then settled back in their seats with their own thoughts.

Suddenly Maria spoke again but in such a low voice, Sydney had to turn her head and lean towards her to hear her clearly. "You know," she said from a faraway place as she stared at the clouds below them, "if I had to do tings over again, I vood do them differently." She paused as if she was ordering events in her mind then she cocked her head and sighed. "My children, they were so sweet and innocent." She shook her head and looked at Sydney.

Sydney thought she detected guilt in Maria's eyes.

"Dey grew up so fast." She shook her head sadly. "Long ago I had two dress shops, one in Buda and the other in Pest. Dey were so busy, and it seemed to me I had to be dere all the time." She looked out the window again. "My husband vas a frustrated, artistic type. He painted a little but he vasn't good enough to sell any of dem and mostly he mooned about, making excuses about vy everyone vas against him. The truth vas, he hid from life behind a bottle." She looked at Sydney sheepishly. "He vas a very bad model for der children and I, unfortunately, supported his habits. Anyvay, he vas home and I vas at business and somehow, I missed dem growing up." She shook her head. "It is the damnedest ting, but now dey seem to adore him, and I am out in the cold." She stopped and Sydney thought she was going to cry but she didn't. Sydney reached over and held her hand.

"It's funny," the older woman said absently, "It's like being in a movie house. Dere are tree frames in the film. One before the light of the projector, one after, and one right on it. If you vatch the frame after it vent through the projector it's like living in the past. You know that type of person, always talking about how good it vas in der good, old days. If you vatch the frame that is not in the projector yet, it's like living in the future. Bot vays when you come out of the movie you vill have seen notting. Only der person who vatches the frame in the light sees der movie. He is de only one who is living in the present." She turned to Sydney a little anguish on her face. "Do you know vat I mean?"

Sydney sat back in her seat, a little depressed. "Yes, I know exactly what you mean."

"I loved dose children and yet I vas always vorried about the future. I vas always concerned about making enough money. I vas always tinking how great it vill be ven I have enough money... enough time. I vas on the job all the time..." Maria choked up and her voice trailed off. Both women were silent. Sydney sat still holding her hand, feeling deeply for the older woman.

Finally Maria gained her voice and spoke again. "Dey grew up and I vasn't even dere. I vas living in der future and they vere in the present, being raised by a drunk." Her voice choked again. "How stupid of me. Now I have money and time, but I have no love." She turned and looked at Sydney. "So I run around der world trying to find something... anyting..." She laughed and looked away. "Ven the children grew up and left der home, my ex-husband found a stupid young girl, who vas looking for her father. She tinks she has found him. Of course, she supports his drinking and his abuse to her. Believe me, he knows how to take adwantage of dat. But someday she vill grow up and that vill be a sad reckoning for him. Me, I have a vorse Hell. I have tree children but I have no connection vit dem." Maria turned away and looked out the window again. Tears rolled down her cheeks and spilled freely on her dress.

Sydney stared stonily into space, her own depression making her unable to console the woman.

For a while the space around them was heavy. Maria dried her eyes dabbing them with a lace handkerchief. "Please forgive an old woman's foolishness. For some reason I felt compelled to tell you dis nonsense."

Sydney squeezed her hand. "I am glad you shared some of your life with me. I have learned a great deal."

Maria smiled at her and dabbed her eyes. "Now, please tell me more about yourself. Not the painful tings, but the good tings."

Sydney smiled and began to tell Maria about the magazine and some of her life in New York. As she spoke her depression lifted.

The time passed quickly as the two women chatted amiably. Suddenly Maria pointed out the window. "Dere it is, der coast of Europe."

Sydney leaned over her to look out the small window. The sight of the endless ocean meeting the land thrilled her and she sat back, smiling, content that she had come.

The stewardess' voice cut through the excitement building in the plane. "...Seats, upright... Tray tables up... Seatbelts on... Landing in a few minutes..." She repeated it all in French. As promised, in a few minutes the plane was approaching the Frankfurt airport.

Maria wrote her name and phone number on her plane ticket and handed it to Sydney. "You must call me ven you get to Budapest and please, tink about seeing Dr. Kodaly."

"I will, Maria, I promise," she lied.

"Please call me Mari, I feel like ve are old friends."

The first class passengers deplaned at once and the two women were on the ground in minutes. Maria turned to Sydney and they hugged in a fond embrace. Maria kissed Sydney on both cheeks and began to cry as she turned away.

Sydney watched her for a few moments as Maria walked towards the gate for the plane to Budapest. She looked like a million other people, five foot two, a matronly waist and a roundish face that seemed to blend in with all the other people Sydney saw at the airport. But there was something special about this woman, some indefinable thing that didn't show on the outside. Sydney hoped she would see her again. At the thought of seeing Maria again Sydney shook her head and smiled. Then she turned and walked towards the gate marked Swiss Air.

Chapter 10: Switzerland

From her vantage, on top of the mountain, Sydney could see the lake in the valley below. It glittered in the sunlight and appeared so close that it seemed she could reach out and touch it. The road wound itself around the mountain and it was another two hours until she arrived at lake side. The air was clean and the sun was warm. Sydney felt exhilarated, her platinum hair blowing freely in the wind as she made her way down the Swiss mountain curves

Sydney braked the bike at the edge of the water, winded, but pleased. She had biked in Manhattan's Central Park but only casually. Here, in Europe, she biked in earnest for long hours at a time and it was beginning to show in her legs and wind.

Along the shoreline were several gleaming, white buildings clustered about in a circle like an old wagon train girded for a fight. Sydney laughed. *"No Indians this far up."* She reached into her backpack and pulled out a wrinkled and weathered map. She scrutinized it carefully. *"Yes this is it, IL Hostel Americano."* (The American Hostel) It was here Sydney planned to stay for a week before her train trip to Budapest.

Sydney looked out over the water then at the sky above. The sky was covered by soft cirrus clouds with a flock of birds flying below them in a perfect V-formation. The air was cool and a slight breeze drifted to the land from the dark lake. The large fir trees that circled the lake bent slightly with the breeze and when the wind picked up they made a mournful sound. Sydney shook her head at the wonder of it. She laughed aloud as she thought of all the people at the Woman's Home building. *Right about this time they're entering their cubicles, like ants scurrying around in their glass and concrete homes, all busily serving queen bee, Theresa.*

"Servus!"

A startled Sydney turned.

"I am so sorry, I didn't mean to disturb you."

She smiled at the intruder. She was a young girl, not more than twenty. She wore jeans, loafers, and a Levi shirt, an exact mirror image of the way Sydney was dressed. She sounded a lot like Maria.

"You Hungarian?"

"Yes, some tings you cannot hide. How did you know?"

"You sound like a friend of mine. By the way you speak excellent English."

She smiled again. "Not so excellent. You new here?"

"I just arrived."

"I did not tink I had seen you before." She reached out her hand. "My name is Magda."

They shook hands. "Mine's Sydney."

"Pretty name."

"So is Magda."

"You are an American?"

"Yes, but I'm not loud, I promise." Both girls laughed.

"What's it like there?" Sydney nodded her head towards the white buildings that made up the hostel. "If it's anything like this lake it would be very hard to leave this place."

"You are right, it is hard to leave. My boyfriend and I have been here for a mont and ve usually don't spend more than a few days at any von place. But dis place is special. We vill have to be leaving soon, though. School begins in two weeks and ve must get back to Hungary."

"Well, that's a coincidence. I have to go to Hungary too."

"School," she said expectantly?"

"No, the opera."

"You're a singer?"

Sydney laughed. "No, just a fan"

Magda looked puzzled.

"A devoted listener," Sydney explained.

Magda smiled. "To answer your question about what the place is like, it is youth hostel vit dormitory rooms. They charge the equal of five American dollars a week. You have to keep your own area and the bathroom clean and as you Americans say, you chip in with the cooking or clean-up, every night." Magda looked across the lake. "Dere are canoes to go out on the lake, lots of trails to walk, and loads of time to meditate. Dere is also a casino on the other side of the lake, but as you can imagine, none of the kids can afford to go dere."

Sydney shifted her backpack and turned towards the largest of the white buildings. The main building of the hostel was a gleaming white, well cared for wooden structure that was built to last, like all the other buildings she had seen in Switzerland. It had a large porch, with rocking chairs strategically placed so the people sitting on them could watch the sun set over the lake. Just now the afternoon sun was hitting the building, turning the windows a flaming red.

"You say you sleep in a dormitory, Magda? Is everybody mixed all together?" Her voice lowered. "I have a condition and I would hate for some guy make a pass at me."

"Make a pass at me?" Magda repeated, puzzled. Then recognition flashed on her face and she showed a smile of understanding. "No, no, you're quite safe, the men here are quite civilized." Both women laughed again. Magda turned serious and touched Sydney's arm.

"Herpes?"

"I'd rather not talk about it."

"I understand."

Magda patted her hand. "Come on inside and I'll help get you settled." They walked up to one of the smaller buildings in the hostel together, Sydney wheeled her bike beside her, and when they reached the building, put the bike in the rack near the entrance then caught up with Magda, who was on the porch holding the office door open for her.

When Sydney stepped inside she got a small shock. It was not at all like she had imagined it would be. Instead of the usual Swiss mountain decor, the inside of the hostel office was like the inside of a Japanese Geisha house. Magda was smiling as if she knew a secret.

"Surprised?"

"To say the least." Sydney put down her backpack, looked around in wonder and then walked to the window and fingered the silk curtains.

"In a minute you'll find out why. Tommy, hey, Tommy, you here?"

"Keep your shirt on," a voice came from the back room. The words were in English, but Sydney noted the accent was far from American. Sydney spotted a lovely oriental painting of children and cherry blossoms across the room, and walked to the far wall to get a closer look.

Just then the beaded curtains parted and an oriental woman stepped into the room and smiled at Magda.

Sydney turned and looked at her. She was a small woman with jet black hair, cut very short, and the darkest eyes Sydney had ever seen. Her body was lithe and slim, and she walked towards Magda with the grace of a cunning panther. She wore a white flower in her hair that enhanced her native beauty. Her face was so totally smooth that Sydney wondered at her age. She greeted Magda warmly, then Magda turned to Sydney.

"Tommy, I vould like to introduce you to a new friend. Dis is Sydney.

The oriental woman smiled and turned to Sydney. The moment she saw Sydney's platinum hair, Tomiko's face hardened and the muscles around her mouth tightened pulling her mouth corners down. In that infinite moment, she was back in Hiroshima.

Chapter 11: Tomiko (1945)

It was a cold, blustery morning and the old man hurried the young girl along the windswept street. The loose, white, cotton clothes he wore whipped in the wind making a peculiar flapping noise. He and the little one had their heads down to break the wind. Both of them had handkerchiefs tied over their nose and mouth to keep out the stench that pervaded the land.

All about them was devastation. Burned-out buildings surrounded them in mute testimony to the civilization that had once been there. Empty windows with broken glass stared, like sightless beggars with haunted eyes, pleading for an explanation. The wind whipped the litter around them in miniature tornadoes, and man-made rocks slowed their progress.

The little girl pressed hard to keep up. Her small legs churned in tiny circles propelling her forward. She was just ten years old, but already wise in the ways of young children. She knew if she obeyed the adults, no matter what they asked of her, she would be safe.

The child had jet black hair that was cut short with straight bangs ending just above her eyes. She wore a miniature kimono, that was as black as her raven hair. It had touches of red and pink, like the roses in the garden that used to be. The little one suddenly thought of her mother tending the roses and almost cried. *I must not cry, grandfather said. I must be a brave little girl.* Nevertheless, tears rolled down her cheeks.

"Just a little further Tomiko, we are almost there." *Aaaaiieeeee, we have come to this,* he thought, *selling the little ones to stay alive. Aaaaiieeeee, and to the barbarians. But the other children, they must live. I have lived my time and I am past time to go and see my ancestors. But they, the little ones, they are our future and I cannot watch them starve.*

It is fitting... the barbarians first destroy us and now they will keep us alive. It is fitting... In the beginning the barbarians were no match for the samurai. We knew only victory. But now... The grandfather looked at the burned-out buildings and shook his head. *Despite what the generals said, they were too strong for us. It is fitting...*

The old man took the handkerchief from his face and pointed. "Look, Tomiko, the river, we are almost there. The smell is better here. You may put away your handkerchief."

Tomiko nodded gratefully. She was getting very tired and the handkerchief cut down her wind.

"We must hurry, little one."

Tomiko wrinkled up her small face and grimaced with effort. "Yes, Grandfather," she said politely.

Soon they were at the river's edge. Grandfather stopped and Tomiko stopped beside him. She looked at the scene in wonder. She had never seen anything like it. Tied to the pier was a large pleasure craft with several European people on board watching the proceedings. There were a great many Japanese people on the shore, pushing and shoving to get to a tall barbarian man with hair so golden it almost looked white. He was in the center of the group of people, laughing and handing them money. Tomiko stared in amazement at the golden giant. *No wonder Grandfather called them barbarians, they look so strange.*

She had never seen a Caucasian before, much less one with platinum hair. Off to the side, near the water, she saw a small group of obedient little oriental girls, standing quietly and looking very grave and forlorn.

Near the water, standing next to the group of small girls was a stunning Japanese woman. She was dressed in the green kimono, made of the finest silk. She was unsmiling, her posture erect and her face very stoic. Her dress was flawless and her hair was carefully and cosmetically placed on her head, held in place by a long silver pin, in the manner of the geishas. Her heavily made-up, white face was also very grave.

It was easy for grandfather to find his man. His platinum blonde hair was visible among all the black heads bobbing about him as he towered above the Japanese that crowded him. He was laughing and counting and giving Yen to the people nearest him.

Grandfather closed his eyes for a brief moment, took a deep breath and holding on to Tomiko's hand, began to walk towards the crowd. When he reached them he began to move the people in front of him to get to the golden haired one. As grandfather pushed closer, the white giant saw Tomiko. He pushed the crowding people aside and reached down for her.

With a nod from grandfather she allowed him to draw her near him. The man held her in his arms and smiled at her. Tomiko could see his yellowed and broken teeth and the scars on his face that bespoke of a rough past. Tomiko saw the strangeness of his platinum blonde hair and got very frightened. She made a face when she smelled him. He had an odor of pork and sour milk. It was then that she realized he was not clean. She was terrified and mortified, and with her arms and legs pushing against him tried to get away.

Laughing, the man put her down and pushed her towards the other little ones. "Aye, little one, yi'll be a beauty sume day. An' yer got spirit too."

Watching the barbarian hold his granddaughter, grandfather recovered his dignity, took the girl back and walked away from the loud pushing crowd. He told Tomiko to stand with the other children and turned and bowed low to the Japanese woman. With great politeness he addressed the lady. "Mama-san, are you with the barbarians who buy the children?"

The woman looked at the man with great sadness. *Such a civilized man must be greatly troubled to be reduced to this act,* she thought. "Grandfather, you must join the others and the foreign devil will settle up with you. Which girl is yours?"

The old man pointed at Tomiko.

The woman was immediately attracted to her and saw the beauty the little girl would become. "Grandfather, do not accept less than 5,000 Yen for her. Now, join the others. When you are finished, bring the girl to me. I will take care of her personally."

With great relief the old man again dutifully joined the crowd.

The woman in green followed him to the pushing and shoving crowd around the laughing foreigner. Immediately they parted and let her through. He leaned down and she whispered in the blond man's ear. He shook his head and pointed to grandfather and crooked his finger to have him come over to him. "G'dai, mate. Yiv got a bonny little gurl there. I'll give ye..." His voice was lost in the hubbub.

Tomiko looked on curiously while her grandfather finished his business with the stranger. Then he came back to Tomiko and took her hand. "Come, little one."

Tomiko trusted her grandfather but even then she instinctively felt a jolt of fear as they again passed by the man with the platinum hair and the crowd of Japanese. She stared at him as they passed, and even from a distance she felt a loathing for him.

They approached the Japanese woman in the green kimono who was now standing away from the others. She bowed so low, Tomiko could see the top of her kimono.

"Honored Grandfather, you have a lovely daughter."

"Mama-san, she is mine and she is not mine. She is the eldest daughter of my eldest son. But, he is no more. Having defended his family and home, he went to his ancestors on Okinawa."

"And her mother?"

"Evaporated in the great explosion."

"Aaaaiiieeee, so many gone. We should not have wakened the sleeping tiger. The barbarians are strong."

"And Hiroshima is now weak and to save some, we must give up others."

"Yes, it is so honored Grandfather, but this flower will be safe. I will watch her as if she were my own. What is her name?"

"Tomiko."

"Come, Tomiko." Gently the Mama-san held out her hand and took the little girl's. "I will take care of you now."

Tomiko's heart sunk. She knew she must be obedient but she could not help herself. "Grandfather," she said plaintively, eyes brimming, "please do not leave me here."

Without a word the grandfather turned and started back towards home. His body was flushed with shame up to the roots of his hair. This dishonorable act made tears run down his cheeks and spill on to his shirt. He raged inside. Every fiber of his body wanted to fling the yen back in the foreigner's ugly, western face and take his grand-daughter back but the vision of the starving children at home stopped him. At every 'Grandfather' the little girl called, his heart constricted, his skin crawled and his eyes watered. Stoically, with measured steps, he forced himself to keep walking from this devilish place. As he walked by the crowd of people were still pushing and shoving around the platinum haired man. His barbarian laughter rang in grandfather's ears increasing the mortification. He had decided. When this family crisis was over, he would cleanse this shameful act by committing harakiri.

Tomiko stood with the Mama-san, and watched her grandfather leave. She was devastated. With every one of his steps away from her, her heart broke anew. He had not told her she was to live with strangers. There was now a hole in her soul that would never be filled. Her tears ran freely down her cheeks and she clung tightly to the geisha's dress and her sanity.

Chapter 12: The Geisha

The Mama-san had never had any children and Tomiko began to fill that natural void. In turn the geisha poured out her love and affection to this young girl that the great Buddha had sent her.

Along with the other children, Tomiko learned the art of dance, polite conversation and the tea ceremony. She was taught the pleasures of men and the art of pillowing. Unlike the other girls, she lived with the Mama-san and was nurtured and protected by her.

The Mama-san had been correct in her assessment of the little black-eyed girl's potential and Tomiko developed such beauty and grace that men would be stunned when she came in their presence. She was in great demand to the tired and jaded businessmen that frequented the geisha house.

The Westerners who ran the geisha house were interested only in profit and began to notice the attention paid to Tomiko. Over the geisha's objections of her youth, the management announced to their wealthier clients that Tomiko would now be available only for private entertainment. Soon Tomiko's reputation was such that it might be easier to see the emperor then have an evening with her.

The Mama-san continued to watch over her charge and wisely invested the considerable amounts of yen that Tomiko was paid. In the burgeoning post war Japanese economy they were soon modestly well off.

Although the Mama-san was no longer active in the dream world of the consorts, she was unfortunately left with a habit from those days. Some of the foreigners that used recreational drugs had enticed her to try some and she was trapped by an addiction to cocaine.

As the Mama-san got older the habit began to sap her health. Tomiko nursed her through her frequent illnesses and even consulted addiction specialists, but the Mama-san was too far gone.

She soon became very ill and finally the Bonze, (the priest) was sent for. After the prayers for the dying were chanted, the holy man left and the two women were alone.

It was dark and quiet and the Mama-san slept a troubled sleep. Tomiko sat by the bed applying compresses to her fevered brow, and holding her hand and remembering. Tears ran freely down her cheeks as she thought of the day in Hiroshima when this lovely lady took her as her own and raised her as she would her birth child.

The old geisha's eyes fluttered.

Tomiko tensed. "Mama-san, can I get you something?"

"Tomiko, daughter of my heart, I have trained you too well to do for others. You must now do for yourself."

Tomiko smiled. "You have trained me well mama-san. I am a mirror image of yourself."

The Mama-san's dark brown eyes hardened for a moment. "Then look well into the mirror, my daughter, lest my fate be yours. Do not let men's pleasures be your own. Especially the barbarian's drugs." She closed her eyes and was quiet. Tomiko thought she had gone back to sleep and turned to leave.

Suddenly the mama-san squeezed Tomiko's hand with surprising strength and spoke again, with fervor. "Listen to me well, daughter," she raised herself on her elbow, "the Japanese love the barbarians and together they make an unholy pair. Since they forced their way onto our shores we have copied them. We copy their ways, their weapons, their business, even their dress. It is not an improvement. When I was young and one of them came among us, the stench was awful. We ran away as fast as we could. Now our own people eat meat the same as they and many of the people of heaven now smell just as the barbarians do. It is an abomination. They and their cartels have flooded our island with drugs and other western filth." She tried to rise. "You, my daughter, must protect yourself from these people."

Tomiko tried to support her but she fell back weakly. "Rest little mother, and have no fear, you have taught me well."

The Mama-san was staring at the ceiling. "Little mother? Mama-san? Aaaaaaaaaiiiieeeee," Tomiko wailed. But it did no good, Mama-san was gone. Holding the Mama-san to her breast Tomiko began to cry from a well of pain deep within her. For the second time in her life she had lost her mother. She lay the Mama-san back on the bed and gently she reached out, and with great love, closed the Mama-san's eyes.

****

It was a month before Tomiko could perform her duties again. During that grieving time she was told over and over again how her clients missed her entertainment, but Tomiko would not be budged. She would do a vigil of mourning and would not return before it was complete.

When she was finally through grieving, she returned to her duties and it was as before except for one thing. Tomiko had always had her Mama-san to take care of the financial side of the pillowing. Of course she could always get someone to take her place for the accounting, but Tomiko could not bring herself to do that. The wound was too fresh and painful. Since she now had to carry large amounts of yen she began to be afraid. There were many ronin (thieves) about, who would gladly lift your purse and slit your throat. With this in mind, Tomiko began to carry a stiletto in her kimono, carefully placed for easy access. She later found out that most of the other geishas had a weapon on their person.

Mama-san was also the bridge between Tomiko and the Westerners. Now she would have to face them herself.

One month to the day that Mama-san had left her, she was summoned, and reported dutifully, to the office where all the business of the geishas was handled by the barbarians. Tomiko had dressed for her appointment in a beautiful white kimono that was speckled with cherry blossoms. Her hair was long, black and lustrous, and she had it coiled and fastened with a silver pin in the manner of the geishas. Her coal black eyes matched her hair and blended with the cherry red of her lips. Her white face had little expression until she smiled. Then her face lit up in girlish delight. She walked with small, graceful steps as she had been taught. Her tiny hands were expressive and could tell their own stories. When she spoke, she used them in small, delicate movements.

When Tomiko entered the office, the secretary rose to greet her and with great courtesy ushered her to a chair. The secretary was dressed in the western style of a silk shirt and a short skirt. She smiled broadly at the geisha. "My name is Reko. If there is anything I can do for you please let me know." Although the secretary was a product of modern Japan she had a great respect for the old ways that Tomiko represented.

"You are very kind, Reko-san." Tomiko bowed, her head slightly to the side in deference to the secretary's politeness.

After a short wait the secretary again presented herself to Tomiko. "Geisha-san, would you do me the honor to allow me to present you."

"Hai, domo." (Yes, thank you)

The secretary led Tomiko to a large oak door which she opened noiselessly. "Mr. Wallace, Tomiko-san is here to see you." Tomiko stepped into the room and Reko politely backed out and closed the heavy oak door.

The man behind the desk looked up and Tomiko stared at him in disbelief. It was the man with the platinum hair. He was older now and had a big paunch but it was him nonetheless. He leaned back in his chair, which squeaked loudly, and stared at the delicate geisha obscenely.

Tomiko avoided the man's eyes and looked at the papers under his pudgy hand. She could not help but notice his fingernails were yellowed and there was a large food stain on the garish, colorful sport shirt he wore. The papers on his desk were not placed in an orderly manner but strewn about the desk haphazardly. Some of them had fallen to the floor and lay near his feet. Their wrinkled and dirty condition indicated that they had been stepped on many times. Tomiko longed to leave.

Wallace stood up, his eyes fixed on Tomiko, a strange look on his face. "So yer the doxie what's by 'erself now," he said in a thick Australian accent. "We'll miss the Mama-san. She was a big 'elp with the other doxies." He got up and walked around the desk and half sat on the edge.

Tomiko's eyes narrowed. *Doxies? Is it possible this barbarian does not know the difference between a courtesan and a prostitute? Since he buys little children and then sells them, I imagine that it is possible.*

"Now that the Mama-san is gone, we'll need someone to take 'er playce." Wallace was leering at Tomiko strangely.

Tomiko's skin crawled. "What does Wallace-san have in mind?" Tomiko said trying to bring him back to the business at hand.

"Call me Pete, luv." His eyes glittered and he trembled slightly as he felt a rush through his body. "When we first got you, you were a little bitty tyke" Suddenly he reached out, grabbed Tomiko by the arm and pulled her towards him. "But, yer nay a wee one now."

She was immediately sickened and shrank away. His smell of pork and sweat was overwhelming just as it was, so long ago, when he picked her up as a child. Again it disgusted her.

He leaned forward and smiled, exposing his yellowed teeth. "Oi don't ordinarily mess with the 'elp but oi'll make an exception in yer case, dearie." He motioned with his head towards the far wall. "Let's use the couch there."

Tomiko resisted and he scowled. Suddenly, with a strong grip on her wrist, he began to pull her toward him. But she pulled back. He stopped and laughed. His barbarian laughter grated on Tomiko and she tried again to break away to leave. With a deft move he grabbed her hair, so carefully dressed that morning, and pulled her toward the couch. The silver pin came out, clattered to the floor and her raven hair spilled out over her shoulders. Wallace felt the falling silken hair on his hand and arm and it excited him.

Now feeling panic, Tomiko tried once more to break away but Wallace held her in place with his strong grip on her hair. She struggled but could not break free. Wallace laughed at her puny efforts and drew her right up to him and put his mouth on hers. The sour milk smell on his breath was overwhelming and Tomiko struggled even harder to get away. He was strong, but with her long nails scratching his face, she managed to push his face away from hers. She spat out the bad taste, her face contorting in rage and loathing.

Wallace touched his face with his free hand and felt the sticky blood. He still had his fist in her long hair and painfully pulled her back to him. When she got close again he angrily hit her a resounding blow to the face.

Tomiko was stunned. She had never been struck before. Her hand came up to the welt that was forming rapidly on her cheek. In her worst nightmare she could not imagine this barbarous behavior.

At this moment there was no smile on Wallace's face. "Now that we know oo's boss ere doxie, let's get on with it." Wallace pushed Tomiko against the wall, reached out and grabbed the top of her kimono then tore it open to expose her. Pinning her small body against the wall with his bulk he circled his arms around her and kissed her so forcefully it bruised her mouth. Wallace leaned back and looked at Tomiko's bruised face, unkempt hair and exposed breast and became even more aroused. Pain and violence always excited him.

Still holding her hair he threw her down on the couch, clumsily lifted her kimono and prepared to rape her. With a quick movement he exposed himself and began to laugh as he fell on her. His laugh was cut short as his beer belly met her stiletto.

As she had practiced a thousand times, Tomiko had deftly drew her knife out of her kimono and thrust it into his abdomen as he came down on her.

"I will do your seppuku for you, you damned barbarian." she hissed.

There was a look of shock on Wallace's face as he half lifted himself off Tomiko. Still partially leaning over her, he looked down at the knife and his abdomen, now turning crimson.

"You fuckin' slut, you've killed me." Wallace stayed in the same position, still trying to comprehend what had happened. Tomiko tried to push him off but his weight held her in place.

Suddenly he reached for her throat and began to strangle her. "You bitch, oi'll take you right to 'ell with me."

Tomiko tried to breathe but she could not. She felt the blood pounding against her temples and the room started to turn black. She felt like she were sinking down a long shaft. Suddenly she stopped fighting and let go. *Just relax Tomiko, it won't take long and then you will be free to join Father and Mother and the Mama-san.*

But the wound was too deep and Wallace began to weaken. As the heart pumped the blood out of his aorta, his strength waned. His hands slipped off her throat and she noisily sucked air in as she gasped for breath. With what energy he had left, he rolled off her and fell to his knees. Breathing in short gasps, he stared at his killer malevolently, hate clouding his face.

Tomiko looked on his wicked face with loathing and contempt. Like a fakir in an Indian market staring at a cobra, she was hypnotized and could not move. She was now sitting on the couch, staring back at him, her hair in disarray, and her white kimono stained red with his blood.

A dark cloud came over Wallace's face and with a shriek of pain and renewed energy he pushed Tomiko back, reached down and pulled the blade out of his abdomen. With a great effort he lifted it over his head and with both hands clutching it, howled a demonic cry and brought the knife down in a deadly arc towards Tomiko's chest.

For a split second she tried to get away but the couch blocked her one way and his massive body the other.

Just as suddenly, she stopped and prepared to accept her karma.

As the stiletto reached halfway to her, Wallace's strength failed him again and he dropped the knife. The blade sped toward Tomiko's face and only a deft move saved her from a massive disfigurement, allowing only a cut on her cheek.

The barbarian swayed back and forth, like a towering tree, staring at Tomiko, his eyes full of hate.

Just then the office door timidly began to open...

Suddenly Wallace's eyes rolled back in his head, and he gurgled and rattled from deep in his chest, and fell heavily on Tomiko's lap, dead.

Mustering all her strength, Tomiko pushed the corpse away from her as the door opened.

"What was that noise?"... Reko threw the door open wide and stood shocked in the doorway just as Wallace hit the floor with a thud. In an instant Reko understood. Quickly, her mind raced and calculated the situation. *Wallace is influential. His government would demand jail time. Can you imagine this little fragile flower in one of our jails? She couldn't even get through this interview. She has to get away from here. I'll cover for her somehow.*

Reko ran to the bathroom and grabbed a towel to staunch the blood on Tomiko's face. When she patted the wound she noticed the geisha was looking down at Wallace. Her eyes were dry and cold, but there was a mask of hate and loathing on her face.

****

The geisha lives in the Willow World. She is taught for many years under the strict schooling of the head geisha who no longer practices that art. She is trained in all the social graces from the simple tea ceremony to the of ways of story-telling. She is trained to entertain men and make them forget their workaday cares. Her every movement speaks volumes. She walks and talks with small, endearing movements and her hair is fixed, curled high upon her head in the manner of the geisha. Her make-up is immaculate, and her features are delicately exquisite. To those geishas who wish to Indulge, they excel in the art of pillowing. To leave this ancient art, except for marriage, is to be disgraced. For those geishas who are samurai, there is no other path, save shame or death.

****

Reko stood by the gate waiting for Tomiko to finish buying her ticket just as she had taught her. She looked her over with satisfaction. In a short time Reko had transformed the geisha to look like a modern Japanese woman.

Reko was anxious to get Tomiko away. The police may still have questions and she was exhausted after all she had done. After cleaning Tomiko up, she had rushed her to Tomiko's apartment in her own car, to avoid leaving a trail the police could later follow. She admonished the geisha to bolt herself in and not to answer the phone or the door. She was to open it only to the secret tap she demonstrated. She then left Tomiko and went back to the office, cleaned up Tomiko's blood, and wiped the handle of the knife clean. She then took the geisha's name off the appointment book. *No good,* she thought, *they would surely spot the erasure.* Reko substituted a new appointment book, carefully copying the old one. It took precious time but her plan must be flawless. She carefully tore each page out of the old appointment book and then shredded them by hand. When the pieces were small enough she flushed them down the toilet. The cover of the book was then deposited in the garden under six inches of soil. She would dig it up and dispose of it later.

While she was cleaning and straightening up Wallace's office, Reko studiously avoided the body which seemed to stare at her no matter where she was in the room.

Finally she stopped and addressed the dead man. "Don't accuse me with your eyes, you barbarian," she said in a low voice. "You could have had a million women, starting with one of your own prostitutes and you had to go and pick one of the ancients. Her bloodlines go back to the first samurai. She would defend her honor with her life, or, as it turns out, with yours!"

After disposing of the towel she had cleaned with, Reko straightened her dress, combed her hair, carefully looked around the office and then called the police.

After a long wait a detective and a uniformed policeman came. The detective asked Reko to stay in her office while they investigated Wallace's room. She was told, 'Under no circumstances was she to let anyone in or out of the building. And she was not to leave the building herself.'

A half hour later the detective called her back into Wallace's office. Everything was the same except they had covered Wallace's upper body with his jacket and the detective was holding the stiletto wrapped in plastic to preserve any fingerprints.

The detective questioned her and she told him she had been sent by Wallace to get him sushi for lunch, which she had actually bought on her way back after dropping Tomiko at her apartment. Tears welled up in her eyes as she tried to continue and the detective asked her to please sit down and compose herself. He apologized for making her continue but the quicker they found out what had happened, the better chance they had to catch the murderer. Reko nodded her understanding, dabbed her eyes and continued....

"When I walked back in the office to deliver his lunch, I found the horrible sight which you now see before you." No, she didn't know who had been there. No, there was no one on the appointment book for that hour. "Would you like to see the book?"

He said yes and she went to her desk and got it. He took it politely, for evidence and asked her if the man was alive when she left the office. "Yes," she said, "he was alive when I left."

The detective gave Reko his card and told her to call him if she remembered anything that might help them, and told her she could leave. Reko walked out, closed the door behind her, leaned on it, breathed a quiet sigh of relief and wiped her brow. She quickly went to her desk, got her purse and hurried out the building to her car.

The detective put his pen and notebook up. He looked at the uniformed policeman and grimaced. "Not much to go on, Yoshi."

"No, Sir."

He stared out the window thoughtfully. "That secretary knows more than she said." He nodded his head and compressed his lips. "...But nobody will miss this ronin. I guess someone really did us a favor. The world's a lot cleaner place without him."

"Yes, Sir."

"You think it was another gang, Yoshi?"

The policeman nodded. "Probably, Sir."

"I'll just bet one of the local boys just couldn't stand these Caucasians cashing in on our girls and wanted to take the streets back. Well, if it happens a few more times, we'll know. Don't let anyone touch anything Yoshi, the scientific boys will be here in a few minutes and then you can wrap it up. I have to go in now and write my report." As the detective left he already knew what the last six words of the report would be, 'Death by assailant or assailants, unknown.'

****

Reko tapped the code on the apartment door. After a few moments she heard a gentle voice from within. "Who is it please?"

"It's me, Reko."

Reko heard the bolt unlatch and the door opened noiselessly. Tomiko bowed her head in greeting and stepped back. She had bathed and was dressed in a borrowed gown. Reko noted with surprise that her hair was done up again, wound tightly and held by the silver pin.

Tomiko sat erect on the couch while Reko paced and explained the plan she had thought out while she was driving to the apartment. She would cut Tomiko's hair, dress her in Western clothes and send her to Reko's sister who lived in Macao. As Reko spoke, Tomiko just nodded, bewildered by the pace of events. "Do you have any money?"

"Hai." (Yes) "My mistress spent most of the money on the barbarian's habit but there is some left over. If I am careful I could get by for a year or two."

"Good. Now, let's get you out of here. The further you are from this place the safer you will be."

Tomiko was so used to others making her decisions she never gave a thought to question Reko. She dutifully prepared to follow the plan.

****

Reluctantly, Tomiko sat at the dressing table with her hands in her hair. Slowly and reluctantly she pulled out the long, silver pin that held her geisha coiffure in place. Tears formed in the corners of her eyes as her hair fell to her shoulders. Reko began to comb Tomiko's long tresses until they shown. Then she began to cut. Tomiko's hair fell in clumps around her feet as Reko cut and combed. It was a geisha's pride and she was being shorn of it, like a sheep. In the mirror Tomiko noticed, with compassion, that Reko had tears in her eyes also.

After the haircut, Reko re-did Tomiko's make-up and cut and painted her nails. She trimmed the bangs just above Tomiko's eyes and with that, she was done.

Reko felt terrible when she looked at the bandage on Tomiko's cheek and the scar she knew was forming underneath. But, if they went to a hospital, embarrassing questions might have to be answered. Reluctantly, Reko decided not to take her there.

Tomiko looked in the mirror in wonder. A strange and different person looked back at her. The dress she had been given was just a trifle large and hung loosely at the waist. A simple belt fixed that quickly. Then a pair of shoes and a bag and the transformation was complete.

****

Tomiko walked back to Reko with the plane ticket in one hand and a small suitcase in the other. She had a slight smile on her face.

She is so innocent, Reko thought.

"Tomiko, let us go over the plan one more time. You will fly to Hong Kong, take a bus to the town and then a rickshaw to Kowloon. Tell the rickshaw driver to take you to the Peninsula Hotel on Salisbury Road. There you will be met by my sister. She will wear a white carnation in her lapel and she looks a little like me. Do you understand?

"Hai, Reko-san, (I understand)"

Reko hugged the guileless, delicate geisha, now turned modern, and both women were crying when

Tomiko climbed down the steps to the tarmac. Soon the slight Geisha was climbing the metal ladder of the TWA DC 6 taking her to Hong Kong.

Chapter 13: Kowloon

Tomiko looked out the airplane window. The blanket of clouds stretched as far as the eye could see. *Surely the gods were amazing,* Tomiko thought. *Only they could make this specter world on top of the world I already know. Astonishing that men could build this winged box and soar it above the clouds. I shall make a haiku out of this experience.*

> The world is made of billowing sea and sky.
> I am part of and from the world...

"Excuse me." Tomiko's reverie was interrupted by the stewardess. "Would you like some sake?"

Tomiko shook her head no. She smiled sweetly at the stewardess. "This place I am going to, Kowloon, do you know it?"

The stewardess sat down in the empty seat next to Tomiko and tried to remember exactly what her training manual had said about Kowloon. "Yes, I have been there many times." The stewardess put her hands in her lap and concentrated on her knowledge of Kowloon. "It is said that Kowloon came into being when the last emperor of the Sung

Dynasty, while fleeing the Mongol hordes, went to the sea to escape. Waiting for his boat to come, he looked up at the mountains surrounding him. 'Lord Minister," he said to his trusted aide there are eight mountain peaks on this peninsula around us. They are like dragons waiting to pounce on us poor unfortunates.

Still trying to curry favor, the minister replied, 'No, My Lord, there are nine. You forgot to count yourself.'

The Emperor laughed, 'Some mountain I am. I am more like a mouse running for his life. In any event, to celebrate our rapid departure, and since these mountains are like the dragons in stories my mother read to me, this place shall ever more be known as Kau Loong (Nine dragons)'

'Kau Loong, yes... Yes, My Lord that is good.'

"So, eventually Kau Loong became Kowloon."

Tomiko tipped her head. "That is a lovely story. Thank you very much."

The stewardess smiled, got up and went back to her station. Tomiko turned her mind back to her Haiku, but before she could finish another line, a disembodied voice came on the loudspeaker. "Please prepare yourself for landing in Hong Kong."

The rest of the day was a blur for Tomiko. She collected her luggage and took a bus to town as she had been told to do. Then she hired a rickshaw and started towards the peninsula of Kowloon. Everything was new to her in Hong Kong and she looked about in wonder and awe. The streets were full of people bustling about, going in a hundred directions. Vendors lined the roads yelling for people to buy their wares in a hundred different dialects. All around her were tall buildings that were like stone pillars reaching for the sky. Hiroshima was like a small village compared to this. Tomiko felt very small indeed.

After a time of dodging people and slow moving cars the rickshaw was finally at the hotel. Tomiko paid her fare and stepped into the lobby behind the bellhop carrying her bags. It was a place of high ceiling splendor that made Tomiko feel even smaller. She was a lonely figure surrounded by people and space.

After a few minutes of anxiety and confusion, a young woman approached her. She looked very much like the secretary, Reko.

"Tomiko?"

Tomiko felt a rush of relief as she saw the white carnation. She bowed low in greeting. "Hai, (Yes) I am Tomiko."

The young woman looked around furtively then laughing, took both of Tomiko's hands in hers and nodded her head. "I am Reko's sister, Kamika. Welcome to Kowloon."

****

In the next few months Tomiko's life changed radically. Kamika had discussed the situation with her sister and they had decided that the best thing for Tomiko's survival was to complete her make-over into a western woman. Fortunately Kamika's husband was an American banker who believed in the complete separation of men and women's roles, and left the two ladies to their own devices. He did however admire Tomiko's grace and delicacy, and when his wife told him of their plan, he secretly hated to see her changed.

The second day in Macao was a shopping day. At first the crowded streets and shops bewildered Tomiko but after a while she caught the rhythm of the place and actually began to enjoy it. The new clothes she tried on were strange and revealing but she trusted Kamika and relied on her judgment.

The next few days went by quickly as Tomiko was instructed in the ways of the modern world. Kamika was constantly amazed at how sheltered the geisha had been. But Tomiko learned fast and after each talk, the two women actually did the things they had talked about. Soon Tomiko mastered the art of the market place and the maze of the shops. She began to venture out by herself and began to look forward to each adventure.

Kamika had her own life and gradually went back to it. Every afternoon she left her charge and went to her passion, the tennis courts. She and the tennis pro, Joe Wilson, worked on her game every day. Slowly but surely she had gained in ability and had finally reached the top of the woman's ladder. Her husband also played on the weekend and since he also played a pretty good game they were a top team in the 'divorce doubles' group.

Kamika's husband was John Paul Rives. He was an American who was sent by his bank, that was headquartered in Sacramento, California, to cash in on Japan's new post war prosperity. He was an athletic man who liked getting up early and working out. After that he would go to the bank and try to fathom a new-fangled gadget called the computer.

He had met Kamika at the bank in Kowloon where he was an officer and she a teller. He fell hard for her and was very nervous as he asked for a first date. He was relieved as she laughingly said yes in her broken English. Their romance blossomed and over the objections of his parents, and hers, they were married the next spring. Despite the dire predictions, they were very happy together.

Now, as he finished the last report for the bank examiner, he muttered to himself, "Someday these Japanese will be in deep shit over their finances. In the States, we couldn't get away with a tenth of what they pull over here." He heard the door open. Kamika stood in the doorway with her racket in her hand. As usual she looked ravishing. "Hi, babe."

Kamika smiled sweetly at him and went to him. He wrapped his arms around her and squeezed tight. Suddenly he said, "Ouch!"

She backed away quickly, concern on her face. With a wry grin and two fingers, he delicately lifted the lifted the handle of her racket that she had left between them, pressing on his chest. They both laughed.

John handed her the racket and his face turned thoughtful.

She half smiled. "What, John?"

He started to speak and then thought better of it and stopped.

Kamika pressed him. "What is it John, say it?"

"Why don't you take Tomiko to the courts with you? I bet, with her balance and grace, she would pick up the game in no time."

"I don't know, John. She doesn't look like she has enough strength to pick up the racket, much less hit the ball."

"Look who's talking! You're a hundred pounds, soaking wet, and you hit the ball a ton."

Kamika punched John in the upper arm, playfully. "You nasty man, I don't weigh an ounce more than ninety five."

"Right," John said sarcastically, grabbing her by her waist and swinging her around. They both fell on the couch, laughing.

Tomiko appeared at the door. "Oh, excuse me, I thought someone was injured." She had heard the noise and quickly went to the living room where the couple was playing. She was still not used to men and women being so informal with each other.

She turned to leave and Kamika struggled to sit up. "No, please stay, Tomiko. We were just talking about you." Kamika blushed slightly while she straightened her skirt and blouse. "John thought you might like to learn how to play tennis. The pro could give you the basics and I would be glad to practice with you. It probably would integrate you into this society much more quickly."

Tomiko nodded and smiled fleetingly, not really comprehending completely what Kamika was saying.

John sat up. "It's settled then. Now, you lazy thing, let's get your man some lunch." With that John pushed Kamika up and spanked her behind, lightly. She laughed, holding her bottom and growled, "Barbarian," and walked happily towards the kitchen. John watched her admiringly.

Tomiko looked on wide eyed in amazement. She wondered if she would ever get used to the ways of these people.

****

When she first got on the court Tomiko was all thumbs. She had trouble even bouncing the ball on the racket. Kamika hid her head in her hands when she observed the first lesson and quickly left, not able to watch. When John saw her on the first weekend he said to his wife, "Maybe this was not such a good idea."

But the pro, Joe Carter, was undaunted. For his own reasons, he took an intense interest in the slight, timid Japanese girl. He saw the grace underneath her awkwardness and stayed right with her on every stroke. Finally she could hit the ball back on the forehand and within a week, the backhand. In a few months the two Japanese women were hitting the ball to each other steadily, with Joe looking on with satisfaction.

The serve and the volley were more difficult but with hard work and determination Tomiko conquered both strokes and amazed the others in the club with the pace and power her small body generated. Although Tomiko had the ability and determination, the tennis pro was the reason for her success. He was tenacious in his desire to see her achieve.

Joe Carter leaned against the fence waiting for the two women to join him. He really looked forward to teaching Tomiko. He laughed as he watched her walk toward him. She didn't actually walk, he thought, she minced her way forward. It was endearing. In fact he found everything about her endearing.

When he first got her on the court he found she was a pleasure to teach. If Tomiko was anything she was obedient. She hung on every word and copied his every move. It was uncanny. Before long he was watching a miniature of himself hitting the ball, with one improvement. Tomiko had exquisite timing. Joe knew he couldn't teach that. It was there or it wasn't. When Tomiko swung through the ball, she met it at the exact point, that would give it its maximum pace. Before long she was hitting in steady rally's with him. One more thing developed. Joe was no match for her beauty and skill and fell madly in love with her.

Joe Carter was an American and the son of John Rives' boss. He was twenty four years old and was playing number two on the tennis team at UCLA when he ran into a small problem. His girlfriend got pregnant, and his mother freaked out. When the girl miscarried, everyone breathed a sigh of relief.

Everyone except Joe's mother. She angrily put in a call to Joe's father in Macao and soon Joe was winging his way towards the Orient and a new job at the tennis club.

John Rives knew Joe came from a good family and Kamika thought it would be good for Tomiko so they encouraged her to go out with him. Soon they were inseparable. Joe could not get enough of her beauty and grace and Tomiko felt utterly safe with his animal strength and the love that Joe exuded. Joe was already a vegetarian so even if he were a barbarian, at least he didn't smell bad. Besides, with all the other Westerners around her, she was almost getting used to it. His father liked her immediately and thought she would exert a settling effect on the young rascal.

When they weren't on the courts they were motor scooting through the countryside or shopping and bargaining in the Indian and Chinese shops along the waterfront. Sometimes they would walk in the rain, oblivious of their wet clothes and the thunder and lightning around them. When Joe finally made love to her, it was like nothing he had ever known. She was so beautiful and gentle, and her touch became a totally new experience for him.

She too experienced something new. In all the entertaining she had done she had never given her heart as she did now. Finally they moved in together and a month later Joe realized he was totally and completely in love with her. He proposed to Tomiko and pledged his life and love to her. After consultation with Kamika and John, and the spirit of her mama-san, she accepted. In three months they were married.

Tomiko continued her friendship with Kamika but now she worked on her game in earnest. She and Joe were on the court every day practicing her strokes and now he improved her serve and her speed and she quickly rose near the top of the ladder.

When Tomiko finally played her closest friend for the number two spot on the ladder, she lost. After the match was over, Joe met Tomiko as she was leaving the dressing room. She had never seen him angry before.

"You tanked that, didn't you?"

"Sorry, Joe, not understand."

"I know you lost the match to her on purpose, Tomiko, but you really didn't do her a favor."

Tomiko looked bewildered. "But Joe, she is my friend."

"Tomiko, there are no friends on the court. To do right by your opponent you have to play your best. That way, they know just how well they played, and how good they really are. It has nothing to do with friendship."

Tomiko looked down, trying to understand.

"He's right, Tomiko, I can't accept that gift." Kamika had just come out of the dressing room and overheard the last of the conversation. "The only way for us to play is for both of us to give it our best. Then we know who really won."

Tomiko nodded, said, hai, (yes) and hugged her friend.

The next time they played Tomiko did not hold back and beat her friend two and four. The next month she played for the club championship and won it just as easily. People in the club shook their heads in wonder. Kamika worried a little about her small notoriety, but when the police didn't come, she relaxed.

Joe and Tomiko settled into a very comfortable lifestyle. They bought a lovely house on the water and were hosts to lively parties and dinners. To Tomiko, the art of party giving was natural and she was an excellent hostess. Joe's naturalness made him a favorite with the people from the club and together they were very popular. Joe and Tomiko prospered.

****

Summer turned to fall and the tennis club went indoors for better lighting, and now Joe worked long hours. There were only four courts, three of which the club players used and the one Joe taught on. He still worked with Tomiko daily but now he also used her for demonstration with the younger students. He also had her compete with the up and coming boys and girls who showed promise.

Tomiko had never been happier. She realized how dependent she had been in her former life, first with the Mama-san and then with her new friends, Reko and Kamika. She had now reached a stage of independence she never dreamed of in her former life. Joe had seen through her subservience and worked on her self-confidence until he knew she could survive nicely by herself.

****

The tragedy began innocently enough when a boy brought a telegram from Joe's sister who lived in California. Tomiko did not get alarmed since she wrote regularly to her brother.

When Joe came home she gave him the message. After he read the telegram, he was shaken and pale.

"It's Mother, Tomiko. She is very ill and my sister wants me home, just in case she doesn't make it. Besides I haven't been to the states in three years and they all want to see what you look like. Including Mother."

"Joe, my place is beside you. Of course I will come."

Joe took Tomiko in his arms, his large Western body, dwarfing her slight frame. "My dearest Tomiko, I want you with me always, but your friend needs you more than I do just now."

Joe was referring to Kamika's present problem. She was pregnant and now she was in trouble. She had told Tomiko and Joe two days ago that her last visit to the doctor revealed a toxemia and that both she and the baby were in danger. The last blood test revealed that her platelet count was dropping fast and that she was in need of a platelet donor with the proper blood type. Tomiko had the type she needed.

John knew an American Army doctor who was with him on Guadalcanal and now was stationed in Tokyo. John contacted him and asked his advice. To John's relief he volunteered to perform a procedure called plasmapheresis where a donor's whole blood was extracted, and her platelets removed. The removed platelets would then be given to Kamika. To John's second delight Tomiko had the right blood type, and also volunteered to help.

It was an uncomfortable process that took at least two hours and it had to be done several times. Joe and Tomiko both decided she should stay to help her friend.

On the day of departure, the couple went sadly to the airport. Tomiko had not been separated from Joe since she met him. Now she faced the prospect of him being gone for weeks. Uneasily, she watched him climb the stairs of the plane. At the top he turned and looked for her. She stood on the wet tarmac and waved gracefully to him. He grinned his boyish smile, waved back and then disappeared into the bowel of the metal bird.

When he was gone, Tomiko turned and walked back towards the parking lot. The misty drizzle wet her face and hid the tears that rolled down her cheeks. When she got to their car she turned back to look at the mighty bird once more. By now it was moving slowly, making its way toward the runway, undulating in an ungainly fashion. Tomiko shuddered, unable to shake the foreboding that gripped her.

****

The Buddhist monks looked oddly out of place in the gray December morning. Their bright orange robes won the battle of color against the gray mist that surrounded them. Their shaved heads bobbed as they chanted the prayers for the dead. Tomiko followed behind dressed in a pure white kimono with a blood red obi. She walked, as if in a dream, behind the two monks, her practiced walk returning to the mincing, pigeon toed step of the geisha. Slung across her back was her lute.

Walking just behind Tomiko, her belly swollen with child, was Kamika. Tears ran freely down her face and she sobbed frequently. John held her hand and walked stolidly beside her, his face grave and drawn. At the rear of the small procession was a minister, his white collar framing a red face.

The small procession entered the cemetery and walked toward the open crypt. A quiet, somber crowd of friends and tennis players awaited them.

The priests stopped and stood before the opening and blessed the crypt. One of them sprinkled water with strands of Kasha grass in it, over the entrance. The other struck a small bell and chanted "Ohm Yamantaka Samaya." When he stopped, he began to speak of Joe's soul being purified of the six stains and finding peace in the Bar-do. While he spoke the other priest, chanted "Ohm," and cast sesame seeds into a fire pot. Puffs of smoke rose as the seeds hit the flame and then blended into the mist above them.

When they were finished the minister stepped forward. In a ringing voice he began. "The Lord is my shepherd..."

When he was finished Tomiko stepped forward and lovingly placed the small effigy of Joe, she was carrying, into the crypt. John placed the urn of ashes next to the effigy. Tomiko stood still for a moment then stepped back, placed the lute on her knee and struck a note. Then in a high pitched nasal voice she sang her geisha song of lament. Her song painted a Japanese haiku of home and family, the joy of love and the pain of death. Most of all, the anguish of loss. When the last note reverberated in the cool mist, only the coldest of heart had not shed a tear.

Showing no emotion, her face chalky white, Tomiko placed a picture of Joe, she had in her hand on a shelf in the crypt between the effigy and his ashes and stepped back. John closed the door of the crypt and walked back to a somber Kamika.

Tomiko stared at the entrance, her heart locked inside the vault.

****

Two days before, the stillness of the night had been shattered by the ringing of the phone. For some reason Tomiko was uneasy as she lifted the receiver. She almost reverted to the Japanese moshi, moshi, but remembered and said, "Hello."

The words still rang in her ears. "Mrs. Carter?" The voice was strained, the accent, British.

"Yes."

"This is Asian Airlines. We regret to inform you that your husband was in an accident. The plane he was on went down in China. We are having difficulty with the government there, but we are doing everything we can to..."

Tomiko did not wait to hear the end of the conversation. Her hand, moving very slowly put the phone down as if it had a mind of its own. For a long while she just stared into space. *Why am I surprised, she thought,* it is my karma to be separated *and alone.* But, it was too late. She had let Joe come past her protective layer and into her heart. She lay on the bed and cried until she had no more tears and then she cried some more. When she finally stopped, the night had turned into day.

****

Kamika held on to the edge of the couch and let herself down slowly and awkwardly as only a large, pregnant lady could do. When she was finally seated she wiggled and smiled. "These barbarians don't know how to make small babies. Tomiko if you're going to have a baby you better find a Japanese man."

Tomiko smiled. "Honto, (It's the truth) you are big."

Kamika patted her belly and smiled again. "Ah, here is the tea."

Reko placed the tray down and sat down beside her sister. She looked fondly at Tomiko. "You're the one who's trained to serve, why am I doing the honors?"

"Ah, my dearest friends, such a long absence from civilization has dulled my abilities. It is a horrible thing to see, but I now pour like an American housewife."

"Buddha forbid it," Reko blurted out, and all three of them burst out laughing.

Tomiko poured and sat quietly as the two sisters caught up on the news since they had last met. Finally Reko turned to Tomiko. "Well, Kamika tells me you have almost become an American. You speak the language well and you now play tennis as if you were born to it. That is good." There was an awkward silence. Reko cleared her throat and spoke again. "What will you do now? Will you stay here or come back to Hiroshima?"

Tomiko spoke slowly and deliberately. "It has been four months since Joe's accident." She paused as if to collect her thoughts. "I have heard from his lawyers. There will be some insurance money." Tomiko hesitated. "There is something else." The other two women noticed a change in Tomiko's voice and both of them leaned forward in anticipation. "Joe was a major partner in a hostel in Switzerland and he left his shares to me. I have spoken to his father and his sister and they both want me to have their shares. His poor mother had passed away while Joe..." Tomiko stopped her eyes glistened. "Excuse me," she said in a soft voice and then continued. "While Joe was still in the air, and she had the remaining shares in the hostel. The attorneys have assured me that her shares were left to him and that they will eventually come to me." The two sisters looked at each other, in amazement, and then at Tomiko.

"A hostel," Kamika blurted, "that's wonderful!" Will you go to see it?"

Reko was more thoughtful. "Tomiko, if you go to live in Switzerland, extradition would be most unlikely. You can probably forget that business back in Hiroshima, forever."

"Yes, forever." Tomiko looked wistfully into space and tears filled her eyes. "Forever is such a long time... without Joe."

Chapter 14: Italy (1945)

Eric lifted his head just enough to peek over the embankment. His blackened face was made even darker by the black beret he wore. He stared at the German guard, walking along the train tracks, hate filling his heart. The German stopped, lifted his rifle and scratched under his arm. He stifled a yawn, held the rifle at arm's length, and stretched.

Nazi bastard, Eric thought, *he's oblivious to us. Well he won't be for long.*

The German soldier peered into the dark around him and finding nothing unusual began to walk his post again.

Eric slid back down the embankment away from the tracks. He crawled for a few yards then got up in a half-crouch and began to run. He quickly made his way back, in the dark, to a group of shadowy figures that impatiently waited for him.

"What is the situation?"

"There is only one guard, Number One. He should not be difficult to deal with. I believe we should go ahead."

Number One nodded and looked at the others. All of them nodded their heads in agreement, except one.

That man shook his head in the negative. "I say we do nothing. The Germans will go into a frenzy and there will be reprisals. You remember the last time?" He turned his head and looked pointedly at another blackened face. "What about you, Beppe, you lost your father last time. And you, Antonio, the Germans shot your two brothers and a cousin." He turned back to Number One. "And, most important, the allies told us by shortwave not to upset the Germans because they needed us for the Invasion and didn't want us getting killed for the small stuff. I say we do nothing."

Eric colored red beneath his charcoal colored face. "It is true there is a certain risk for us and our families but I have lived with these butchers for years and if we do nothing they will get stronger every day. For every one of them we get we will save a thousand later. If we lose a hundred in the process then we must look at the numbers and be glad. As for help in the invasion, there will be more and more of us as the time grows near. I say we blow up the train and take as many of the Huns to Hell as possible."

Number One looked around the circle. All were nodding in grave assent.

Number One compressed his lips and pulled his mouth corners down. "It is agreed then. Andiamo! (Let's go!)

The moon peeked from behind the clouds and for a moment Eric could see his fellow partisans clearly. Their blackened faces showed no emotion for the clandestine work they were about to do. They were all dressed differently so they could melt back into the city and countryside from whence they came, without notice.

Number One turned to Eric. "Since you already have an acquaintance with the guard in question, would you do the honor of dispatching him to Valhalla?"

"I'll need a distraction."

"Paolo, go with him." A young blond haired boy nodded his head in assent. "Check your watches." All the men looked at their luminous dial watches that had been dropped by the British. "Twelve fourteen... check!" All of them set their watches to the exact time together. "The train gets here at exactly twelve fifty-five." All heads nodded in agreement. He turned to Eric. "After the explosion, we will form a perimeter against the Germans until you get out." He looked back at the others. "Then we all leave and go back to our homes and stay there. Do not tell your wives or families anything. The less they know the better." He looked around the circle, locking eyes briefly with each man. "Understood?" They nodded back in agreement. He tapped Eric on the shoulder. "Go, and God be with you."

"Yes. Come on, Paolo." Eric crouched again and began to move quickly back towards the tracks. Paolo followed like a shadow, behind him. When he got there, Eric silently scrambled half way back up the embankment and stopped. Paolo was right beside him.

Paolo put his mouth next to Eric's ear. "Must be something big, eh, Eric? I mean Number One asking us to blow up this particular train."

"Yes, something big, very big, very important. But first we must get this guard and put him out of commission." Eric realized the boy was nervous, but so was he and there was no time to waste. He started to wipe the black from his face while the boy watched, his face wrinkled in curiosity. When he was done Eric got up on one knee.

"Listen, Paolo, these Nazi bastards are efficient but they are also greedy and punctual." He looked at the luminous watch. "In a few minutes the guard will call in as an officer passes by. Then we will have thirty minutes until the next call in. First we have to approach him, get him off guard, and then dispatch him to Valhalla. After that, we have to plant the explosives. If we time it right there will be a big commotion when the guard doesn't answer for the next call. The train is due in thirty-five minutes so we have just five minutes to avoid them and then, poof! By then they should then be too busy to bother about us." Paolo nodded his head in agreement.

Eric started crawling towards the top of the embankment then stopped and looked back. Paolo quickly came alongside him. Putting his mouth near the youngster's ear he whispered, "I will go over the embankment and walk along the tracks towards him. He will make me halt and I will make some conversation with him. When I light my cigarette, make a diversion of some kind. When he turns to investigate... You just leave the rest to me. After I am done you come down quickly with the explosives and we will plant a surprise for Herr Hitler's Henchmen." He looked at Paolo intensely searching his eyes for any sign of cowardice. He thought he found none.

Paolo smiled and patted the pouch with the British explosives. In his heart, he prayed he would do his part without fail.

Eric pointed to a place on the embankment. "That's where you go." He gave the boy a fleeting smile and a thumbs up, then quickly went up over the top and slid down into the night. Paolo looked after him trying to see his form in the darkness.

Suddenly he was very lonely. Paolo began to get nervous and hear noises. A bead of sweat appeared on his forehead. He looked around in the dark, but other than a slight rustling of leaves he was alone.

Paolo fought down the panic and crawled up the rest of the embankment to his position. Slowly he raised his head until he could see the guard. The German was slowly walking his post. The guard was so close Paolo could hear him humming a German folk tune. By a dim light on the small building next to the tracks he could see the rail lines going north and south. They seemed to stretch to infinity.

The guard turned and started walking back towards him. Instinctively, Paolo lowered his head and hugged the ground. He lay there for a few moments his heart pounding. Finally, he lifted his head again. The German had not seen him and was still coming towards him at a leisurely pace. Paolo's heart slowed and the pounding in his ears stopped.

He took the German's measure. He was about six feet tall and as blonde as Paolo was. His uniform fit very snugly with both his wrists and ankles showing. *He's still probably a growing boy,* Paolo thought. He knew Eric was going to kill him and the thought of it made his stomach flip. He lay his head down and anguish filled his heart. A tear formed in the corner of his eye. In his mind he could hear Eric say, *"It's him or us, Paolo."*

Suddenly the guard whirled about, crouched and raised his rifle. "Halt!" he barked.

Paolo's head snapped downward.

"Who goes there? "

"Nicht schiessen, Kamerade, (Don't shoot, friend) I'm just going to work." Paolo began to breathe again. It was Eric.

The German cast a suspicious eye at Eric. "This area is forbidden to civilians, let me see your papers."

Eric searched his pockets. He absently pulled out a pack of cigarettes and held the pack towards the German. "Englisher cigaretten. (English cigarettes) They are called Players. Would you like one?"

The German's eyes got wide. Ach, mein Gott, (Oh my God) Players! Where did you get those?" The German boy reached out and snatched the cigarette, but his eyes were still suspicious. For a moment he took his eyes off Eric and looked lovingly at the cigarette. "They give us horse shit to smoke." He put the cigarette to his nose and lovingly smelled it. Then he looked pointedly at Eric. "Don't forget the papers."

"All right, all right, I've got them right here." He patted his coat pocket. "Want a light?"

The German pointed the rifle barrel at Eric's middle, his finger on the trigger. "Yes, but I also want the papers... now!"

"Ja." Eric lit the match. The flare of the match lit up Eric's face clearly. He puffed and suddenly the match went out and it was dark again. He saw the German stiffen. "Sorry." He lit another match for the German. He was playing a life and death game for more time. *Where was Paolo. Come on boy, do it.* Eric took a puff and glanced up at the embankment. *I can't keep this up much longer, Paolo. Come on boy, do it. Do something and do it now or I'm done for.*

Paolo lay on the embankment paralyzed with fear. He thought he would be alright, but they were actually going to kill that young boy. When he helped with the mass he had heard so many times, *'Thou shalt not kill.' Was this different? Did God now give him a dispensation because this soldier was a German? Does a different God let him speak, sing a song, move his feet?*

Paolo's heart constricted and his body shook. Every fiber of his being wished to run. He longed to be in his mother's arms away from any thought of killing. She did not want him to join the partisans but he told her he was a man and he must do his part. He wished he had listened to her. It was not to late he would go to her now.

He looked at his hands. They were shaking violently. He put them down on the ground to stop the trembling. Paolo dropped his head and he flushed and felt the heat of shame on his face. *Coward!* he thought, *I am nothing but a coward.*

Shaking like a leaf in a summer storm, Paolo got to his feet. Tears streamed down his face. "I must go home," he muttered. He turned to leave and started to slide down the embankment away from Eric.

The German was getting nervous and his hands began to shake. He threw the just lit cigarette down and poked the barrel into Eric's stomach. "Get your hands up, now! I will call my captain." The German put his whistle in his mouth.

Eric was sweating profusely but tried to keep up the bravado. *This boy is too smart,* he thought. Eric was trying to think of something, anything, to get an advantage.

The game is over unless Paolo does something. And now! Come on boy, do something, do it now.

Eric said a silent prayer, but was answered with silence. It was now or never. He would have to go for his knife but he knew the German would be faster.

The German pulled his bolt back and the cartridge slipping into the chamber made an ominous sound. The rifle muzzle came up toward Eric's head. "Hands up or I shoot your head off, now!"

Suddenly the German's head jerked. From the dark, just behind him, there was a shout. Both Eric and the German were startled.

Paolo had started down the embankment to run away but stopped halfway. In the dark one could not see but suddenly his face changed from that of a child to a man, a man with resolve. With a clenching of his fists Paolo turned back towards the railroad tracks. When he reached the top of the embankment, without thinking, he shouted, jumped off and noisily began to roll down towards the bottom.

Instinctively the guard turned toward the noise. In a fraction of a second he realized it was a trick and tried to turn back. He was too late. In a practiced move, Eric bent over and unsheathed his stiletto from its case at his ankle. He then stepped in, caught the gun barrel on his forearm and thrust the blade home into the German's abdomen. All this was done in complete silence. The look of surprise on the young German's face froze there as the blade entered his body. With his adrenaline pumping, Eric lifted the blade up until it was stopped by the German's breastbone. The British had taught him well.

The German tried to cry out but the scream caught in his throat. In a vain attempt to keep his intestines in place he dropped the rifle and grasped his belly with both hands. They spilled out over his fingers and he went into shock. Suddenly his eyes rolled back into his head and he fell silently, dead before he hit the ground.

"For the Jews, Nazi." Eric spat on him.

"You okay, Eric." Paolo came up, breathing hard.

Eric looked grim but gave Paolo a fleeting smile. "I thought you'd never come. That was the longest ten minutes of my life." He put his hand on Paolo's arm. "Wait!" They both listened intently. "Good, no one heard us."

Eric turned back to Paolo and grasped his shoulders. "Paolo, you saved my life. I owe you one."

Paolo smiled, his young heart swelling with pride at the praise. He was grateful Eric did not know how close he had come to running away.

Eric pointed at Paolo's pouch. "Let's plant the plastics and go. But first..."

Eric lifted one arm of the dead German and began to drag him. Paolo quickly got the other arm and they hauled him across the tracks to an overgrowth of brush. After they put some branches over him Eric smiled and said, "Okay, let's get some fucking Germans."

They had been taught well by the commandos. Quickly and expertly they went about planting the British explosives along the rails and then covered them with leaves and branches. Eric then wound the thin, almost invisible wire into the plastic and carefully laid it on the ground. As he walked backward towards a concealed place near the body, Paolo lifted the wire and smoothed out the snags and twists. Finally the two men reached an obscure area near the copse of trees. Eric crouched down and tied the wire to the positive and negative poles of the detonator he had carried under his jacket.

Paolo stood guard at the edge of the trees, his heart pounding in his ears, gun at the ready. He tried to avoid looking at where they had laid German's body but his eyes kept coming back to where the body was. A great sadness again filled him. He was only a boy, Paolo thought, just like me. In another place another time they might have even been friends.

Eric's voice broke the stillness. "Paolo, go on back, I can handle it now."

"No," Paolo said, "you may still need me."

Eric nodded, glad for the company and also, the lad just might be right. He looked at his watch, the luminous hands ticked off the moments. Nine minutes and thirty seconds to go. A lifetime!

Paolo ducked back into the darkness as a German's voice shattered the stillness. "Spread out and find him. If he is not dead, he vill be. He vill be summarily shot for leaving his post. I vill do it myself."

"Kapitan, kapitan. There was a scuffling of feet and a clanking of weapons. "Over here, sir."

Eric muttered, "Goddamn it, they found the guard. Just today they had to change their routine." Eric heard the faint whistle of the train in the distance. He looked at his watch. *Six minutes to go. Another lifetime.* "Paolo," he whispered, "go on back."

Paolo gritted his teeth and shook his head stubbornly. "No, Eric, you may need me."

Eric watched the captain intently as he wiped the sweat forming on his brow. The captain was a small man with a swaggering gait. He held a riding crop that he would use on his men if they didn't move fast enough. Just now the bright light of the station was above him and Eric could see a large dueling scar going from the side of his nose across the right cheek of his ferret-like face. His mouth was a thin line of cruelty.

"Achtung, (attention) all of you, line up on the sergeant."

Eric's hand tightened on the detonator. Another whistle, this time closer. Beads of sweat were now coursing down his cheeks, making tracks in the grime on his face. Eric looked at his watch again. Four minutes. Another mournful whistle as the train chugged towards its fate.

"Spread out and walk towards that embankment. Don't ask any questions. If you see anyone, anyone other than a German soldier, shoot to kill."

The train whistled again, this time, louder. It was coming closer to the station. A quick glance at the watch. Three minutes. *Oh, God, no! Lord, give me just a few more seconds.* The Germans were combing the brush, coming right towards them. *They're just a few steps away. There's not enough time.* Eric prepared to run.

Suddenly Paolo stood up and took a step towards the Germans. Eric looked at him, shocked. He started to tell the boy to get down but suddenly he realized what Paolo was going to do.

The boy stopped and turned back to Eric. His face was peaceful, almost serene. His prayer beads were wound tightly in his fist. "Eric," he whispered, "my mother lives in Palermo. Numero Fifteen, Via de la

Rosa. When this madness is over, see her, and tell her I wait for her."

Eric reached to him with his free hand, unable to speak. Paolo touched just the end of Eric's fingers with his own and then turned and began to run and shout.

Immediately the Germans saw him. "Halt, halt!" Short bursts of gunfire rang out and then, silence.

As if to underscore the tragedy, the train then made its last mournful whistle as it pulled into the station.

Tears streaked down Eric's face and mixed with the sweat on his grimy features. "Your people will know your sacrifice, Paolo, Lo giuro." (I swear it) The train's wheels made a screeching noise of metal on metal as the engineer began to apply the brakes. Finally the great iron horse ground to a stop. White steam came from under the belly of the train obscuring the soldiers forming around Paolo's still quivering body alongside the track.

For a moment everything was silent and still except the whoosh of the steam. Then with an angry, defiant gesture Eric thrust the handle down and the world exploded in ghastly sound and fury. The first ball of plastic exploded, enveloping the engine with fire and blowing it off the track. The second explosion went off just below the ammunition car and began a series of catastrophic explosions much larger than the first two. Eric was fascinated. He stared at the fireball unable to think or move. It was larger and more destructive than any he had seen before. One by one the cars exploded until they were all on fire. The entire train was a smoldering, burning wreck, and German soldiers, with their uniforms on fire, were screaming like they were in the deepest cave of Dante's Inferno.

Eric stood up and his fascination turned to satisfaction. The Germans who had shot Paolo had moved far enough from the flames not to be engulfed by them but could only stand by helplessly, shielding their eyes from the blinding light and heat. The captain shouted orders at them, but they seemed so frozen in horror that they were paralyzed.

The captain then started kicking and pushing the men back to reality. He was shouting at the top of his lungs, trying to organize the men to continue the search.

When the noise of the explosions died down, Eric could hear him clearly. "You men, spread out quickly. You must catch the ones who did this. Und I vant dem alive! Dere vill be a two week pass for the man who gets vone."

Eric quickly gathered his wits about him. He crouched as low as he could and began to make his way out of the woods towards the town. As planned, the rest of the partisans dispersed at the first explosion. Time and again Eric had to stop and hide as the patrols came near him. It was when he heard the barking of the dogs that he really became afraid. Eric redoubled his efforts, eluded the dogs, and moving in a large circle, finally approached the town from the other side. Partisan headquarters was a basement on Intrepid street. Eric quickly made his way there. Too late! German soldiers were already standing in front of the basement steps, their guns trained on the other partisans looking dejected as they were hustled out of the cellar. *The Germans must have already known,* Eric thought. *Paolo was dead so he couldn't have told them, so they must have either a traitor, or a spy, in the group.*

Eric turned down an alley, not knowing where to go next. When he had fled from Latvia, he was sent directly to the partisans. They had put him immediately to work so he knew few other people in the town. He felt trapped. He knew the Germans had found the detonator by now and had given their dogs his scent. Eric saw a soldier cross in front of the alley. Then another. The barking of the dogs in back of him was getting louder. Slowly but surely he felt the net tightening around him. Eric ran, quickening his pace as the barking became louder. The soldier holding the police dogs was being dragged along as the dogs had now picked up his scent. Eric was getting panicky. He knew what would happen if he got caught. *Hell might be more pleasant,* he thought. Just ahead was the opening of the alley that went to the main street of the town. He ducked into the alley. His heart stopped. *A dead end.* There was nowhere else to go. Eric tried the first door he came to. It was locked. He ran across the alley and tried another. It opened. He dashed inside and latched it behind him – *just in time* – as he heard the dogs barking in the alley.

It was dark and quiet inside the building. Eric looked around quickly. There was a table that had hundreds of candles burning. Icons looked down at them in an eternal stare.

Eric looked closely the statues. They were of a woman holding a bearded man. The Christ, Eric thought. The supine figure laying in the woman's arms had a wound in his side and a crown of thorns on his head. Both statues were weeping. *I know this work. It's a copy of the Pieta by Michelangelo.* Eric shook his head. *You see Jesus, inhumanity can happen in any century.*

It now began to dawn on Eric that he was in a church and that he may have a refuge here. *Maybe I could hide here for a while and then escape.*

As his eyes adjusted to the darkness he noticed there was a priest and an old woman kneeling in front of the candles. They both had their mouths open in surprise as they stared at Eric. Quickly, the priest grasped the situation and his wits, and beckoned Eric to come with him. Eric jumped when he heard the loud banging on the door he had just locked. Seeing he had no other choice, he quickly followed the priest.

The priest opened a closet door reached in and took out an article of clothing. He handed Eric a black hassock, pointed to another door and whispered, "Into that room and put this on, my son, and then come back to me. Try to be calm and don't be afraid. I will go to the Germans and talk to them." He stopped and put his hand out. "Rub this incense on you, it may throw the dogs off."

Eric looked into the priest's eyes and saw there the heart of a patriot.

Eric quickly obeyed him. He silently washed his face and hands at the sink and then put the hassock on. Quickly he rubbed the incense all over himself praying it would work on the dogs. When done he took a deep breath and forced himself to calmly walk back into the nave of the church. As he walked towards the alter, he had to stifle a laugh. *I wonder what old Rabbi Feldman would think if he saw me dressed like this?*

The old priest took him to the confessional and had him sit down. He had already put the old woman in the confessional and she sat across from him separated by a screen. Through the screen, he could see the outline of the old woman who was now a part of the deception. The knocking was getting louder.

"Do you know the words of the confessional?"

"No, Father."

If the soldiers come near the confessional, the woman will say several things and finish by saying, 'I firmly resolve with the help of your grace to sin no more and to avoid the near occasion of sin.' When you hear that, you say very firmly, 'I absolve you of your sins, in the name of the Father, the Son and the Holy Ghost.' Can you remember that?"

Eric's head was spinning. "Yes, I will remember."

By now the knocking had become louder and more insistent.

Shaking a bit, Eric sat down while the priest went to the door. "I'm coming, I'm coming," the priest called out, "Please be patient, I am no longer young."

With that he opened the door and German soldiers spilled into the room, their rifles at the ready. The dogs also tried to enter, but the soldier who had them held them back, but with difficulty. Suddenly the captain appeared at the doorway and struck one of the dogs with his riding crop. The dog yelped and slunk away, then the captain strode in angrily.

"Priest, we are tracking a dangerous agent who blew up an ammunition train. We have his companions but we want the bomber."

"As you can see, my son, we do only church business here. I fear you must look elsewhere."

The captain's face got red. "I am not your son!" The captain stared contemptuously at the priest but then calmed himself. He began to look around the church. He looked back at his men and gave them a quick nod. "Hoffman, Klepper, search the place."

"I assure you, Captain, you will find no one who doesn't belong here."

"Who is that in the confessional?"

"That is Father Innocenti, tending to one of my flock."

Eric could see that the old woman was trembling. Then he realized he was trembling too. Sweat beaded out on his forehead. He was certain she would dash out of the confessional and denounce him. But she sat still, bent over, praying.

The captain cocked his head and walked towards the confessional. When he came close enough for him to hear, the woman began the act of contrition.

When she reached '...to avoid the occasion of sin', the captain was right outside the door.

As soon as she finished, Eric said in a calm voice that surprised even him, "I absolve your sins in the name of the Father, the Son, and the Holy Ghost."

"Eric was surprised as she mumbled back, "Yes, Father, thank you Father."

The captain turned and yelled toward the open door. Corporal, bring me the lead dog.

The corporal moved quickly into the church and up to the captain. "Ja Kapitan."

The captain abruptly grabbed the leash and turned toward the confessional.

The Priest protested. "Captain, you cannot bring a dog into the church."

The captain's lips turned up in a smile that was more a sneer. "Why not Father? He is one of God's creatures." The captain walked over to the confessional. Eric and the old woman bent their heads in prayer. Eric's heart was beating a loud tattoo that pounded in his ears. The dog sniffed a few times and then looked up at the captain and wagged his tail. The incense had worked.

Angrily the captain pulled the dog back and went to the door. "Priest, ve vill scour the neighborhood. If ve do not find him ve vill be back. Dere vill be guards on each door so escape is impossible. If ve find him in the church, it vill not go vell for you. Goot day to you." The German clicked his heels and he, the dog and his men quickly left.

The door slammed shut and all was quiet again. The priest crossed himself and then busily made his way back to the confessional, a finger on his lips. He opened the door and looked down upon the old woman. She dissolved in tears. She looked up at the priest with fear in her eyes. "Padre mio," (Father, mine), "a lie in the house of God? Calumny. What will happen to me?"

The priest helped her up by the elbow.

By this time Eric had joined them.

"My dear child, God will bless you for what you have done today." He lowered his voice. "Now you must go home and speak to no one about these events. God would not look favorably upon a collaborator."

She smiled through her tears. "What events?" The priest hugged her and the old woman genuflected, crossed herself and began to waddle out of the church.

The priest looked after her with satisfaction on his face. "She is a good woman. She will not speak of what happened here tonight."

The priest turned to Eric. "Well, Father, you did very well for your first confession.

Eric smiled and scratched his head. "I don't know father, after that she may not go straight to heaven. The old priest laughed. There was a noise outside and the priest's face turned serious.

His voice lowered. "We are still in danger, my son. Come with me and we will get something to eat and figure a way out of this predicament."

Eric touched his arm. "Father, I cannot get you involved in this. They are not human. If you are found protecting a partisan..." Eric hesitated afraid to say, *and a Jew.* He decided not to. "In that instance your habit will not protect you."

The priest stopped and turned to Eric. "My son, it is not the habit, but God that protects. Come, we will let God himself decide. But first you must taste my spaghetti a la chiesa. It is my own recipe."

Eric would not move. "Father, I must protest, my name is..."

The priest turned quickly and held up his hand. "No, my son, I already know your name. It is Father Innocenti. You are in the church now. You are a pastor, sent by God to help me shepherd my flock. Your name is Father Innocenti, and we will know you only by that name.

Eric's brow wrinkled with concern. "But the old woman..."

The priest smiled broadly. "Don't worry about her. I will see that she remains silent. "Andiamo, (come now) we must feast first and then find you a place to sleep. Then we will figure out what to do next and how Father Innocenti will get his proper papers."

Eric blanched. *If that damned captain had asked for my papers.* A small smile reached his face and he swallowed hard. "Thank you, Father."

For the next few days Eric nervously watched for the return of the captain. Except for the serenity of the priest he surely would have bolted the church. As it was, he felt trapped, and like a small animal in a trap he unhappily awaited his fate. Each moment of the day Eric waited in fear for the other shoe to fall.

If the Germans bothered the priest he never showed it. Every night, after the evening meal, the old priest began to talk about many things. He had a captive audience and made the most of it.

At first Eric was annoyed at the old man's going on about the ways of men and the secrets of the earth. Then slowly he began to realize it was not prattle. He began to fathom the depth of knowledge the old priest had and he began to enjoy his confinement beyond any expectation. In their nightly talks, the priest soon revealed he was a learned and experienced man in math, botany, and the sciences. Each evening, after dinner, the priest would go to the ancient cellar and bring up a bottle of Chianti wine. The bottle would always be sealed with wax and be seated in a small woven basket. The first night the priest took the bottle out of the basket and showed it to Eric. The bottom was round and when he put it on the table it fell over. Eric caught it as it rolled to the edge.

"This my son, is the gift to the world from the people of Fiasco." He laughed. "As you can see they were excellent wine-makers but very poor planners. The wine is fit for the gods but the bottle, well, the bottle is a Fiasco." Eric laughed along with the priest as the priest poured the claret colored liquid.

At these nightly meetings the priest continued to reveal his extremely bright and facile mind. And little by little he began to reveal the story of his life.

151

The priest filled Eric's glass until he put a finger near the top.

"Father Innocenti," he began expansively, "my life actually began at the battle of Belleau Wood, in the Great War. I was a young man, in the prime of life, who foolishly left medical school to join other foolish, young men, in an equally foolish war. Of course when my superiors found I had the barest of medical knowledge, they made me a medic, gave me a bag of medicines and set me to work on the wounded." His voice lowered and his eyes got vacant. "Day after day, the bombs rained death down on us until the landscape was a desolate desert, where nothing could live or grow. The air was constantly filled with gunpowder and the sun would struggle to get down to a man-made Hades. Each monotonous day became just as the day before until I thought I would go mad. Then an incident happened that changed my life. I am sure that God spoke to me through the mouth of a nun." The priest's voice got very soft and Eric had to lean forward to hear him.

"On one particular, harrowing day, the bombing had been very intense, lasting for most of the morning. The battle had raged back and forth on the battlefield, for the three days previous and the litter men had not been able to bring back all of the wounded. Their cries for help and water were pitiful. For a short while the bombing slackened and we got a chance to go out and get some of those wounded boys.

They carried one particular lad in and laid him on a blood soaked mattress on the floor next to my station. The wounded boy was blonde and blue eyed and so handsome he could have been in the cinema. A bullet had severed an artery in his leg and while he lay out in a dirty field all night the leg had gotten gangrenous. We did what we could to save him but as the day waned, he began to sink fast and become oblivious to the world. Finally a surgeon came, took one look at him, shook his head and left.

By the afternoon the boy was raving and the gangrene began to stink so badly I had to ask one of the orderlies to take him outside, for the sake of the others. Anyway we all knew he could not last much longer. The orderly put him outside and made a lean-to of a pup tent, to block the sun.

Later that day I was walking past the boy and saw a nun leaning over him in that small tent. Where she came from I could not tell you, but nevertheless, she was there. She was a Sister of Charity with the large hat they wear and a clean, starched habit. How she kept it so immaculate in all that filth was also beyond me. You can imagine what a contrast she was to the surrounding scene. None of us had had a bath in weeks, much less a clean uniform.

When I approached, I noticed she was leaning over the boy with a cloth, sponging his wound and talking softly to him. He had stopped his raving and was quietly listening to her mellifluous voice. He had calmed with her ministrations and was fiercely holding on to her habit and his sanity. I was fascinated and stood by for a while watching her.

Finally I could stand it no longer and walked over to her to tell her she was wasting her time and that she would better serve the men by attending one of the less wounded.

As I walked near I could see she was bathing the gangrenous wound. The warm air had made the smell nauseating and there were maggots all around the wound. It was too much. I put my handkerchief over my nose and tapped her on the shoulder. "Sister," I said, "I wouldn't do that for a million dollars."

The sister never stopped working but turned and looked up at me with a look that I shall never forget. It was a look of love and caring and piety that I hope to someday have in my heart. Then she spoke with a voice so sweet she must have truly been an angel, and simply said, "Neither would I."

Then without another word she went back to cleaning the pestilential wound.

The room was silent as the old priest leaned back in his chair remembering the thoughts of long ago. After a while is eyes came back to the present and the shadow of a smile crossed his face. "Needless to say, the good sister made a deep impression on me that I still try to live up to.

After that insane war was over, instead of going back to Medical school I joined the Church. After finishing Seminary and taking a battery of tests, I was picked by the Vatican for the diplomatic service. I was then trained by the Jesuits in their most prestigious colleges, and after some years, I was sent to the United States.

When I had conquered the lavish halls of the White House, including the President and Mrs.

Roosevelt, I was then sent to Latin America. This was a different world. All around me I saw the disparity of the opulent wealth of the church and the grinding poverty of the faithful. Soon I began speaking out about the riches of the church and the squalor of the believers. Then I left the easy living in the palaces of the rulers and began to live my life with the peasants. I exchanged my hassock for denims and worked right along with them in the fields. Those around me began to call me 'Cura delagente' the priest among us."

I tried to make them stop but they would not. Naturally, the church heard about it, and not surprisingly, did not like it. The Vatican sent for me to come back to Rome, but without defiance I told them it was harvest time and I could not come just then. The church then lashed out. 'You will return or face ex-communication,' I was told. With a heavy heart I went back to Rome.

When I got there I was told by a representative of the office of the faithful that I was 'Flirting with heresy,' and that, 'To regain your sense of balance,' I was going to be sent to a small church right here in Rome, so I could be under the watchful eye of the Vatican.

"I think it was more to shut me up than regain my balance. Nevertheless, here I have been for nearly ten years, and yes, I love it here." Suddenly the priest got a defiant look in his eyes. "But I still, and always will, hate injustice. The Germans have rekindled my distaste for that. As for my colleagues in the church, who made me come here, I will leave it up to God to judge them."

Eric was profoundly affected by the story and realized he was in the presence of a powerful and intelligent man.

To Eric's delight, there was a fine meal and a different topic every night. Soon he saw why the Vatican had chosen this man for advancement. His mind was agile and he seemed to be able to put unrelated events in juxtaposition to make his listener see a new perspective. Also he had perfect recall and Eric soon realized that he had a photographic memory and an imagination to match. And the Priest could bring all the things he had ever learned, and lay them at Eric's feet like an scholarly feast.

"The church can be wonderful my son. It offers hope and salvation. But it can also be like an old crone, ignoring the obvious pain of man while it sticks its nose in every phase of a man's life, from his pocketbook to his bedroom. They say everything is God's business. I say render to Caesar what is his and the rest to God.

Even now the church turns away from Jesus' own people and turns its back as the Germans devour the Jews."

Eric felt his body flush with anger, but could only nod in assent.

As captivated as Eric was by their nightly meetings, he kept his vigil on the German guards. Ten days into his new life, and to his immense relief, he noticed that they were gone. His comfort was short lived though as their place was soon taken by the German captain in the form of daily visits. He came every day, but always at a different time. He would always enter, sit in a pew, watch Eric for a few minutes and then leave as suddenly as he had come.

Eric felt trapped. Somehow, for his own sake, and the sake of the priest, he had to leave.

That night the priest poured the wine as Eric sat back and unbuttoned his belt. "Father, if you ever give up the God business, you can open a restaurant in Paris."

The priest smiled. "And you would be my best customer."

In the short time Eric had been there, he had learned many things and always looked forward to their nightly meetings. Fortunately, the priest enjoyed teaching as much as Eric loved learning. His schooling had been interrupted by the war and he enjoyed even this informal schooling.

But all things must come to an end and Eric knew it was time to leave. His heart was heavy and he hated to go but he sensed the captain was now toying with him. He probably knew by now that there was no Father Innocenti. When he got tired of the game he would surely turn Eric over to the Gestapo. It would not go easy for Eric with all those German lives he had taken at the train. He realized he had to depart, and soon.

The next night when they sat at the dinner table, Eric did not touch his food. This was not like Eric and the priest studied him knowingly. Suddenly Eric blurted out, "Father, I must leave. The captain watches me daily now and I feel his net growing tightly around me." Eric nodded his head towards the front of the church. "Why do you suppose the captain does not arrest me now. Surely he is suspicious."

The priest sighed. "For one thing he is not Gestapo. And for another, the Italian government has told the Germans not to interfere with the church." The priest was quiet for a few minutes and then he spoke in a voice so low Eric had to lean forward to hear him. "During my long life I have had no wife to comfort me. No children to love and cherish. But God has given me his own children to love and comfort. And he has given me you."

Eric was surprised to see a tear form in the priest's eye. "Dear Father Innocenti, even for so short a while, you have become like a son."

The air was heavy with silence. Eric was touched and his own eyes welled up with tears. "I too have become very fond of you, Father, and I will hate to leave you." With a brusque movement Eric wiped a tear from his cheek.

The priest looked about as if to make sure that they were alone. "I have been listening to the BBC on the short wave every night. The Allies have landed in France and Italy and as we speak are coming up the boot to Rome to free the country. They would have been here by now but they were bogged down at a mountain town called Monte Cassino. The Germans were using a monastery there as an observation post but the allies have bombed it into oblivion and the church is very upset. In any event, the allies have now driven the Germans back towards the border. The Italian government has surrendered, but the Germans have taken over the army and are forcing the Italian soldiers to fight." The priest shook his head. "The Italians have no stomach for this war and they will quit as soon as they can. Unfortunately for them, the Germans are now interspersed in the Italian army and they won't let them surrender. Mussolini promised the Italian soldiers fame and glory, but the allies give them bombs and bullets. The Germans, ah, they are fanatics. The captain is a classic case. Like the inspector in Les Miserables, the world may fall down around him, but he will go after you no matter what."

Eric stood up. "Then I must leave tonight."

The priest nodded. "I agree, my son." He got up slowly and went to the fireplace. Carefully he got down on one knee, his face showing some pain. He reached down and took the end of the rug and pulled it back. He smiled up at Eric and lifted one of the floorboards. Then, putting his left hand on the floor, he reached down with his right and lifted a leather case out of its hiding place. He placed the board back and rolled the rug back over it. With a few groans, he slowly and carefully got back to his feet. Eric watched in fascination as the priest ambled back to the table and sat down with a grunt. He rubbed his knee and uttered a few Italian oaths, then he nodded his head, put the leather case on the table and slowly pushed it towards Eric. "This will help you get away."

Eric opened the case. It was full of bank notes. Eric stared at it for a moment and then pushed it back towards the priest. "Father, I cannot take this. It's a fortune. It belongs to you... the church... probably the poor. I cannot take it."

"Are you one of the rich? Yes, it is the money for the poor, but what better way to use it then to help you get away. You, who have risked your life and given so much... and will continue to do so. God will bless this money and you. You can and you must take it. It is a long way to Switzerland. You will also need this map and this compass."

The priest then reached into his hassock and pulled out a rolled up map. Then from another pocket he brought out a compass. He pushed the map and the compass towards Eric.

Eric shook his head in wonder. *Apparently the priest has prepared for this moment.* "Switzerland?"

"Yes," the priest said nodding his head. "We have friends there who will ask no questions. One of the women of the church has volunteered to help guide you there." The priest shook his head sadly. "Her husband was killed by the Germans and she has hate that gives her wings. She will cloak your mission in normalcy. Just a man and his wife traveling, looking for work."

The priest stood up, straightening first one knee and then the other and began to pace.

Eric watched him intently.

The priest clasped his hands behind his back and hunched a little, deep in thought. "Our big problem is the captain. He will be after you like a shot as soon as he sees you are not here." The priest straightened up and looked at Eric. "I can hold him for a little while with some story or other, but not for long. You had better get started now." The priest walked out of the room and returned in a few moments with clothing in his hand. "Here, put these on." He smiled. "I think you will be less conspicuous in work clothes."

Dutifully, Eric left the room and put on the peasant clothing. When he was finished he looked at himself in the mirror. He smiled at his gaunt image. *"This is not the scared little schoolboy I used to be,"* he mused. Suddenly the priest's image was beside his in the mirror.

"Let the stubble on your face grow and you certainly will pass for an Italian worker." The priest smiled. "With a little work on your nose you will even look Italian." Eric touched his large Roman nose and both men laughed until their sides hurt.

The next night the two men waited impatiently. The captain had not been to the church for two days and they feared that he would show up at any time.

The door creaked open and a woman stepped inside. "Ah, Anna, you have arrived. Welcome, welcome."

Eric glanced at the woman in surprise. She was a handsome woman in her early thirties, with dark eyes that penetrated when she looked at you. Her long black hair was covered partially with a kerchief. The peasant clothing she wore did not hide the pleasant, curves of her body. Eric had to laugh to himself. *It is best I turn away, lest I forget my vows.*

On second look, Eric noticed there was a vacant, hard look in her dark eyes. *One would best not take liberties with this woman.*

She put down the backpack she was carrying and genuflected slightly as she addressed the priest.

"Father, this is a good night to travel. The clouds hide the moon and the roads are dark. We should leave soon."

"Yes, Anna, just let me say goodbye." He turned to Eric. "Innocenti, this is Anna. She will guide you to the border."

They both nodded to each other.

"When, and if, you cross into Switzerland you will be free. Another of our group will meet you there and get you settled." Unless you come back, or choose to join their underground group, the war will be over for you. If I know you, you will join them. If you do, then perhaps we shall meet again. If not, look me up after the war. I might need a priest." Both men laughed while Anna looked at them strangely.

The priest handed the leather case to Eric and pointed to a battered suitcase he had prepared for him.

Eric again gave a gesture of protest.

The priest forced the case into Eric's hand. "Don't argue. Take the money, you will need it."

The priest took the woman's hand. "Anna, be careful. As soon as the Germans see Innocenti is not here they will be after you." She nodded, quickly said goodbye and went to the side door of the church.

Eric stood before the man who had risked so much for him not knowing what to say. "Father, I..., I..." A tear trickled down Eric's cheek. He embraced the priest and turned to leave. He stopped and turned back. "I love you, Father and I will never forget you."

"Go with God, my son." Tears also filled the priest's eyes.

The priest watched the pair go to the side door and leave. It was painful to see Eric go. He went to the alter and with difficulty kneeled and clasped his hands. He looked up at the image of Mary and the Child. *Dear Jesus, Son of God in Heaven, You and I have been on this warpath for a long while now. Anna and this boy have just joined us. I know it is wrong for me to possess things. And I know I have taken vows of poverty. And I have never asked you for anything for myself. But I do wish to ask one thing of you. Please, dear Jesus, keep them safe and let Anna come back to us. And most of all, let the boy see you and come to you before he loses his immortal way.*

As the two gray figures strode quickly down the street, away from the church, the priest bowed his head, crossed himself and continued to pray fervently this time aloud. "Dear Father in Heaven, I ask nothing for myself. Please give Innocenti and Anna your protection and guidance... In the name of the Father, Son and Holy Ghost."

Slowly straightening both knees as he stood, the priest arose and walked back into the room where he had said goodbye. Suddenly his heart froze. There on the table was the map and the compass. The priest crossed himself, and despite the pain, went back on his knees to pray for the fugitives.

****

It was dark and quiet on the country road. Eric could barely see Anna, but before long he could hear her labored breathing. His own breath was heavy as they kept up an intense pace to get as much of a head start as they could. After an hour, Eric began to stumble just to keep up. He was very glad to finally hear Anna say, "We must rest a few minutes."

Clouds hid the moon and the light was dim. Eric could make out her form in the dark and walked over next to her. She had sat down at the edge of the road, her back against a small tree. Eric sat down at right angles to her and let his head rest back against the trunk. In a few minutes his breathing returned to normal. He realized his limbs were sore and he stretched his arms and legs. Suddenly the woman stood up and walked off a few paces. Eric sat upright and peered into the dark. He heard a slight rustling and then the sound of water. He sat back with a smile. She was relieving herself. He got up on his aching feet. *I better do the same.* He walked off a few paces in the other direction opened his pants and urinated. It seemed to take forever. In all the excitement, he didn't realize how full his bladder was.

When he got back Anna was ready, her backpack shouldered. He picked up the battered suitcase and got ready to leave. He hated the suitcase the priest had given him and would rather have a backpack like she had. But, as he had told him, they would then look like tourists instead of the peasants they pretended to be.

She looked at Eric with a fleeting smile. "Let me have the compass."

Eric reached into his pocket. Nothing! Frantically he searched his case. Something deep inside him told him he had made a dangerous mistake. Suddenly he became panicky. He went to his knees and searched the suitcase thoroughly. In frustration, he turned it over and spilled its contents into the grass. No compass, no map. Eric was crestfallen. He was so angry with himself he could only make signs to Anna in frustration. Finally he found his voice. "Anna, I would suggest now that you go back and let me fend for myself. It was my stupidity and I must suffer the consequences."

"What's happened is in the past. Now, we must re-think our position. Since we will now have to travel during the day, we can go cross-country and will not have to stick to the roads. In some ways that is a blessing. But, as for me going back, no. It is my job to get you to Switzerland and I will do so. We must travel quickly. It is still about a hundred and fifty kilometers to the border. But, since we now travel in the daylight we can make twenty to thirty kilometers a day. At that rate it will take at nearly a week to get to the border. Unless we get lucky and find some transportation.

I understand some Germans were killed in your skirmish. The Huns are fanatic about getting even when some of theirs are killed. They will hunt us to the death."

She smiled at Eric. "Oh yes, before I forget. When we make it to the border and you get into Switzerland, when you are approached by the partisans, your password is, Winston. They will answer, Roosevelt." Eric just nodded, already breathing hard at the killing pace the woman had set.

****

The priest quickly crossed himself and got to his feet. The pounding at the front door was getting louder as the soldiers applied their rifle butts to the wood. Dimly he could hear the shouts of "Open up," through the heavy oak door.

"I am coming, I am coming," he muttered to himself as he moved to the door. When he unlocked and pulled open the heavy door, two German soldiers rushed in their rifles at port arms. Quickly they looked about and then rushed down the hall in different directions. Then the captain stepped in and began to shout orders. "Search the entire church. Bring anyvone you find to me alive, especially the other priest."

"This is an outrage, Captain, I shall report this to your superiors."

"Giving refuge to the enemies of the state is far more serious, Priest. I suggest dat instead of your interfering dat you cooperate."

As soon as the priest said it, he knew it was a mistake, but it slipped out and now was too late. "What is it that you are looking for, Captain?" *Damn, I could have played dumb for at least thirty minutes more.*

The captain's eyes narrowed. "Vhere is the other man?"

The priest thought quickly. "You mean Father Innocenti? He is off on church business."

"Yes, und I am sure dat business vill be transacted far away from here." The captain tapped his riding crop. "Maybe in Free France? Or better yet, Svitzerland?"

A flicker of concern crossed the priest's face. "I have no idea what you are talking about."

"Yes, of course, no idea," the captain said, his voice laden with sarcasm.

The two soldiers returned to the room. The corporal clicked his heels and reported. "No one else is in the church, Captain." He held up Eric's hassock. "We did find this, Captain... and this." He handed the map and compass to the captain. The captain smiled malevolently and spread the map on the table. He looked at the priest with the light of triumph on his face. "I notice there is a place on the Swiss border that is marked. Are you planning a vacation, soon, Father? Or is Father Innocenti having a holiday. Maybe in Switzerland?"

****

Eric was almost grateful to see the sun set in the Western sky. Slowly, the sky began to turn dark blue, then black. Birds silently flitted across the darkened cirrus clouds as more and more quickly, the great orange orb slipped behind the earth. When it was totally dark, Anna stopped, turned into a field and beckoned to Eric. They walked together towards a copse of trees, a hundred meters from the road. When they got there Anna took her pack off and untied a blanket from the bottom of the pack. Eric took his blanket out and soon they were seated on them protected by the trees.

A brief smile flitted across Anna's face as she handed an apple to Eric she had taken from her pack. Eric shook his head. "I am too tired to even chew." Cobwebs filled his head and he lay down and in a few moments was in a deep, dreamless sleep.

Eric woke with a start and sat bolt upright. For a few moments he did not know where he was. Then he knew. The sound of the gears grinding were familiar and irritating at the same time. "The Germans," Eric muttered. He quickly got to his feet and looked for Anna. She was already standing at the edge of the trees watching the truck intently. He silently joined her.

"It's them," she said quietly without looking at him.

"How did they know where to look?"

Anna turned and looked at him with a faint smile. "They know we will head for Switzerland or France, besides..." She tossed her head back from where they had come, "they have a map. But don't fret, it would not take long for these animals to get the information out of an old man," she said tiredly. Eric suddenly felt terrible. Anna walked over to the blanket and sat down cross-legged and closed her eyes as if meditating. "We will stay here. When they leave the area we will continue." She spoke with her eyes still closed.

Eric sat down next to her. "Anna, you don't have to risk your life like this. Point the way for me and go back. I can find my way, alone." Then as an afterthought he said, "The priest may need you."

Anna opened her eyes dreamily. "Innocenti, it is not so easy what we are doing. You are in a web of protection. The partisans have established an underground and escorted many people to freedom. Without them you probably would be caught and...." She drew her finger across her throat and closed her eyes again.

"Why do you do it, Anna, why do you risk your life?"

Her eyes opened suddenly, then narrowed and flashed with anger. "That captain," she said ominously, "the one the priest said is after you. A few months ago he came to our house with his jackboot thugs and took mi esposo, (my husband) Tito. They took him outside and beat him unmercifully. All this while making me and our bambina, our little girl, watch. Somehow they had found he was connected to the partisans and wanted the names of the others. The beating would also

169

warn the other villagers what was in store for them should they follow that path."

She looked down at the ground. "Tito would not talk. After a while he lay in front of me, a bloody pulp. I confess to you, Innocenti, if I knew the names of the others I would have told the Nazis. But Tito, he would not utter a word. Finally the captain tired of the game, pulled out his pistol and simply shot him in the head." She looked off in the distance, her mind fleeing to a different place.

Neither one of them could continue and the silence closed in around them, broken only by snatches of a bird's final song and the crickets serenading the night's arrival. Anna rocked back and forth tears spilling from her closed eyes. Eric longed to comfort her, but knew he could not. He sat watching her, nurturing his hate.

For a long while Anna sat with her eyes closed, resting her bruised mind. Eric stood nearby staring into space. Anna finally lay down and began to sob softly until she was asleep. Eric stayed on guard until cobwebs finally filled his head. Nodding, he promised himself he was just closing his eyes for a moment. He sat down, put his head on his arms and fell fast asleep. He woke with a start just few minutes before dawn.

It was still dark but in the distance he could see the sun spreading its light just beneath the horizon. Eric got up and stretched his sore muscles.

Anna was also up by then and watched him thoughtfully. "As soon as it is light enough we will go," she said quietly. They both waited impatiently as the sun began to spread its illumination over the land.

As soon as they could, they set off at the same blistering pace as the day before, but this time they avoided all well-traveled roads.

The partisan network had set up safe places for people fleeing the Nazis. Downed fliers, diplomats, German soldiers who would no longer fight and those judged enemies of the state were funneled through a series of select people to the Swiss border. The Germans did not know the safe houses but they did know about the crossing places and patrolled those areas heavily. Only the hearty and the determined could survive the last dash over the mountains to freedom.

It was already dark when the two fugitives slipped into a barn near the border.

No one greeted them but there was food and water left in a pre-arranged place. Eric was too tired to eat and barely picked at his food.

Anna watched him carefully. "Innocenti," she said quietly but firmly, "tired or not, you must eat... to sustain your stamina. Tomorrow you will need your strength to climb the mountain. You will be alone and you must be alert and strong."

"Yes, Anna, I will eat after I rest a bit." He lay his head on the ground not even bothering to use his blanket. Soon he was breathing evenly.

Anna watched Eric relax his body and something stirred within her. For a moment she looked puzzled and then she put down her plate, grabbed her knapsack, and crawled near to him on all fours. She sat up next to him and began to hum while she took a brush out of her knapsack and began to comb the tangles out of her hair. After a hundred strokes her hair was as lustrous as when they first set off. She then reached over and got her blanket, spread it out over both of them and lay down next to him. In his sleep, he turned to her and put his left hand on her breast. Comforted she smiled and snuggled back against him until they were like two spoons in a drawer. She was soon fast asleep in his strong arms.

Eric woke two hours later, already drunk with the perfume of her. He was uncertain but the urge was too great. His instinct was to ravage her but he restrained himself and began to move slowly. Gently he began to kiss her behind the ear and down her neck. Anna responded favorably by pushing backward against his now erect manhood. Finally he could not hold back and he turned her roughly towards him.

Her hair spilled on the ground framing her face. Her shining black eyes bore into him full of promise. He bent over and kissed her full on the lips. The wakening kiss was soft and moist and overcame them both.

Eric carefully unbuttoned her blouse as Anna deftly removed her pants. She helped him with his shirt and he quickly undid the rest of his clothes.

They lay against each other for a moment drinking in a host of sensations.

Finally he bent his head down and kissed her breasts and she shuddered. He gently touched her loins and she shuddered again. She was moist and his fingers reveled in the warm, wet feeling. Tears came into Eric's eyes from the sheer beauty of the moment. Another long kiss and then neither one of them could contain themselves. Eric rolled on top of her and Anna guided him inside her. For a few moments they rocked back and forth and then an explosion went off in Eric's body. He continued to move for a few moments and then started to slow down but Anna's movements kept him in place. Knowingly, he just hung on and rocked along with her. Finally she began to shudder and then she erupted. Eric held her while her body gyrated. At last, she slowed and he collapsed on her as she hugged him close to her body. Their sweat mingled as Eric gave her a last lingering kiss.

After a while they both dressed slowly, luxuriating in their new-found feelings. Eric walked to the barn door and opened it slightly. The cool night air was refreshing to him.

Anna came up to him lay her head on his back, circled her arms around him and gently hugged him.

Eric reached back and patted her hair. "Will you come with me... over the mountains?"

Anna tensed and stepped back. Her face hardened a little. "I cannot. I have a child I must care for."

"Can you not send for her."

Anna smiled, centering herself. "You are letting a time of passion cloud your mind. You do not know me, nor me you. We shared a time of pain and hardship and stole a few moments of love. I have my child and family and this work of bringing people, like you, away from the tyrants. I cannot just leave it."

Deep inside Eric felt relieved. This was not a time to make commitments. He looked into her eyes, by the dim light, and saw that they were vacant again. He felt her pain and was glad they shared the night. She had been alive, at least for a little while.

They started out again at a blistering pace before the sun came up. The terrain became hilly and soon they were at the foothills.

While they were moving for the past few hours, Eric had been eyeing the great Swiss mountain in front of them. This was a mass of stone that was thrust up from the earth by a long-gone earthquake. The mountain dominated the world in that section, stretching enormous heights into the sky. Eric had climbed many mountains in his youth but this was different. It was both monstrous and steep. Eric stopped and shook his head as, even in the distance, he could see the craggy slopes and rocky projections. *This mountain is a dangerous adversary even when no one is chasing you.*

Anna also stopped, joined Eric, and they stared together at the forbidding mountain. She pointed toward the summit half hidden by clouds. "This is the mountain you must climb. We picked this difficult terrain because it is hard to guard. But the price is a steep and difficult climb." She paused, then continued. "After you get to the other side, walk down for a kilometer or so and light a small fire with wet wood. Do you have matches?"

Eric nodded.

"Good. Use the water in your canteen to wet the branches you will find. Someone is always looking for a smoky fire and the partisans will soon come to you. Then you will know you are free."

Eric knew their intimate time was over but he hugged her anyway. She was cold and unresponsive.

She twisted out of his embrace and spoke sharply, "We still have some kilometers to go. Come let us go rapidly to get there."

They walked at a rapid pace but by now Eric's body was getting used to it and he kept up easily, not even breathing hard. Just before nightfall Anna slowed the pace and announced simply. "We are here. This is the beginning of the mountain you must climb."

As the sun moved toward evening, Eric stared again at the top of the mountain that separated him from escape. He knew the terrain was rough but his desire was greater and he knew he would conquer the climb to freedom.

The sudden sound of a dog's bark froze them both. Anna spat venomously. "That son of a whore has found us. We must hurry."

"But where, they have dogs."

Anna's lips were a thin line of resolve and her eyes were alive with fire. "Follow me and do exactly as I tell you." She began to run and Eric followed just behind her. More dogs joined in the barking and the sounds urged them on.

In the dimming light Eric could see where Anna was heading. In front of them was a small creek that ran down the mountain. Anna was heading straight for it.

When they got there Anna urged him into the water. Go upstream as fast as you can. The dogs will not follow. They will lose the scent because of the water. I will stay here and try to throw the captain off. I will tell him I am looking for work."

"Anna..."

"Va, (Go) quickly."

"I...I will never forget you."

"Vada..." Go.

Eric touched her hand and quickly went into the water. It was cold and ran swiftly down from its home at the top of the mountain. The water slapped against his knees as he struggled, half walking, half running against the water's energetic flow. After a few hard minutes he looked back. Anna was out of sight, but the sounds of the dogs appeared closer.

Eric looked to his right and saw a small thicket of trees. The branches were plentiful and the leaves were thick. The sounds of the dogs were loud and he knew the Germans were very near. He scrambled out of the water and picking a tree in the center of the copse of trees, he swung on a low branch and hoisted himself up and started moving up the branches. When he was high enough he realized he was shaking, half with fear and half from the freezing water. He willed himself to stop.

In a few minutes, the dogs and soldiers were all over the creek where he had just been. The dogs and soldiers seemed to come from everywhere all at once.

Eric curled himself and held on tightly to the stout branch. He heard an authoritative voice yell, "Halt!" Everyone stopped and the captain appeared. Then he saw Anna.

Oh, God he's got Anna.

The captain had her by the arm and was dragging her towards the soldiers.

Eric froze and stopped shaking. As they got closer the barking got louder.

When he reached the soldiers the captain forced Anna to her knees. "Whore, pig. Vich vay did he go?"

Anna hung her head, staying very still. She would not speak.

The captain unbuckled his sidearm pulled out the Luger and brought it up all in one motion. He pointed it at her head.

Anna turned and looked up at him, her face alive with contempt.

Slowly he lowered the gun but did not put it back in the holster. His voice softened. "Ve have been chasing you vitout sleep for two days. All of us are tired und cranky. Vy don't you tell me vere he is und ve can all go home. He is a Chew, for goodness sake, a worthless Chew."

Anna slowly raised her head. Even from where he was Eric could see her face was bruised, one cheek so swollen it distorted her face. She looked at the captain with eyes from another place. Even from this distance Eric realized she was already some-where where the captain couldn't reach her. Anna bent her head down again and made the sign of the cross on her chest. Suddenly she stood up and spat in the captain's face.

The captain began to shake with rage. In a sudden fury he raised his arm up and brought it down, violently. Eric cringed as he heard the thud. Anna crumpled to the ground. Eric's stomach churned. His mind lurched. *I must stop this.* He reached for the branch and began to let himself down.

The sound of the gun seemed to reverberate to the ends of the earth and back again.

Eric stopped, one leg hanging down, and stared in disbelief. The captain stood, his jack-boots spread far apart, with Anna crumpled at his feet. His luger was still pointed at her head, a wisp of smoke curled from the end of the barrel.

Eric's heart constricted, then he was enraged. He longed to leap from the tree and tear away the man's arm that held the hateful pistol, but some stronger power kept him in place. He brought his leg back to the branch.

Slowly the captain holstered the luger, still staring at the body. His men looked away. Even the dogs were quiet. Eric's head hung down and tears stained his cheeks.

"Sergeant!" the captain yelled. One of the men snapped to attention.

"Ja, herr Captain."

"Spread the men out in formation." He looked down at the body. "Leave the whore here." He looked around at the men who were still staring at him strangely. "Come on, all of you, go find him. I don't care how dark it is. I vant that Chew. Find him now," he shouted.

The captain held Eric's hassock to the nose of the dog closest to him. The dog whined and sniffed the garment. "Find him dog and I vill feed his heart to you. Go and find him you damned animal!" The captain kicked the dog on the flank and the dog yelped and skulked away, tail between his legs. The captain then turned to the men and screamed at the top of his lungs, "All of you, go! Find him... now!"

The sun took an eternity to set and another eternity for the soldiers to leave. When they were gone, and it was finally dark, Eric dropped down out of the tree and ran to Anna's body. She lay just as the captain had left her. Her right arm pillowed her head as if she were in repose. The rest of her body was curled in the fetal position. Her eyes were open wide as if in surprise from the sudden fury that killed her. Eric looked down at her and wept. Slowly he went to his knees and reached out to close her eyes with his fingers. He bent his head and prayed silently, tears running down both cheeks.

After a few minutes Eric took her hand and kissed it, his head still bowed. "Anna, I must say goodbye," he said softly. "But now you and I are bound together for all time. I am eternally in your debt. Whatever happens to me I will always love you."

He stood up, clenched his fist and looked up at the dark sky. "Somehow, someway, if God will let me, I will avenge you." He looked down at her again, knelt and kissed her cold forehead, then he stood up and started running up towards the top of the mountain.

Chapter 15: Switzerland

Cumulonimbus thunderclouds darkened the sky and soon it began to rain as Eric trudged towards the top of the craggy peak. The climb was cruel and before long he was cold, wet and hungry. Fighting gravity, he slipped continually in the wet mud and was cut by sharp rocks and branches. When daylight came he made better progress but now he was in constant fear of being seen. Towards mid-day he heard the shouts of men and the barks of dogs. "Damn, it's the captain!"

At first he hid among the bushes and boulders but it was scant cover for him. At the base of the mountain the trees were plentiful but as Eric got closer to the top the trees thinned out until they were far and few between.

As the voices and barks came closer, he redoubled his effort and scrambled towards the summit. *So close. So close. For Anna's sacrifice I can't fail now.*

When he finally reached near the top, the light was just dipping down toward the west. A layer of clouds hid the light for a while longer, and then the clouds parted and the sun appeared. It warmed the earth, but Eric felt like he was trapped in a world made of glass.

A shot rang out and broke the majestic silence of the mountains. It reverberated through the peaks finally dying down to a whisper. Eric fell to the ground with a sharp pain in his shoulder and lay still, trying to think against the darkness closing in on him. Adrenaline pumped through his body and he trembled and shook. *No, God, I'm so close...*

Gradually, he forced himself to stop and assessed the damage. Blood was seeping from his left arm, at the biceps, through a hole in his jacket. He squeezed his left hand. It was painful but he could move it. He moved the shoulder. It moved easily. *Thank God, no broken bones.*

Eric searched for the shooter and found him. He had his hand curled around his mouth and was yelling to his comrades but because of distance or a strange quirk of acoustical shadows they couldn't hear him. No one came to support him. He shouted again. Nothing. After a short wait he began to move towards Eric, his rifle at port arms.

"The hell with them," the soldier said aloud, "I'll get the Jew myself."

Eric lay still, his face turned to the side and his eyes almost shut. But they were open just enough for him to see through the lashes.

After an eternity the soldier came up to him and looked him over. Eric lay deathly still. Once again the soldier cried out for his friends. Still no answer. He cautiously poked Eric a couple of times with his toe and still got no response. Then he put the barrel of the rifle under Eric's body and turned him over. Suddenly Eric came alive. He grabbed the end of the rifle. The soldier's finger was on the trigger and he instinctively pulled it and the rifle went off, firing the bullet into the ground. Holding the hot rifle barrel with his left hand Eric growled with pain, then with his right he grabbed the stiletto at his ankle, and with an unerring move thrust it up at the soldier's belly. The German's eyes widened. He dropped the rifle and staggered backward, his hands over the wound. He wavered then went to his knees all the while staring at Eric.

Eric stayed on the ground glaring at the soldier, his blade was red with blood. The knife trembled in his hand.

The German then took his hands away from the wound and stared at them. They were covered with blood. "Gott im Himmel," (God in heaven) he said then his eyes rolled back and he fell face down in the mud.

Eric quickly got to his feet. Ignoring the pain in his arm, he stripped the German of his uniform and hid the body as best he could, placing it behind a large boulder. He then covered it with branches and leaves that lay nearby. He quickly put the private's uniform over his own clothes, picked up the rifle and put the steel pot and helmet on his head, and pulled it down enough to shield his eyes. He then squared his shoulders and started up towards the summit. The uniform was tight and his arms and legs stuck out but he had seen other soldiers in the same condition and he knew that he would not stand out.

But the German's blood on the front of the tunic? For that he would have to trust to providence

When he got high enough he looked down and saw that there were other soldiers below where he had been. Eric was puzzled. *Why couldn't they hear the dead soldier when he called?* The only thing he could think of was that sound was blocked by the mountains or it was God's will. Either way he was still not out of danger.

"Hey you, look over there," a sergeant barked. Other soldiers came near him suddenly and Eric froze.

Keep a cool head, he thought to himself. Eric snapped a "Ja sir" (Yes, sir), and pretended to look where he was told. Several more times other soldiers came up to him and gave him orders or joked. Eric held his hand over the blood spot and no one was the wiser. Apparently the uniform was a perfect cover. Eric understood German and spoke fluently so he simply obeyed orders, or joked back with the others if the humor was light. He feared greatly his Latvian accent might give him away and he trembled with fear and anxiety, but with each passing moment that he was undetected he gained more confidence.

Gradually the others turned back and Eric was finally alone again. He scrambled up towards the summit in haste on all fours, sometimes stumbling and scratching his hands and face.

Soon Eric was close to the summit and for the first time he knew he would make it. After a mad scramble towards the top he reached the highest crest. He turned and looked back down the mountain and found he was still alone. With joy in his heart and a prayer for Anna, Eric then turned back and walked down into Switzerland.

Chapter 16: The Italian Partisans

For a long while Eric walked until he reached a grassy field. He turned and looked back up to where he had been, spat, uttered a curse, and threw away his helmet. Anna had told him to just keep walking for a kilometer or so and then make a smoke fire. The underground would be sure to find him. He walked the kilometer, found some wood urinated on it to make it moist and lit the fire. He sat down and realized he was exhausted and couldn't make another step if he wanted to.

He went to his knees, thanked God and lay down. He was asleep in an instant. The grass he lay down in was damp and cold but Eric didn't feel it. He slept the sleep of the dead.

****

Eric woke with a start. He reached for the German's rifle and then stopped. He realized he was surrounded. He forced his mind to focus on the men around him. His heart fluttered with fear when he first thought he had been caught by the Germans but he calmed down when he saw no uniforms. They were armed, though, and not very friendly looking.

He looked for his rifle and cursed silently that it was not nearby. *There are too many of them anyway.*

Hey, he thought, *these might be Anna's friends.* He felt a jolt of depression when he thought of her.

Eric sat up. *They have be the partisans. I pray to God they are. No problem, Anna said they would find him and they have.* He relaxed, but just a little. He got up on one knee and all the men shifted their positions. Eric could see their fingers tighten on triggers. A giant fellow with a large black beard confronted him.

"Who are you?" The giant said loudly.

"Let him get up, Maurice." The lazy voice came from in back of the circle of men.

It was then that Eric noticed him. He was sitting on a boulder, cross legged, with an amused smile on his face. Even from where he was Eric could see that his black eyes held no humor. Those eyes told Eric he would kill in an instant. He sported a scruffy beard and wore the same black beret as the other men but his was severely slouched over one eye. It was evident to Eric that he was the man in charge.

The cold smile left and he spoke again. "What are you doing here, little man, this is not your side of the border." He did not remove the cigarette from his mouth when he spoke and it bobbed furiously.

When he stopped talking the smoke curled up around his eye giving him a permanent squint.

Eric was thinking as quickly as he could.

Maurice backed away a little and Eric stood up. "I have come from Italy. I was brought here by a woman named Anna."

The man on the rock sat bolt upright. "Anna? Where is she?"

Eric was startled at his reaction and realized immediately that this woman meant something special to this man. His insides squeezed as he hung his head and looked away. "She is dead."

"Dead?" He said incredulously. "Dead? How?" He slid off the rock and lowered his weapon.

"The Germans came looking for us. They caught her. She wouldn't talk and they simply killed her."

The man came towards him in a rage. "Killed her?" He raised an angry fist under Eric's nose. "You Nazi bastard, maybe it's you who killed her." He dropped his gun and a knife appeared in his hand.

Eric stood his ground, and thankfully Maurice restrained his friend. He struggled in the big man's grip. "Let me go, Maurice, I must avenge Anna."

The big man held him easily. "There is plenty of time for killing, Aldo, let him speak, he may be telling the truth."

The man burst into tears and Eric realized he was in deep torment. *Anna was more than a friend to him*, Eric thought. He spoke quickly. "This uniform is not mine. I killed a German pig for it so I could get past their lines." Eric opened his shirt. "You see I put the Nazi pig's clothes over my own." He closed the shirt and continued. "Anna and I have been dogged by the Germans since we left Brescia."

Aldo stiffened and Maurice nodded his head. "You see, Aldo, he knows where Anna came from."

"Finally they caught up with us. She made me walk in a stream to disguise my scent so the dogs could not track me. Then she said to leave her. I didn't want to, but she assured me she would be alright. She said she had dealt with the Germans before. They had dogs and my scent from some of my clothes so I had to go."

Eric looked down and shook his head. Then he continued. "After I walked for a few yards in the water I saw them coming in the distance. I scrambled up a tree and watched. When they came closer, I saw they had Anna. The leader, a captain, began to mistreat her and I started to come down to give myself up so they would free her. Before I could get down, Anna spit in his face and then the bastard shot her."

The men were silent. Eric looked down at Aldo who was on his knees, sobbing.

Maurice held his shoulder. "If it's any consolation her death was quick and painless. Anna made the sign of the cross just before he fired. I stayed in the tree until they left and then I went to her. Of course she was dead. I closed her eyes, said a prayer for her and then left. I began to climb up the mountain to find you, as she had instructed. One of the Germans caught up with me and shot at me when I wouldn't stop. That's how I got this wound." Eric gingerly took his arm out of the sleeve of the jacket and showed the wound. "I lay still and when he came to inspect his handiwork I got the jump on him and killed him. I had no choice. I took his clothes and then I climbed, walked and ran and finally reached the top of the mountain crossed it then ran down until I was exhausted. I walked a kilometer then made a fire as Anna had instructed, and then I fell down and slept. The next thing I knew all of you were here."

Aldo was still on his knees weeping. Eric's instinct was to go to him and console him, to tell him he loved her too. But he knew if he did that, they would not be able to control him.

Finally the weeping man lifted his head, completely spent, and spoke to Eric. "You will show us where she is." Eric shook his head and started to get up.

Maurice spoke angrily. "Aldo, your grief has addled your brain. The Huns want this man probably because his head is full of names and secrets. A few days with the Gestapo and they would know all our birthdays and who we slept with last night." Aldo sat down heavily. The big man turned to Eric. "My name is Maurice, what is yours?"

"Eric."

"Eric, what?"

"Eric Shapiro."

"Juive?" (A jew?)

"Oui." (Yes) Maurice looked Eric over, carefully.

Eric stared back. This guy sure is big. By the clothes he wears he must be a farmer. The beret they all wear must be like a uniform. Maurice had a large beard and a pleasant, peasant's face. Eric could tell there was no guile about this man. *I'll bet what you saw on the outside was the way he felt. He's easy to laugh or to anger. But he has an uncommon amount of common sense. He's a steadying influence on this mercurial Aldo. And I notice that Russian burp gun never leaves his shoulder.*

"Where did you get the uniform? Maurice asked."

Eric told him again exactly what had happened.

Slowly his gun came off his shoulder.

Eric was tired of the game and began to get angry. "Listen..."

"Shut up!" His gun came down and pointed at Eric's middle. Maurice's eyes narrowed and bore through him. "You only have one more question to answer. What is the password?"

"Winston! And yours?"

"Roosevelt." Maurice grinned and his gun went back to his shoulder. His smile stretched from ear to ear. "Welcome to Switzerland, Eric." He stuck out his huge hand in greeting.

In the middle of the handshake, suddenly and abruptly, in the distance, a lone figure came over the top of a hill. "Aaaayeeeeeeeeeyaaaa," he was yelling like a madman. As he spotted the band of men he began to run towards them. He stopped, did a jig and began to fire his pistol in the air.

Maurice let Eric's hand go and cocked his gun. "That idiot Vicenzo has gone mad. He will give us away. I must bring him down and then we must leave."

Vicenzo stopped threw up his hands and danced some more. Finally he threw his gun into the air and fell on the ground, rolling in glee. Aldo had stopped weeping and looked at the crazy man with interest. "Wait a moment Maurice."

The big man slowly put the gun down.

"Listen to what he is saying."

Vicenzo's voice was hoarse and cracking but Eric began to understand him.

"The Germans have surrendered. The war is overrrrrrrr." The crazy man fell to the ground in another paroxysm of joy and rolled over and over in pure abandonment.

Eric was stunned. *No more shooting, no more killing. No more hiding, no more fear.* He sat down and began to sob as the men around him began to imitate Vicenzo in an even noisier celebration.

Aldo sat down next to Eric and gently touched his back. "My Anna was the last victim of this war. God wanted her with him, in heaven today." He made the sign of the cross. With that Eric broke down completely and began to weep profusely. Aldo patted his back and the two men sat there, disconsolate, while the madmen danced like furies around them.

****

Aldo lead his partisans to allied headquarters. They arrived in ragged but proud formation, guns on their shoulders. They were welcomed as comrades-in-arms and given food and new clothing. Eric then received proper medical attention for his wound.

Other than some stiffness the arm was back to normal in short order. The physician told him he was fortunate the bullet had missed the bone.

After two weeks the men began to leave for home, each one armed with fifty thousand lire and a letter of commendation signed by General Eisenhower.

Eric approached Aldo. "My friend, why do you not go home? You live the closest and yet you tarry. Are you afraid to face your wife?"

Aldo laughed. "Eric, mio amico (my friend), It is my duty to stay until all my men have gone. Then I will go home." For a moment he was thoughtful. "There is no wife and my family is gone. The Germans took care of that. There was only Anna..." He brightened. "But, I shall find a plump lady who wishes to look at this ugly mug for a while, and bed her for a month or two... maybe, three."

Eric's face turned serious. "I hate to leave you, my friend, but I must go. The Nazis took my parents and my sisters. They are probably not alive but I must search for them, anyway." Eric's voice dropped. "The last I saw of them was when I was leaving on a truck. They took me for slave labor to Italy. And my family? Only God knows where they are." Eric spoke, his eyes focused in the past. "The Germans were herding all of the people from my street, like sheep, to waiting trucks and then cattle trains." He repeated his fear. "Only God knows where any of them are." His voice trailed off and his eyes were distant. "I have no choice. I must search for them."

Aldo smiled. "The Allied generals wish for me to give a detailed account of our movements during the war." He laughed. "When I tell them you won the war all by yourself they will give you half of Germany in gratitude."

Eric laughed back. "And here I thought you won it."

Suddenly Aldo's face looked grim and his voice lowered. He spoke angrily. "I will tell them of Anna and her great sacrifice. I will also find her child and send him to live with my Mama."

"You can find the child by finding the priest. Go to the church in the square in Brescia and ask for the priest there. Tell him Father Innocenti sent you. Tell him what has happened to Anna and then ask him for the child." Eric hesitated then grasped Aldo's shoulder. "Anna will live forever in our hearts, Aldo."

Aldo's face brightened. "We must not be so morbid. This is a time for celebration." He took out a pencil and paper. "I will be with the Americans to lobby for war trials. We must punish and eradicate the Nazis. Then I will go home to Naples. I want you to come and visit me there... after you search, I mean. And I pray to God you find your family." He smiled. "Maybe you can bring me your sister, when you find them. I would be honored to meet her."

Eric smiled but shook his head sadly. "I don't think she will be very plump. Better you should find your own girl."

"Hah! You just don't want me for a brother-in-law."

The grinding of truck gears announced the transport vehicle was arriving.

Eric nodded his head towards the truck. "Aldo, I will miss you. You have become more like a brother to me." The men embraced then shook hands. As Eric lifted his duffle the saw a tear in the corner of Aldo's eye. *These Italians are so emotional.*

But he felt moisture in his own eyes. He walked to the truck threw his duffle in the back and hoisted himself over the tailgate. As the deuce and a half lumbered, grinding in first gear, towards the gate, Eric looked back at his friend. He was waving and then suddenly stopped, clenched his fist, and stuck his thumb up in salute. Eric returned the salute and then settled back for the bumpy ride to town and then the train to Latvia.

Later, as the train lurched across Eastern Europe, Eric tried to imagine the fate of his fellow Jews. He had heard the Nazis had loaded the cattle cars with hundreds of men, women and children and sent them to the concentration camps. No food, no water, no toilets. Only death awaited them. Eric felt no guilt for the Germans he had killed. *"I only wished I had killed more of them."*

Chapter 17: Latvia (1946)

Europe was devastated. Eric could not believe the destruction he saw from the train window. Although he had been in the thick of battle he now saw the bigger picture of the allied onslaught.

Bombed out buildings seemed to line the train beds in all the major cities. *Hitler must be writhing in the deepest part of Hell,* Eric hoped. Only in the countryside did things appear somewhat normal.

All along the way the people were sullen and seemed to go about their daily tasks like automatons. After the joyous celebrations he had seen the last two weeks in Italy, this part of Europe seemed like a drab painting by a madman, dark, foreboding and desolate.

****

The train hissed and screeched to a halt. When it finally stopped, clouds of smoke billowed from under its belly. The sign said Riga. His heart was pounding, he was in Latvia. Home at last.

Eric threw the duffel over his shoulder and stepped off the train through the steam. It was strangely quiet in the station. People moved about but made little noise. Gone was the boisterous cacophony of sound Eric remembered as a child. When the people spoke, they spoke in whispers. No children romped through the station with parents chasing them. *To quote Wolfe,* Eric thought, *maybe you really can't go home again.*

Eric's home was near the station and he decided to walk there. He stepped out of the station into cold rain. With a gesture of annoyance he pulled his coat up around his neck to keep in the warmth.

As he made his way through the streets he realized the depth of the devastation up close. The Germans and Russians had used the town for a battlefield and when the Germans left they practiced scorched earth as much as possible. It made little difference to them that the people needed food and shelter for the coming winter.

I remember what the Germans said, '*Weren't the Latvians like the Poles untermenchen (less than human) anyway?*'

Eric finally reached his street. His hopes were raised. Here the houses were intact. He began to believe against all hope that he might find some of his family still alive. Afraid of what he might find Eric approached the house slowly. When he reached the front door he stared for a moment at the polished oak door and the brass knocker. Then a flood of feelings and memories came crashing in on him. *I'm home. I'm really home!* He shook his shaggy head not really believing he had arrived at Riga and home. Eric looked through a window. *There are lights inside. Dear God, let it be my family.*

Eric put down the duffel and absently brushed at his hair. With his heart pounding in his ears he walked up the three steps and knocked at the front door. The noises inside suddenly stopped. But, he thought he could hear hushed voices.

Then the door opened just a crack. He saw an eye, then a disembodied voice said, "Who is it? What do you want?"

"I am Eric Shapiro. This is my home. Are my parents here?"

The door closed abruptly. Again there was more hushed conversation behind the closed door. Suddenly the door opened again, and this time Eric was confronted by a bulky man dressed in peasant clothing. He was muscular from the hard work he had done through the years. His large, meaty hands were wrapped around a Russian rifle.

He squinted at Eric, his bushy eyebrows half hiding his malevolent eyes.

"Listen, Jew, you don't live here anymore, we do." He smiled, showing rotted and blackened teeth. "The time is past when you Jews can suck the blood of poor Christians. The Red Revolution has come," he said proudly, "go out and make your own daily bread, but do it somewhere else." The door started to close.

Eric felt revulsion but stuck his foot out and stopped the door. "What are you talking about? This is my house. Where are my parents and my sisters?" Eric's voice was raising as he spoke and the man, showing a little fear at Eric's anger. He lifted the Russian rifle and pointed it at Eric.

"Go on get out of here before you join them." He smiled mirthlessly. "They got a one way ticket to Auschwitz. You won't find them here or there. Go somewhere else."

As quick as a cat, Eric dropped his duffel, ducked past the rifle and grabbed the larger man at his shirt collar. In an instant, the look in his eyes changed from defiance to terror.

"Listen you pig, you're lucky I don't break your neck." Eric pushed him to the floor his rifle clattering down the stairs. "I am going to the authorities and I advise you, and your herd, to leave here before I get back." Eric grabbed his duffel and jumped down the three steps. He kicked the rifle into the street then turned to leave. He hesitated then turned back. The man was still on the floor cowering. "And, by the way, while you were here, helping to turn my family to dust, this Jew was in the woods killing the Nazis that devastated your country."

Eric threw the duffel over his shoulder and stormed down the street, his heart was now pounding with anger. He had passed a policeman on the way to his house and now headed for him. He asked, and was told, where the housing authority was and headed there immediately. He did not see the policeman's amused smile as he left.

Eric stopped in front of the official building. It was gray and dark and there were many people milling about. He pushed his way to the guard at the front door. "Strangers are living in my house. I need to see someone to get it back."

The soldier was young and obviously ill at ease with all the people surrounding him. "Sssorry, Sir, I'm only here to keep order. You'll have to speak to the Sergeant, Sir."

Eric was exasperated. "Well, where is he?"

"I'm right here. What is your problem?

Eric whirled about while the private snapped to attention. Facing him was a man in a sergeant's uniform. His face was craggy but clean shaven. His eyes were bored and dull from years of dealing with bureaucracy. *This is one that would jump from the Nazis to the Russians without batting an eye,* Eric thought. "Some people are living in my house."

"Yes, well there is a lot of that just now. Since the new regime took over, I mean. Lots of people and too few houses. Have you seen the minister of housing?"

"No."

"Go up those stairs and see the receptionist. Tell them the sergeant of the guard sent you."

"Thank you, Sergeant."

As Eric climbed the stairs the sergeant winked at the private. "The minister will keep him busy," he whispered. He laughed heartily as he pushed his way back through the crowd.

Eric's heart sunk as he reached the top of the stairs. There were more than fifty people in the room. He made his way towards the secretary and got on a line to her desk. After a fidgety hour, he finally reached the young woman. "Someone is living in my house," he told her angrily, "I want to see the minister."

"Don't yell at me. Half the people in this town want to see him. Take this number and sit down. We will call you."

Eric felt sheepish and apologized. *Of course, it's not her fault.* He took the slip of paper and looked around for a seat. There were none. He leaned back against the wall and watched the door to the minister's office. One, sometimes two people an hour went through the door. *At this rate, it will take a week for me to see him,* Eric thought.

At five o'clock the receptionist stood up. "We are closing now." A collective groan came from the crowd of people left in the room. "You can all come back tomorrow." A few angry epithets came from some of the people as they threw their slips down and stormed out. The rest of the group sullenly followed them out the door and down the stairs.

Eric looked around the room. He smiled to himself as he slipped into a small door at the wall opposite the receptionist. *I am a partisan again,* he said to himself, *waiting to surprise the enemy. Some things never change.*

He left the door slightly ajar and waited quietly in the darkened closet. He watched through the crack under the hinge and saw the girl tidy her already spotless desk and then sit down and light a cigarette. In a few minutes Eric was rewarded. The door opened to the minister's office and a man stepped out. He was in his mid-fifties and moved with a strut to his step. His hair was thinning and graying and the bulge over his belt showed he was obviously battling corpulence. In a city of scarecrows, he seemed well taken care of. Eric opened the door and stepped out.

"Excuse me, Sir."

"What is this. Where did you come from?" He glared at the secretary and she merely pulled her mouth corners down and shrugged.

"I don't mean to bother you, Sir, but I have been waiting all day and I have no place to go."

The girl leaned back and took a puff. "Shall I call the guards, minister?"

Eric noted her familiarity. "No need for that, Sir. Just tell me how to get my home back and I will gladly leave."

"Wait, Carla, this man has courage and ingenuity. I like that." He turned to Eric. "What is your name?"

"Shapiro, Sir. Eric Shapiro."

The minister froze. "Shapiro? A Jew? There are no houses for Jews in my district. If it weren't for you people there would have been no war and no housing shortage. You are only getting what you deserve. Now, you are paying the price for your duplicity."

Eric saw red and raised his voice. "I started no war and I demand my home back."

The minister turned to the woman. "Carla, now you can call the guards."

The minister folded his arms and glared at Eric as the secretary left the room.

Eric stared back knowing he could snap this poppinjay's neck in a flash.

Suddenly the minister dropped his arms and walked behind Carla's desk. He sat down in her chair with a satisfied look. "You know, Shapiro, soon we will have all Latvia Juden rein," (Jew free) "as our German comrades used to say. Why don't you get smart and leave Latvia to the Christians? Just go to Israel. They will welcome you there.

"Mr. Minister, where did you spend the war?"

The minister turned red.

"Just as I thought. Well, this Jew spent it fighting in the woods with the partisans, just so you could be German rein, and have a decent place to live."

Just then the door opened and two soldiers burst in. They leveled their rifles at Eric.

The minister smiled a mirthless grin with hate in his eyes. He had collaborated with the Nazis but had kept his role hidden. Apparently nobody knew. Sometimes, though, just like now, someone would say something and he would get afraid.

He thumped the desk and ordered the soldiers, "This Jew was just leaving. Deposit him at the city dump." The soldiers each grabbed Eric under the arms. "And you, don't come back."

Eric stared at the Minister. "I see Hitler lives after all," he said with closed fists.

As they were escorting Eric out of the building the older of the two soldiers whispered in his ear. "I knew your father, Dr. Shapiro. He was a great man. The Nazis killed him and these Red pigs are no better. You had best leave. All this will come right in time, but right now, it is best that you go."

Eric froze on the stairs and turned to the soldier. The younger guard stopped also, and let them talk.

"And my mother and sisters?"

"The Nazis had no use for old women. The pretty sisters, that was another matter..." The old soldier shook his head. "I am sorry, I thought you knew."

Eric was shaken. "My whole family, gone." He shook his head as he started back down the stairs. He knew the old soldier was right, he must leave.

Eric boarded the train going to Italy that night. Somehow, somewhere, I must start a new life.

Later that evening, as he sat in the dark, the train's mournful whistle touched a chord in him and his eyes filled with tears.

My dear mother, so kind and good, gone. My father, a loyal Latvian, who fought in the first World War and doctored the people in this city for half of his life, devoted father and friend, gone. My two sisters, God only knows what has happened to them. For the first time in his life, Eric knew total isolation and abandonment.

Chapter 18: Italy

"Ten thousand lire! Man, you must have an iron cock."

Eric smiled and combed his long, black hair down over his face, then parted it. He turned to his friend, his hair still partially covering his face. "Just part of the service, Aldo."

Aldo nodded his head and made an all knowing expression. "These rich American women, all they want to do is fuck and spend their husband's money. They all say their husbands are too busy making dollars to pay attention to them. It's a vicious cycle." Both men laughed and then sang in unison, "Americani Poverai." (Poor Americans).

Eric looked back into the mirror and combed his hair back, away from his face. He had curly black hair that came down over an intelligent brow. His eyes were coal black and he had a thin, aquiline nose. His wiry muscular body moved easily through life and he had an indefinable something that attracted people to him. His work clothes now were ski clothes, sweaters and a sweat band that held his hair back.

Six months ago Eric had left Riga, alone and disconsolate. For three months, he wandered the streets of Europe's cities looking fruitlessly for his sisters. Finally running out of funds he contacted Aldo. His friend understood and said he would gladly give him a place to stay until he got his life together. Gradually, Eric began to be his old self and the two bachelors began to live the Bohemian life. When their money ran out, they were forced to consider working again.

"Maurice said to be at the hotel at ten o'clock. He says the manager himself interviews so I had better bathe."

Eric pinched his nose. "I think you better."

In a half hour, the two men parked their bikes and walked into the Grand Hotel. Maurice greeted them in his undersized bellhop uniform.

Eric, always impressed with his strength and gentleness, was glad to see his old friend.

"This would be great if you both get on here. We would be the Three Musketeers, again."

"Yes," Aldo said, "we could change the name of the hotel to the Third Partisans Group." They all laughed together.

Maurice pointed. "Go through that door and the receptionist will direct you."

"Grazie, (Thanks) Maurice."

"Buona fortuna." (Good luck)

The two men entered the door and were greeted by the secretary. Aldo was called in first and came out in just a few minutes. There was a big smile on his face. "I'm in. When I told him I was second cook at the Royal before the war he said, "You can you start today." Better eat somewhere else Eric, the food here may start going downhill." The two men laughed. "I have to get a uniform and learn the ropes, so I will see you later. Ciao." (goodbye) Whistling an aria from The Elixir of Love, Aldo happily turned and left. Eric continued to wait.

In a few minutes a disembodied voice said through the speaker on the receptionist's desk, "Donna, send the next man in."

The receptionist pointed to the door and Eric walked into the room. The man at the desk was reading papers intently, and without looking up, motioned Eric to be seated,

Eric sat down and looked around the room. While the manager continued to read the document, Eric noted the room was rich and masculine. He ran his fingers gently over the arm of the chair. It was old, the leather was cracked but was surprisingly comfortable. He nestled back in his seat. A companion couch sat against the far wall. Eric smiled imagining the sofa was a disapproving big brother to the chair. The walls were decorated with Persian carpets and copies of old masters. After a few minutes Eric slowly began to realize how tastefully the room was done. It was good to see that some people were interested in more than money.

His eyes went to the mahogany shelves lining the walls. They were crowded with books and periodicals written in Italian, French and German. A copy of Paris Nights magazine was open on the desk, a slender pair of women's gloves lay carelessly on top. *I guess the manager is a ladies man.*

Eric's eyes went to the man at the desk. He wore a rich black suit with a pure white shirt and black tie. It was hard to tell from where he sat, but Eric judged him to be a thin, active man. He had thick black hair that grayed at the temples. His face was calm and he had a large Roman nose that centered his handsome, Italian face. *This was a self-made man.* Eric knew they would get along. He just hoped there would be a position open for him.

Eric looked out the window. Snow had started to fall and the sight of the flakes gave him an unexpected feeling of melancholy. His mind flitted back to winters past. Fireplaces, skaters whizzing around on the frozen lakes, and his older sister holding him up as the skates, with a mind of their own, tried to go their own way.

"Mr. Shapiro?"

The voice was distant but Eric knew it was for him and he forced his mind back into the room. "Excuse me, the snow out there reminded me of... never mind, you were saying, Sir?"

The manager tipped his chair back and looked out the window, understanding. "Yes, whenever it snows my head gets full of family, and Christmas, and good things to eat. I know just what you mean."

Immediately Eric was sure that he would like this man.

The manager picked up the papers he had been reading. "I have looked at your application. Whatever we have open you are over qualified for. You really should be in graduate university, studying rocket science or something."

Eric smiled. "I think the war was like a large bowl that put all the people inside, mixed us up and made us all homogenous. It was the great leveler. I starved and froze with the high born and peasants alike. I will be content to have a regular job now and do some catching up. Perhaps I will study later. When one loses his Mother, Father and his Sisters to the Nazis, it is difficult to just resume your life."

The manager nodded. "Yes, I understand." There was a palpable silence in the room. "Well perhaps we have something here for you... I see that you have skiing as a hobby. How good are you? Could you teach?"

"In 1936, I won the collegiate downhill at Grenoble and was considered for an alternate for the Olympics that year. Later I was told that political considerations kept me from going." Eric's face turned cold. "That meant I couldn't ski for Latvia because I was a Jew."

The manager's face was troubled. He said in a low voice, "I am sorry my friend." He shook his head slowly. "Sometimes I feel that I want to apologize for my fellow man, as if by my living in the same world as they, I am somehow responsible for the reprehensible things they do."

Eric smiled wanly. "I think I know what you mean. Sometimes, when I am in bed and the night is long, I stay awake and stare at the ceiling feeling guilty that I survived the holocaust. It is as if a million fingers point at me and say "Why you?""

"But, you know even the bastion of democracy, the United States, pulled the same underhanded thing in the '36 Olympics. It seems one of the American runners was a Jew. And the head of the American Olympic team, one Avery Brundage, wouldn't let this Jewish boy named, Marty Glickman run for the USA. I guess that was to satisfy Hitler. But, Hitler got his comeuppance anyway when the negro runner, Jessie Owens won the medals in Marty's place."

For a while the room was silent. Then the manager stood up and walked to the side of the desk and half sat on the edge. "The hotel owns a ski resort in the mountains. The ski instructor takes the tourists to the mountain and looks after them. He gives them lessons, settles arguments and blows their noses. The salary is modest but I understand the tips are good. In the best Italian tradition, you will not have to report the tips. In the summer you will work at the resort and help the tourists with their summer vacations. Agreed?"

"It sounds alright, but I am rusty. I will need a few days on the slopes to work the kinks out."

The manager stood up and extended his hand. "You can take a week at the resort and do anything you like. Your pay will start immediately. Welcome aboard, Eric."

Eric stood up and said thank you. The two men shook hands and he left.

For a long time the manager stood staring at the door. Finally, he sat down in his chair and hung his head. A half hour later the door opened and the receptionist came in holding a steaming cup of coffee in her right hand, the left supporting the bottom of the cup.

"I thought you might like some coffee, sir." She noted there were tears in his eyes. "Is something wrong?"

The manager looked up, with tears trickling down both cheeks. "That man Eric, he is alone in the world. His entire family, killed by the Nazis." His head lowered again. "We should have done more, Marta, we should have saved more."

The woman looked down, as if in a funeral, and nodded to acknowledge his pain. "I know you saved more than a hundred souls, sir. Downed airman, deserting Italian soldiers, Jews by the score. You did more than most."

Without looking up the manager nodded his head. Quietly, the woman turned and left the room. After a few moments the manager lifted his head and stared out the window at the falling snow, cleansing the earth.

****

Eric walked out of the elevator into the lobby of the stately hotel. He looked up admiringly at the vaulted ceiling with the great pillars holding it up. *The architect meant to make a room to overwhelm, and he certainly accomplished that.* From then on, Eric always felt dwarfed when he entered the great room.

He had not felt happier since the war had ended. The manager had given he and Aldo an airy room in the help quarters. As the man had said, 'the salary is modest, but the tips were very good.' The young women tourists were looking more for romance then they were for skiing and in fact, he had lately recruited Aldo to help him with the ladies who wanted more than just the ski slopes.

Eric looked at his watch as he walked briskly towards the desk. He thought he would pick up his mail, run a couple of miles, shower and start getting everyone ready for the first run to the slopes. *Good, only one guest checking in. I'll get my mail and take off,* he thought.

The desk clerk saw him and smiled, then turned back to the man checking in.

"I can give you a double away from the street noise, sir."

"Goot. Vun never knows if he might have a companion for der evening."

Eric froze and his heart turned to stone. He began to tremble with anger and pain. It was difficult to breathe. That voice! It couldn't be. He steeled himself and carefully walked to the side of the desk to get a better look at the man.

The man was looking down and writing on the card the clerk had given him. Eric could not get a clear look at him. No, it couldn't be, this man is larger. But that voice...

"Goot, danka." (thank you) The man lifted his head and Eric froze again. It was him! Slightly older and more corpulent, but it was him, the captain!

Eric blushed with fury. It was all he could do not to attack the man right there. He shakily walked back to the stairs to collect himself. When he got there his knees turned to jelly and he had to sit down on the stairs or fall.

"Shall I have someone help you with your luggage, sir?" the desk clerk volunteered

"Nein, I vill do it myzelf."

Eric's face was grim. Slowly, the strength came back to his body. In a split second, Eric firmly resolved to exact revenge. It was quiet in the hotel. He would follow him up to his room and kill him. His mind searched wildly for a weapon. No need, he thought, *I will be glad to strangle him with my bare hands.* He once again saw the oft seen vision of Anna curled in the fetal position, eyes open wide, eternally dancing in his head.

Eric watched from a distance as the captain walked to the elevator. He waited until the captain entered the elevator then quickly ran to the desk. "What room did you give that man, Georgio?"

"410," Why?"

Eric began to race towards the stairs. "I think I know him. Forget I asked." *That was stupid, now I have involved Georgio. Got to get up the four flights before he does.*

After the second floor Eric began puffing for breath. Floor two... three... He was slowing down. Can't be late. With a renewed effort he bounded up the stairs to the fourth floor. When he got there he fell to the concrete floor on one knee. Breathing deeply to catch his breath, he soon recovered. Eric then carefully opened the door to the corridor and peeked out. The dial above the elevator said the elevator was still on the third floor, but it was moving. *Good, not here yet. I will wait by the elevator door and would give the captain the surprise of his life... Death!*

Eric quickly opened the door to take a good position. As he slipped into the corridor his heart sunk. A door from one of the rooms opened. A small child threw a ball into the corridor and began to chase it. "Charles, wait for us," a female voice said from the room. Just then the elevator door opened and the captain stepped out. At the same time the woman left her room and looked up the corridor for the boy. "Charles! Charles! where is that boy?" she said with some frustration.

"He is right here, madam, The captain picked up the ball as the boy ran up to him, stopped and stood in front of him, staring up at his face."

Eric backed up and slipped back through the door into the stairwell. He kept the door open a crack, eyes glued on the captain.

The captain held the ball out to the boy. The lad took it absently, still staring up at the large man.

The woman caught up with them. "Thank you very much, sir." She took the boy's hand, while he was still staring up at the captain and jerked him. "Don't you dare run away like that." That broke the boy's attention and he dropped her hand and broke away and mischievously ran down the corridor.

The woman began chasing him once again, and the captain laughed, picked up his case and walked to his room.

Eric had calmed by now and thought better of attacking him. He waited until the captain got into his room. *Just as Georgio said, 410. Good, I've got him.* He closed the corridor door and slowly walked down the stairs to the floor below. I will think this through and then do what I must.

Eric opened the door to his room quietly. Aldo was still sleeping. The two men had become very close since he had come back to Italy. Aldo's sleepy personality and Eric's bright outlook clicked, and the two men got along well.

Eric sat on the edge of the bed, his mind racing and his chest bursting with this new turn of events. He shook Aldo. "Paisan, paisano, (Pal, pal) wake up."

Aldo turned over and muttered in his sleep.

Eric stood up. *No time to waste,* he thought. He quickly went to the bathroom and filled a cup with water. He walked back to the sleeping Aldo, hesitated for a moment and then splashed the cold water on his face.

Aldo jumped to a sitting position, sputtering and fuming. "Gran Dio en ciel!..." (God in Heaven)

"Aldo, calmativi, per favor." (Aldo, stay calm, please) "I wouldn't have done that to you but this is important and you wouldn't wake up.

Aldo glowered but a small smile played on his lips. "It better be important, paisano, or you're a dead man." Aldo pivoted to the side of the bed and put his feet on the floor. He shook his head and the water flew. Aldo reached to the night stand and with a practiced move took a cigarette out of its pack and put it in his mouth. He lit it and it dangled carelessly in his lips, the smoke curling up to his squinted eye.

"Well?"

"He's here."

"Who's here? Mother of God, you are making less sense than usual." He dragged impatiently on the cigarette.

"The Captain is here."

Aldo tensed, his face turning black. "What captain?"

Eric turned away and almost sobbed, then he turned back to Aldo. "The bastard that killed Anna."

Aldo's face turned bright red. The veins at his temples started to beat a visible, rhythmic tattoo. His eyes were wild and his voice was venomous. He started to rise. "I will take his head off!"

Eric touched his shoulder and gently pushed him back on the bed. At first he was surprised to see that Aldo sat back so easily. Then he noticed that Aldo seemed to be in a state of shock. *He must have loved her deeply, far deeper than I did*, Eric thought.

Eric turned away and looked out the window. He spoke absently. "When I first saw him I too was enraged. Since then I have calmed down some. My first thought also was to kill him and rid the earth of this vermin. But the more I think about it, the less I want to go to prison for dispatching him to Hell."

Aldo turned and looked at him blankly. "It would be worth dying for to rid the earth of that human filth. But, I will hear what you have to say first. Well, what do you think we should do?"

Eric stood up and paced. Then he stopped and turned towards Aldo. "The captain is a ladies man. I heard him say as much at the desk downstairs. Who do we know that is attractive enough to act as bait and has enough balls enough help us."

A puzzled look came over Aldo's face, then it lit up and a smile spread across his handsome face. "Ah, Maurice's girlfriend, the Americano. Si, Dolores from Pittsburg. She is gorgeous and Maurice says she is a little crazy, and that she will try anything once. I am sure she would do it."

Aldo jumped up and reached for his pants hanging on the edge of the bed. "You go talk to her and I will watch the pig."

Eric turned away and began to speak in a slow pace again, head down. "No, Aldo, I am not letting you near him. Let's first think this thing through. I don't want to go to prison nor do you." He looked up. "And we certainly don't want to get Dolores in trouble. This is not her fight." Eric stopped. He snapped his fingers. "I've got it. How about this?" He turned to Aldo. "The captain doesn't know you. Why don't we follow him and see what his habits and interests are. Then we could have you meet him, accidentally. After a while you can introduce him to Dolores. She can bring him somewhere and then..." Eric snapped his fingers.

Aldo nodded slowly. "Simple and efficient." He looked up at Eric. "I have lost my skills. Maurice is right, I cannot see past my anger. You are now the leader of this Partisan group." Both men nodded and then grimly set about their deadly business.

****

Aldo tensed as the elevator opened. Eric turned away, put his newspaper in front of his face and muttered a simple, "That's him."

The heavy-set man walked to the desk and said something to Georgio. The clerk reached to one of the pigeon holes and handed several pieces of mail to the captain. The fat man looked at them briefly then stuffed them in his pocket and turned to leave. He sauntered toward the bar. Eric and Aldo followed at a discrete distance. The captain stopped at the entrance looked around and then entered the bar. Eric paused and turned away. He whispered to Aldo, "Go on in. If you get an opportunity, make his acquaintance." Aldo took a step towards the bar and Eric stopped him with a hand on his shoulder. "Aldo, calmatavi. (stay calm) I don't want to lose you for a pig like that." Aldo affectionately touched Eric's hand, nodded his head and walked into the bar.

The captain was already seated at a table when Aldo walked into the room. He headed for the bar and said hello, affably, to the bartender, sat down on a stool and ordered a drink. After a few minutes he turned and surveyed the room. The captain put a cigarette in a holder and began to light it. Aldo left the bar and casually walked over to the table. He put his hands on the table and leaned over. He smiled and said something Eric couldn't hear. It was maddening.

The captain smiled and took out his box of cigarettes and handed one to Aldo. He held his lighter up to the cigarette and flicked it a few times, until a flame appeared. The captain held it steady for Aldo. The Italian took a big drag, thanked the captain, and turned to leave. The captain said something and pointed to the empty chair. Aldo stopped, smiled and sat down.

"We're in," Eric muttered. He leaned towards the two men behind his paper, but could hear nothing. The night dragged by slowly. At first he thought he would be conspicuous, but the lobby was crowded and no one paid any particular attention to him. He had bought a newspaper and sat in a chair where he could look over the paper and observe the two men. Several women came by to say hello to Eric, but got a curt goodbye.

Aldo and the captain ordered several rounds of drinks and soon were chatting amiably. After, to what Eric seemed an interminable amount of time, they both stood up and shook hands.

As the captain left the bar, Eric buried his face in the newspaper and the corpulent man walked right by him and went to the elevator. He pressed the button and waited patiently. Finally the elevator opened and he got in and disappeared. Eric breathed a sigh of relief.

In a few moments Aldo was in front of him. He was not smiling. He indicated for Eric to follow him and they walked toward the front entrance of the hotel.

The two men left the hotel and walked down the street. Neither one spoke for a few moments. Finally Aldo began. "He is our man alright... An ex-captain in the German army... Here on business." Aldo seemed distant, as if he had seen an accident and was trying to forget it.

Eric nodded his head. "I know he's our man. I would never forget that face. Did you make any arrangements?"

Aldo stared straight ahead. His voice seemed distant. "No."

Eric stopped, stunned.

Aldo continued calmly. "He is going back to Germany tomorrow."

Eric's heart fell and he was instantly depressed.

Anger contorted his face and he flushed. "Well, damn, Aldo, we have to do something now, tonight!"

Aldo also stopped and turned to him. "And you tell me I'm impatient. No! We'll do nothing now. He will be back at the end of the week, and he is very anxious to meet the young woman I told him about, the Americano."

Eric sighed and began to walk again. "Good," Eric said thoughtfully, "in the meantime I will talk to Dolores. I'll tell her just enough to pull it off. The less she knows, the better." The two men were somber as they walked aimlessly into the Italian night.

Eric stopped and looked up at the millions of stars lighting the heavens. "E lucevan le stella," (The stars are shining brightly) Eric said.

"Bene," (Good) Aldo answered, "it is well that it is a night for lovers, it will hide the hate in our hearts.

Chapter 19: Italy

The phone rang just as Joe stepped out of the shower. "Damn," he muttered as he wrapped the towel around his dripping body, "wouldn't you know it. I'm coming, I'm coming," he said to the empty room. Joe lifted the phone and put it to his wet ear. "Pronto," (hello,) he said, expectantly.

"Joe?" The voice sounded close to tears.

"Yes, this is Joe Wilson," he said puzzled.

"It's me, Dolores, Dolores Black."

"Dolo! What a surprise. Are you in Italy?"

"I have been living in Italy for a year now. I called my mother today and she told me you were here, too. She also told me you had some difficulty at home but she wouldn't tell me what it was. I am sorry." She waited expectantly, as if she expected him to tell her what it was.

"Yeah," Joe said sadly, and then abruptly changed the subject. "Dolo, is something wrong? You sound awful."

"Oh, Joe, I think I got into something over my head. And you were always so level headed,... that's why I called you. Please help me, Joe."

Joe thought to himself, *Level headed, me? Riiight.* "Of course, Dolo, tell me what's going on? Where can we meet?"

Dolores gave him the address and the best way to get there. Joe dried himself and slipped into jeans and a sweat shirt. He put his tennis shoes on without socks and dashed down the stairs, two at a time. In a few minutes he was on his Vespa scooter maneuvering through the narrow streets looking for the Via Vanetta, the street where Dolores lived.

Joe found the street, pulled up at the right number and parked the scooter. He looked up and marveled at the old building. The villa, Dolores had rented, dated back to the sixteenth century. It was built by the Medici as a country get-away from their own city.

From that distant point in antiquity, the villa had changed hands many times. Just now it was owned by a man with a heart of stone. He was a penny pinching slave to his purse and would do nothing to preserve this proud, old sixteenth century lady. But the rent was cheap and Dolores reveled in its ancient charm.

Joe went quickly up the worn steps. As he skipped up the stairs two at a time he marveled at the way the marble stairs were worn in the center and level at both sides. He reverently thought of the millions of feet that had preceded his, both royal and common.

When he reached the top, he tapped at the only door present and heard a muffled, "Come in."

Carefully he opened the door and gingerly stepped in. A voice called out, "Just make yourself at home,

Joe, I'll be right out." Then as an afterthought, "I hope it's you, Joe."

Joe smiled broadly. "It's okay, it's me."

Joe stared out the window and tried to remember exactly what Dolores looked like. Her brother Al and he were forwards on a Pittsburg high school basketball team and the only time he ever saw her was when he came over to pick Al up and sometimes on Sunday when Al's mother would invite him for Sunday dinner. His mind flitted back to those Sunday dinners and he remembered Dolores as a skinny kid with braces and a flat chest. She would come to the games and bashfully hang around the players. After a while Al would tire of her, and run her off. Absently he wondered how she would look now as he wandered around the room looking at the pictures on the wall.

Dolores had painted the room a light pink with reddish baseboards. Ugh! There was a high arch over the windows and the stained glass reached from just off the floor to a foot below the ceiling. Now, God, that's just beautiful, Joe thought. On the home-made shelves, Dolores had put up, there were antique pieces that she had searched for all throughout Italy. It was easy to see that she had a good eye for form. Original paintings by unknown artists adorned the walls. The couch Joe finally sat on was a vintage midnight blue, and its companion easy chair, that sat across the room, was checkered dark and light blue.

When Dolores finally entered the room, it lit up. She was nothing like Joe remembered. The braces were gone and in their place was a smiling, sensuous mouth. The skinny body had been replaced by a handsome woman with the measurements of a playgirl. The serious eyes of a moonstruck teenager were now deep blue and sparkling. She went right to Joe and he stood up just in time to receive her embrace. It was warm and full of promise.

"Oh, Joe, it's so good to see you. Thank you for coming to my rescue." Dolores pointed to the couch. "Please, sit down." Both of them sat down on the couch. Dolores turned to face him.

She turned her head slightly and looked past him to the window at the darkening sky, then turned back, but this time she averted his eyes.

Joe waited patiently.

She smiled sheepishly and finally looked directly at him. "Joe, I am so selfish, thinking only of myself. How are you?" Joe nodded. "Your dad? I heard your mother was sick again. Please give her my best."

"Thank you Dolo." Joe felt a sudden pain for his mother and the anxiety he caused her because of the trouble he had just been in lately. Quickly he changed the subject. "What is this problem your having."

Dolores dropped her head. Her voice began so softly that Joe had to strain to hear her. "I met this man here, in Italy. His name is Maurice. He is just wonderful and I really love him." At the word 'love' Joe felt a slight constriction in his chest. He shook it off. "He has a friend in the local Mafia, named Aldo." Dolores was raising her voice and her delivery became staccato. She was clearly very nervous.

"Apparently they ran into an old enemy, a German, that killed Aldo's girlfriend..." she hesitated, then added hastily, "...during the war." She looked back out the window, this time her eyes were vacant, unsettled. "Aldo wants revenge." She looked back at Joe. This time he saw fear in her eyes.

"They want me to decoy the German so Aldo can confront him." Her eyes brimmed. "Oh, Joe, I think they want to kill him. I'm scared." She leaned over and put her head on his shoulder and began to cry.

Joe felt the perfume of her enveloping him. He could not help but think how good she felt there.

Dolores pulled away and looked down. "Just look at me crying like a big baby. Joe reached for his handkerchief, hoping it was clean. She dried her eyes and handed it back to him. Joe mumbled for her to keep it.

Clumsily, Joe stood up, glad to get away from her charms. "Why don't I speak to your friends and see what they have in mind."

Dolores stood up. "Oh would you?" she said excitedly, "that would be great." Then her face fell. She looked sheepish again. "They might be very angry. They told me not to tell anyone..."

Joe smiled. "I'm not just anyone, I'm family."

"Oh, Joe, mille grazie." (A million thanks) Dolores stood up and threw her arms around him. At that moment he did not feel like family.

Joe separated himself, with difficulty, and picked up his helmet. "Set the meeting up and call me. Make sure you tell me where to go and I will meet you there." He walked to the door, Dolores just behind him. He turned to her with a serious face. "In the meantime you stay out of trouble." Then he smiled. "See ya."

Impulsively Dolores embraced him again. Joe felt her body next to his and felt like he was going to melt. He gently separated himself and turned to leave.

At the door she called his name and said, "Thank you again." She blew him a kiss as he turned to walk down the stairs.

Joe was more than glad to get away from her without showing his feelings.

The next day Joe got a call from Dolores to meet her at the Grand Hotel. As he walked through the lobby he looked for her. No Dolores. Then he saw the entrance to the bar. He stepped through the door and there she was, sitting at a table, nursing a glass of wine. Joe swallowed hard. She looked better than the day before. Dolores was dressed in jeans and a T-shirt that caressed her body just right.

Joe pasted a smile on his face and went to her. He stuck out his hand to shake hers but she would have none of it and quickly got up and embraced him. The natural perfume of her body was overwhelming and threatened to suck him in again, but he resisted it and forced himself to concentrate. *Maybe later,* he thought, all the while remembering the recent problem he had been in.

Dolores sat down, turned to business and quickly briefed him. She said Maurice and Aldo were very angry when she told him that she had said something to him but, they finally calmed down and now they were willing to speak to him. Joe just nodded and Dolores quickly chugged the wine nervously. When she finished her drink she nodded and they both got up and walked out of the bar to the elevator.

Joe started to feel tense. *What the hell am I getting into?* This was certainly a long way from Pittsburg, USA. He had thought about carrying a gun, but that seemed too melodramatic. *Anyway, these guys weren't the enemy,* he hoped. He settled for being on his guard.

Dolores was very nervous and he was glad when the elevator reached the fifth floor. She quickly got out and Joe followed her down the hall. She tapped twice on the door and a muffled voice said, "Entrare." (Come in) The door was opened by a giant of a man and Dolores stepped in with Joe right behind her.

The room was smoky. It was a typical middle class, Italian hotel room with faded wall paper that was peeling. *This could not be the famous Grand Hotel,* Joe thought. Then he realized, this was the hotel workers quarters.

There was an old couch and two chairs and a bed with the standard brass headboard and footboard. An unshaven man lay on the an unmade bed, smoking. Rudely, he glared at Joe but did not get up. *A bad beginning,* Joe thought.

The colossus who had opened the door looked very strong. He pecked Dolores' cheek and then, without warning turned Joe around and began to frisk him. Joe protested and confronted the bigger man.

Suddenly the man on the bed sat up and a pistol appeared in his hand. "Just relax, mister. Rules of the house say no guests get to use guns." The big man turned Joe back again and continued frisking him. Dolores stood by looking sheepish. When he finished, he nodded to the man with the gun. The man smiled mirthlessly and put the weapon back under the pillow and lay back down again.

"Have a seat," the big man said. Joe sat down on the edge of the couch. Dolores, looking very uncomfortable, stood off to the side, shifting her feet.

The door to another room opened, and a third man dressed in ski clothes, walked in and came directly up to Joe. The man was smiling and relaxed, and stuck out his hand. Joe reluctantly took it. He spoke with an East European accent. "My name is Eric. You will excuse this American movie cloak and dagger stuff but there is some serious business to be done and we must, be sure of our man." He pointed to a chair. "Please, have a seat and we will explain."

Joe sat down, uneasily. Eric sat down on the chair opposite him. The big man remained standing by the door and the smoker got up to a sitting position. Dolores shifted her feet uneasily.

Joe took the measure of the three men and knew at once he could not take them. In addition, the one by the door had placed himself strategically so he couldn't leave. Dolores smiled encouragingly at him and he smiled back, but his eyes remained non-committal.

The man in the bed got up and began to speak, the cigarette bobbing in his mouth, ashes falling to the floor. "What is your name?" he said in a thick Italian accent.

"Joe."

"Joe what?" he said abruptly.

"Joe Wilson." he said patiently, measuring his words.

Dolores spoke up angrily. "What's the difference what his name is, Aldo. What all of you want to know is will he keep his mouth shut. I have known him all of my life. He will. Just ask him what you want to know, he will give you a straight answer."

Eric smiled at Dolores. "Dolores from Pittsburg," he said engagingly, "if we told this young man we were going to kill someone, in cold blood, he would be revolted, and rightly so. Probably, he would go straight to the police. But," he turned to Joe and riveted him with his eyes, "if we told him the intended victim was a murderer, on a scale he could not imagine. And that he had sent thousands of men, women and even little children to concentration camps and then on to gas chambers, where they were efficiently slaughtered like dumb cattle, then he might be more willing to join us."

Joe was listening carefully, his eyes moving rapidly from Dolores to Eric.

Eric continued to look at Joe, his black eyes penetrating. "Listen, Joe, this man who we want to deal with was a captain in a deaths head commando group, the Eisensatzgruppen. Their sole purpose was to round up Jews and other people the Germans thought were untermenchen (sub-human) and either shoot them, gas them, or bring them to concentration camps."

Joe had seen pictures of the concentration camps and shuddered inwardly.

Eric continued. "When I was with the partisans, this captain, tracked me across Italy to the Swiss border. He was relentless. The fact that the war was lost by now to the Germans meant nothing to him. The other exterminators, like the captain, tied up the entire European rail system just to deliver Jews to the death camps. They all knew the war was over but they kept on killing anyway." Eric's face was flushed and grave. "Even their own troops were denied necessary supplies by rail to fight the war." Eric's voice lowered. "If they could only get one more Jew to exterminate it was to be done at any cost."

The air was charged and Eric turned and looked at Aldo. "The guide the underground had given me for my escape to Switzerland was Aldo's fiancé." He nodded at Aldo who sat back down on the bed again, his face black with hate.

"To give me a better chance to escape, she and I split up. Unfortunately, the Nazis caught her. While this was happening I was in hiding in a tree, but had a clear view of them. She was captured by the very man who we are now talking about. The captain had very persuasive interrogation methods." Eric's voice lowered. "He beat her unmercifully, but still she would not betray me. Tiring with her reluctance he pulled out his Luger and shot her in the head and left her in a field for the dogs. By the way, he had killed her husband a short time before and now left her only child an orphan."

There was silence in the room. Dolores began to cry softly. Joe tried to speak but his voice betrayed him and he croaked. He cleared his throat. "I can understand your anger, but what does this have to do with Dolores?"

Aldo sat up, his cigarette still in his mouth. His right eye was squinting from the smoke curling up to his face. He spoke with no emotion on his face, his eyes as cold as ice. "The captain is a lady's man. I promised him a lady for a night, on the town, and then in bed. Dolores will take him on the town, I will put him to bed." Joe shuddered inwardly again. Aldo sounded ominous.

"What kind of danger will she face."

Eric spoke. "Not much." Maurice will be driving the rented car and just look at the size of him." Joe laughed nervously as Maurice contracted his right arm showing a powerful biceps.

Aldo continued, his voice still low and ominous. "We will be following their car. At the appropriate moment their car will stop. Maurice will make sure he will have car trouble. Dolores will get out and we will step in. Before we even talk to the Nazi, she and Maurice will start back to town. They will have done nothing and seen nothing. Dolores will be done with it.

Joe smiled, understanding completely. "Of course this is all speculation, a story to entertain me, a gullible American. None of this will really happen."

Aldo looked at him, puzzled.

Eric smiled. "Of course. It's all a joke. We would never do such a foolish thing."

Aldo smiled, realizing this line of talk took Joe out of the picture as a conspirator.

Joe got up, shook hands with Eric, nodded to Aldo and turned to Dolores. "Dolo, let's you and I talk for a few minutes." Eric got up and walked to the door. Maurice looked at Aldo and then Eric. Eric nodded his head and Maurice opened the door. He smiled fondly at Dolores and let them out.

Joe and Dolores walked slowly down the hall to the lift. Joe was silent and thoughtful. When they got to the elevator, Joe began to speak. His voice was clear and forceful. "The risk seems minimal." Joe nodded his head towards the room they had just left. "They seem ruthless and determined, so I would imagine they will follow through. It will be a conspiracy to commit a crime, so you would be involved despite what they say. I really can't advise you to do this."

Dolores pursed her lips and nodded her head slightly. "Joe, when I came here it was to get away from my family and taste freedom. I dropped out of college because everyone seemed to just want the security of a big bank account, a home with a picket fence and two and a half kids. I want more than that. Here is a beast that needs to be separated from decent society." She shook her head vigorously, setting her hair to bobbing. "Not only will I do it, but I will be proud to do so."

They embraced and Joe was glad the lift had arrived so she would not see how really nervous he was.

****

Eric paced the floor. His brow was wet with sweat and he had changed clothes twice in the last two hours. He needed to do it again. He wiped his brow.

Aldo walked into the room in his white cooks outfit, the smell of the kitchen still on his clothes. "Well?"

Eric's face was grave. "It has begun. They are already together. We will intercept the car at the agreed place. Maurice is driving as planned." Eric sat on the edge of the bed and wiped his brow again.

Aldo cocked his head and looked at his friend. He looked troubled. "What is wrong, Eric, you have killed Nazis before. Aldo turned and threw his cook's jacket on the head of the bed.

Eric looked up at Aldo's back. "That was war. This is murder."

Aldo whirled on Eric. "Murder? This beast is the king of murder. He could teach the Devil to kill. Did you not tell me yourself he cut down Maria like a slaughtered calf." He crossed himself trying to contain his sudden anger. After a moment he calmed a little then walked to Eric and put his hand on his shoulder.

Eric looked up at him with troubled eyes.

"Eric, mi amici, (my friend) he is not fit to live among us. He needs the killing. Do not worry, when the time comes, I will do it and then he will die with Maria's name in his ears."

Eric shook his head and stood up with resolve on his face. "Aldo, I will do my part... as planned. "Prossimo, lascili vanno al nostro destino." (Come, let us go to our destiny) The two men looked deep into each other's eyes and grasped each other's forearms like Roman gladiators.

Chapter 20: Murder?

The Renault sped through the night and soon left the lights of the city. As they accelerated through the quiet of the countryside, Aldo was silent and Eric contemplative. The only hint of Aldo's nervousness was the chain smoking he did on the drive to the appointed place. Eric noted he lit the new cigarettes with the last one he half-smoked. Finally Aldo spoke.

"We are getting close." Eric slowed the car as they rounded a large curve. "There they are just ahead," Eric said softly. He could see the dull glint of the moon off the black metal and the smooth, man-made shape of the German car against the irregular shapes of nature.

The sky was clear and the moon was at harvest. Eric could clearly see that their plan was unfolding like clockwork. Maurice had the hood up and was bent over the fender, tinkering with the engine while Dolores was in the back seat with the captain.

Eric put the lights of the Renault out and quietly eased the car forward for the last twenty yards. The captain was busy pawing Dolores and the two men pulled up unnoticed. Slowly and carefully they got out of their car. The night was silent and aside from the voices from the car, only the crickets spoke.

Maurice signaled and quickly went to the front door of the Renault and slid in behind the wheel. He waited stoically. Aldo and Eric split up and went to opposite sides of the Mercedes. Dolores and the captain were still in the back seat and she was pouring a drink for him. He was laughing and fondling her breast. She looked past him and saw Aldo. She pulled her dress strap over her shoulder and then put her hand on his knee as she handed him the glass. He sat back with a satisfied look on his face. He took a long drink and threw the glass out the open window. The glass struck Eric, fell to the ground and shattered.

Dolores laughed and blocked the captain's hand as he again reached for her breast. His mouth corners turned down and he looked like a petulant school boy. "Sorry, my Captain, nature calls. You have made me drink too much," Dolores said as she slid toward the door.

"But don't go away yet my love. Let us finish our business." The captain felt a rush as Dolores opened the door. He lurched towards her and pawed at the back of her dress. "No, don't go yet," he said, half smiling, half serious.

She laughed as she pulled away and stepped out of the car.

The captain's face turned to surprise as Aldo, his face like a piece of granite stone, slid in and took her place.

For a split second the captain could not comprehend what was happening. "Vat is dis?" then his brain tried to kick in over the drink and he reached for the Mauser he always kept strapped to his leg.

Aldo watched the move and quickly put his stiletto to his throat.

The captain stopped abruptly.

At that instance Eric slid in on the other side, reached down and snatched his Mauser.

The captain's eyes went wide and his voice, high and excited, exploded, "You!"

"Yes, me, Captain. You have been looking over your shoulder for years," Eric guessed, "and tonight your past has caught up with you."

The captain looked around wildly as the other car started up and Maurice and Dolores sped away as planned.

The fog was leaving the captain's brain and he fought to gain time.

"I, I vas only doing my job. It was orders... from higher up..."

"Yes, and some Jews are among your best friends." Eric was smiling sardonically.

"Vy, yes. I have lots of Jewish friends."

"Get out of the car." Aldo's voice was menacing. "Slide out towards me."

"I vill not move." The captain crossed his arms akimbo.

"This is for Anna, now move!" Aldo hissed and moved the blade across the captain's throat leaving a bloody wake.

The captain touched his throat with his fingers. "You have cut me," he said incredulously.

"Move, when I tell you, you fat pig." Aldo hissed again.

Frightened, the captain carefully slid out of the car while Aldo held the point of the stiletto at his throat. When they were both outside Aldo turned him roughly and stood at his back. "Cover him," he said to Eric who had come around the car and stood quietly, feeling sick and wondering what Aldo was going to do next.

He did not have long to wait. Aldo grabbed the captain's hair and pulled him to his knees.

The captain howled in protest.

Aldo tightened his grip and stuck the point of the stiletto into the skin next to the captain's Adam's apple. "Quiet pig!" The captain stopped abruptly. Aldo took a large handkerchief from his pocket and handed it to the captain. "Put this in your mouth." His brow now covered with sweat he reluctantly obeyed the instruction. Aldo let his hair go, put the knife up and quickly drew tape from his pocket, tore off a piece and taped over the captain's mouth and wound it around his head. A second piece was torn off and Aldo put his hands behind his back and expertly wound it around his wrists. There was no doubt in Eric's mind that Aldo had done all this before.

The captain was trembling and tried to speak but all that Eric could hear were garbled, muffled sounds. Aldo grabbed his hair again. The knife again appeared in his hand and this time the point was placed against the captain's abdomen. Over the liver just as Aldo had been taught by the English instructor.

Eric knew this was a quick but painful death.

"Listen pig," Aldo hissed, "I am Mafiosi, so trust me, I have killed before, but never with such pleasure."

The captain's eyes bugged out, wide with terror. He tried to break away but Aldo held him fast. More strange, pleading sounds came from his taped mouth.

Aldo's eyes narrowed to small slits. "This time Anna's blood cries out for vengeance, and I am her avenging angel. And I will avenge all the others you have murdered." The captain turned his head some and looked at Eric for mercy. Eric turned away. With a mighty effort the captain tried to rise up but Aldo held him by his hair, firmly in place.

"Tell the Devil to find you a nice, hot place, pig. Aldo dropped to his knees and looked at the captain at eye level. "For Anna," he hissed. He tightened his grip on the knife at the captain's abdomen and started it moving forward, slowly. Sounds tried to escape from the captain's throat but the handkerchief stopped them. He tried to move his arms but the tape held them firmly. Aldo kept sliding the stiletto slowly and carefully into the captain's liver.

Eric could not look and turned away. A feeling of cowardice came over him and he wanted to run but he forced himself to turn around and look again.

There was a strange look on Aldo's face as he continued to slide the knife into the Captain's abdomen, very slowly. The captain let out a muffled scream and lost his fluids and still he tried to get away. Aldo was too strong and continued to hold him firmly. "Remember her name as you descend into hell, Nazi. Anna! Anna!"

In complete and total terror the captain managed to swallow the handkerchief and loosen the tape. His last scream filled the night and echoed through the trees as the knife went into his abdomen up to the hilt. Suddenly, the light went out of the captain's eyes and he crumpled to the ground.

Eric turned away and walked to the closest tree. He wretched, but could not throw up. Aldo stood over the body, soaked with sweat, his heart pumping and his eyes wild. He had killed before but always dispassionately. This was different, this was personal. Finally a more normal look came back into his face. With a sardonic smile he reached over and wiped the blade on the dead man's coat.

Aldo slowly stood up and stared at the captain for a long while. Then he screwed up his face and spit on the body. "Nazi bastard!" He spit again. "Decent people will no longer tremble at the sound of your jackboot."

Aldo and Eric dumped the body in the deeper woods and then got back into the Mercedes. Aldo began to wipe the steering wheel with his handkerchief. "Maurice will come soon and take us back to town. Wipe your fingerprints off carefully, we don't want to leave a trace for the polizia." (police)

Aldo was silent for a moment and then a smile slowly spread across his face. "Being Mafiosi has its advantages. This car will be picked up tonight and taken to a chop shop. There it will be broken down and sold for parts. And if we are lucky, no one will find the captain's body for months, if ever. Relax, mio amico, (my friend) Anna is avenged."

Eric nodded grimly, still sick at his stomach.

****

Joe was waiting as they walked into the room. Eric sat at the edge of the bed and stared into space. Aldo poured a drink and offered one to Eric. Absently, he took the glass.

"Well?"

"It's done," Eric said, focusing his eyes on Joe. He downed the whiskey in one gulp.

Seeing how disturbed Eric was Joe sat down next to him and put his arm around his shoulder.

Eric dropped his head and stared at the ground.

Joe patted his shoulder and said in a low voice, "It'll all come out alright, Eric."

Aldo angrily ground out the cigarette he had lit. "I will be back later," he said his voice cracking with emotion as walked out the door without looking back.

Eric lifted his head still staring into space. He said to no one in particular, "I fought the Nazis for five years and killed many of them, but this was different. This was cold blooded murder." Eric stood up and paced, his head down eyes closed.

Joe remained on the bed and was thoughtful. "You know, the way you feel about this, maybe a change of scenery might be good for you. Besides, if the police dig hard enough they might just find a connection between you and the captain.

Eric stopped and looked at Joe. "If I left now, and the police found the body, they might get suspicious."

Joe stood up. "Not if you merely made a job change. I have a hostel on a mountain near Ubecht in Switzerland." He smiled weakly. "The place could use a manager and ski instructor.

Aldo walked back into the room and nervously lit a cigarette. Apparently he had been listening. "You know, Eric," Aldo said in a tight, clipped voice, "that just might be a good idea."

Eric looked at his friend. "What about you Aldo?"

Aldo smiled a broad grin. "Ah, mio amico, (my friend) I am a much better liar than you. Besides, if both of us disappeared..." He exaggeratedly shrugged his shoulders and pulled his mouth corners down.

Eric nodded his head and sat back on the bed. In a few moments he was in deep thought. Almost to himself he said, "Yes, and Dolores must stay put for a while too." Then he looked up and brightened. "Yes, it is best that Dolores stay here as if nothing had happened. And if no one calls her or questions her, she is in the clear and can continue to live here, or perhaps, even go back to America." He turned to Joe. "She may even want to go with...." Eric stopped afraid he had said too much. Instead of continuing he stood up and grasped Joe's hand. His eyes were on fire. "Yes, my friend, I will go to Ubecht. I really do want a change of scenery."

Chapter 21: Switzerland

The sun was just setting as the Swissair touched down at the Zurich airport. As the plane taxied towards the terminal, Tomiko watched the beginning gentle rain touch the wings and roll off. She looked with fascination as the ground crew began to scurry around the great bird. When the plane came to a stop she busied herself to deplane. Standing in line she waited patiently until she got to the stewardess who was saying goodbye to the departing passengers. Tomiko nodded her thanks to the stewardess then walked through the covered walkway towards the terminal. A tinge of fear walked with her.

She had written the hostel and was answered right away by an Eric Shapiro. He told her in his letter that he had been hired by Joe as the manager and that the place was running smoothly. He also said he was devastated when he heard of Joe's death and that he would be there to pick her up when she came. He said he would wear a red carnation and requested she wear a white one for identification. She fingered the carnation as she walked towards the unknown.

As Tomiko made her way to the baggage carousel a friendly, smiling man approached her wearing a red carnation. "Mrs. Carter? I'm Eric."

Tomiko stared up at the dark haired giant. He was well over six feet and muscular. His face was rugged and tanned and he had white circles around his dark eyes made there by sun goggles and ski slopes. *He looks like he lives on skis,* she thought. He wore a bulky wool sweater and ski pants, topped off by a dark blue sweat band that kept his black locks from spilling over his eyes. *His eyes,* Tomiko thought, *they have known great pain...*

Tomiko bowed her head slightly to the left and, with a geisha smile, nodded a greeting. She offered to shake hands, western style, but Eric gently turned it, bowed low, and kissed the back of her hand. Tomiko, not used to such deference from a European and blushed to the roots of her raven hair.

After they exchanged pleasantries, Tomiko followed Eric to the baggage carousel where he expertly salvaged her luggage. In a short while, her hair blowing in the wind, they were speeding out of Zurich towards Übecht where the hostel awaited them.

****

Eric eased the gearshift into second as the small, convertible Fiat whined and protested against the steep grade of the winding mountain road. When the final curve was negotiated, Tomiko looked down from the top of the mountain and saw her Swiss home for the first time. Involuntarily, she sucked in her breath as the beauty of the place overtook her. The moon was full and silver and shining so brightly it made the night into day. It shone on a wide shimmering lake with gleaming white buildings that made up the hostel. In back of those buildings rose an immense mountain that had a jagged ridge and was topped by a year round cap of snow. The mountain was even higher than the one she was on. Evergreens dotted the far shore of the lake and twinkling lights from the hostel danced on the water like fireflies on a summer eve.

Tomiko had to admit to herself that this was every bit as lovely as anything she had ever seen in Japan and she suddenly felt less lonely. She was startled out of her reverie by Eric.

"Well, there it is, your new home." Then he blurted something that had been on his mind since he received her letter. "It has been my home for quite a while and I hope to stay on with you."

Tomiko nodded silently, respecting the intense feeling she got from Eric.

The beauty of the place did not diminish as they got closer. As the Fiat rolled to a halt, among the bicycles in the ordered parking lot, Tomiko noted the gleaming fences and bright, white buildings., she thought, *Someone is taking loving care of this place. I'll bet it's Eric.*

Eric quickly walked to the passenger door, but he was too late. Tomiko had already let herself out and was slowly turning, drinking in the beauty and peacefulness of the hostel. He stood by and watched her quietly. Finally, she stopped with a sigh and reached for her bag.

"I'll get that," he said, and was quickly by her side." He reached past her to get the bag and as he did he brushed against her. For a moment he felt giddy as the perfume of her stirred him. He immediately pushed it down. "I'll have your things brought to your house, Mrs. Carter."

Tomiko nodded and began to follow him as he strode through the front entrance.

As Tomiko entered, she immediately noticed the deer heads hanging on the wall over the front desk. The young woman behind the desk put down her magazine and cigarette and smiled sweetly at Eric.

Well, everything is not perfect, Tomiko thought. Mentally she made a note to have the deer heads taken down and no smoking signs put up.

Chapter 22: Ubecht, Switzerland

By the time a year had passed Tomiko had not only became aware of her multi-faceted duties as owner of the hostel, but learned to rely on Eric for his expert abilities.

Magda opened the door to the office and beckoned to Sydney to come in. "Tommy," she said loudly, "you have a guest here waiting to get checked in. Come out to the desk."

"All right, I'll be right there." In a few moments the door opened and Tomiko entered the room. She greeted Magda then turned to the guest.

"Tommy, this is Syd..."

Tomiko stared at Sydney's platinum hair and shook her head. She felt suddenly faint and grabbed the side of the desk to support herself. Both women went to her at once. Magda held her shoulders and gently walked her to the couch. Sydney stood by helplessly. Finally she reached out, and took Tomiko's hands and rubbed them. "Can I get you some water?"

Tomiko shook her head. "No, it's just... Your hair, it's just like... Please don't mind me." She looked contritely at Sydney. "It's just... for a moment, you reminded me of someone,... someone from the past I thought I had forgotten."

Sydney smiled as if the matter would soon be forgotten but she promised herself she would ask more about this when Tommy recovered.

Tomiko stood up shakily. "Please forgive my unforgivable manners." She bowed her head formally. "I am now recovered fully." She extended her hand. "My name is Tomiko. Everyone here calls me Tommy. I would be honored if you would call me Tommy, too."

Sydney took her hand. "I'm Sydney but my friends call me Syd."

"Syd just rode up on her bike Tommy. She needs a bunk for the night. She turned to Sydney. You're in luck, Syd. Tommy's the best cook in the mountains and if she likes you, you don't even have to peel the potatoes you eat."

Tomiko had recovered by now, and the three women chatted easily until the shadows in the room grew long. Finally, Tomiko stood up, drew the shade back and looked at the tranquil, glassy lake. "It is getting late. I must organize the dinner for tonight."

Sydney rose. "I can help."

"No, tonight you are our guest." She smiled and turned to the young girl. "Magda will do the cooking."

Magda threw her hands up in mock disgust.

"See, it is just like the Hungarian army. If dey see you, you have to work. If you hide, you're safe." She tossed her head and put her nose up in the air. "I'll be in the kitchen if you need me."

Tomiko looked wistfully as Magda left. "She has been such a big help to me since she has been here. I will miss her when she leaves. I have offered her a permanent job, but she wants to finish her studies. And I certainly approve of that." She beckoned to Sydney. "Come, I will show you where you can put your things. It is not luxurious, but I think you will find it comfortable."

Tomiko opened the door and Sydney heard the familiar, comforting, squeak of the dry hinges so common in the mountains. Feelings of her childhood flooded her mind and body. Then she stepped outside and there was the grand mountain that dwarfed the hostel. *It's simply wonderful but a bit overwhelming.*

Tomiko was watching her reaction.

"It's magnificent," Sydney said in awe.

"Honto, excuse me, yes, it is the truth. It is magnificent. My Joe found this place without me. It is a tribute to his love of beauty." For a split second she looked crestfallen. "I miss him," she added wistfully. Sydney understood immediately and her heart squeezed with longing for Paul.

The two women walked down the path to the dormitory. They could not have been more different in appearance. Tomiko was small with raven black hair cut short with bangs just above her eyes. She had cream colored skin and stood no more than five feet tall. She was very thin and walked with delicacy and grace. Sydney felt awkward next to the diminutive Tomiko. She felt like she towered over her but was actually only four inches taller.

Sydney was now suntanned to a toast brown. That skin color was accented by her platinum hair that glistened as it brushed her shoulders. She looked like a suburban California girl biking her way to a tennis lesson. Wherever she went, she moved gracefully athletically and with purpose.

Inexplicably, maybe because opposites attract, they were drawn to each other. Perhaps, on a subconscious level, each of them recognized the others pain.

As they walked down the path Sydney spied the tennis courts. They were clay courts and even from a distance Sydney could see that like the rest of the hostel, they were well taken care of. Immediately, she was glad she had brought her rackets. "Who plays?"

Tomiko looked up from the path, mildly surprised. "The guests do... And I play some myself," she added modestly.

When they reached the dormitory, Tomiko opened the door for Sydney. Once more she heard the familiar, homey squeak of the hinges. Sydney looked around with a graphic artist's eye. It was a large, open building with twenty or so beds. Several children were playing tag, glad to be rid of their bossy parents, and the car, and the constant traveling they had done that day. In the meantime, their parents busied themselves getting the bunks ready for sleep. Suddenly, one of the children brushed by Sydney, and just as suddenly another one ran right between them bumping into Tomiko. "Slow down, kids," Tomiko called quietly after them.

"Kinder!" (Children) another voice said firmly and the two youngsters stopped dead in their tracks.

"Danke," (Thank you) Tomiko said to the large woman who had spoken.

"Bitte." (You're welcome)

Tomiko looked at the now sulking children, then turned and looked around the room. She smiled at Sydney. "Let me see, where shall we put you?" Suddenly her face lit up and her black eyes danced. She leaned over and whispered, "I think we can do better than this for you. Come, let us leave."

Sydney was puzzled but said nothing. She hiked her back pack up on her shoulder and followed in Tomiko's wake. They left the dormitory, but this time they turned away from the lake and started walking up the mountain. The sun was slowly settling over the lake and as they went up the air turned sharply cooler. Sydney stopped and put on her sweater, but the smaller woman seemed impervious to the cold.

Sydney was glad to be stretching her legs after her long ride and luxuriated in the walk. She could not help but wonder where they were going since the dormitories were now back where they had come from. She decided to simply trust Tomiko's judgment.

Suddenly she stopped. "Tommy, shall I get my bike?"

Tomiko kept walking. "It will be quite safe where it is."

With her longer stride Sydney quickly caught up with Tomiko. She felt the chill of the wind off the mountain. "Tommy, I have an extra jacket in my pack, would you like to borrow it?"

Tomiko smiled. "We Japanese are taught at an early age to be stoic. There are so many people on our islands that privacy is a luxury. To show discomfort is to display bad manners. Unlike your society, even using the bathroom is done with others present. We are taught that even with others there, we are alone. One learns to be mentally disciplined in such circumstances. Thank you, but I will not need the jacket."

Sydney shook her head knowingly and smiled. "I know what you mean. I have a nosy sister. Privacy was a luxury with her around."

They got one quarter up the mountain and Sydney stopped and looked up. "It absolutely overwhelms the senses," she said reverently. She shook her head and they started back up the steep grade. Soon Sydney began to feel the climb. "How... much... further..., Tommy?" Sydney was gasping for breath.

Tomiko stopped and looked up the winding road and pointed. "Not far, just up there."

Sydney looked up, still breathing hard. Suddenly she lost all consciousness of herself and stared at the sight. Nestled up against the mountain's bosom was a home. Not just a house but a dwelling that was all angles, made of wood, stone and glass. It was magnificent. The architect had made the house an extension of the mountain. An extension of granite, surrounded by wood and stone. All Sydney could think of were the many pictures she had seen of Frank Lloyd Wright's creations. "Wow!" Sydney exclaimed, "that's unbelievable. Who's is it?"

"It is mine." Then quickly she added, "It belongs to the hostel." Then she further added, "It was built by Joe."

Sydney shook her head in affirmation. *What a day. I wonder what's next?* She was now content to be quiet and conserve her strength. Despite her bicycling in the mountains, this sharp climb took her breath. In contrast, Tomiko seemed to be completely at ease.

Finally they reached large, winding, wooden steps that went upward to the front door. Sydney marveled, *This house has been built right into the mountain by a long gone adventurous man, who left this magnificent mark on the Earth. This Joe must have been quite a man.*

Now the going was easier. Finally the two woman reached a planked platform with a guard rail and a wooden bench. They were there.

Sydney dropped her back pack and sat down hard, trying to catch her breath. Tomiko leaned against the railing, completely at ease, smiling and observing her new friend. "You will get used to the climb after a few attempts."

"And I thought I was in good shape," Sydney gasped between breaths.

When her labored breathing slowed, Sydney stood up and looked past Tomiko at the hostel and the lake. "Tommy! It's breathtaking!"

Tomiko turned and looked. "I know," she said absently, with a small smile playing on her lips. Then she turned back to Sydney. "Welcome to my home."

Sydney walked to the railing. Looking down she could see the wooden stairs and the winding trail they had come up. Beyond that was the road leading to the hostel, and then in the background she could see the gleaming white buildings and the sun setting behind them. Further back was the shimmering lake with the cirrus clouds reflected on its surface. Ducks making asymmetrical rows of small V's, paddled through the water in search of food. A small canoe with a man and woman in it, made its way across the lake towards the hostel. Only the caw of the birds and the drone of insects broke the stillness.

Sydney said almost to herself, *"I could stay here forever."* Then she muttered, "If forever wasn't so near."

Tomiko heard her and thought, *This young woman is troubled.* She made a mental note to talk to her about it later. "Come, let us climb the stairs to the house."

Sydney approached the cabin with delight. She could see it was made up of logs from the same trees that made up the forest. It seemed to jut out of the mountain as if it were thrust out by forces contained in the mountain. The great glass windows that looked out over the hostel and the lake, angled back from the roof to the base of the building. *How does she clean the glass?* Sydney wondered. The deck sprawled away from the cabin and was braced directly into the mountain.

"Your home is just as beautiful up close," Sydney said quietly, almost reverently.

Tomiko opened the front door and let Sydney in. "Tomiko!" Sydney exclaimed, "It's even more beautiful than the office!" Sydney looked about the room. Japanese art abounded on the walls of the rooms that were separated by strategically placed shoji screens. Large futon sofas and the tables next to them were exquisitely carved and artistically hand painted in silver, gold and red, in the style of the Japanese. The large glass windows looked down at the hostel and the lake where one could watch the sun set and the moon rise. The only token to the modern world was the record player, hidden by an exquisitely carved entertainment center's doors.

"Tommy!" Sydney exclaimed, turning around completely, "it's almost too much!"

"I am glad you like it. I hope you will do me the honor of staying here while you are at the hostel."

Sydney felt overwhelmed by her hospitality. "I can't take such advantage of such generosity."

"It will be my pleasure. Besides, as beautiful as it is, it gets lonely at times. I will be glad to have your company." She beckoned to Sydney and both women walked into a room off the living room. It was a bright sunny bedroom with a window looking out over the lake. The twin beds had mahogany headboards with dressers and end tables to match.

The bedspreads were bright, depicting the flowers of spring in a burst of color. The room was spotlessly clean.

"This is your room. The bathroom is there."

Before Sydney could answer, the telephone rang. Tomiko excused herself to answer it. When she left the room Sydney went back out on the deck. Even without trying to listen, she could not help but hear the last part of Tomiko's conversation. "No, Syd is with me. It is such a long walk back I think I will just fix something here. Oh, by the way Magda, tell Eric to close up the office and we will see you all tomorrow."

Sydney had walked to the edge of the deck railing and was looking up at the large moon now climbing overhead. She turned and leaned her back on the railing. Gradually, she moved her head back and her eyes slowly rose to the top of the mountain. "My God, what a rock. It's massive. I can actually feel energy coming from it."

Tomiko smiled as she stepped out onto the deck. "There is also a legend that goes with the mountain. I suppose all mountains have a legend. If they do not, they should have. Would you like to hear it?"

Sydney nodded eagerly.

Tomiko sat down on a lounge chair and looked out over the lake. Sydney sat down next to her and listened intently as she began to speak.

"The mountain's name is Julietta. It was named after a young girl who lived by the lake five hundred years ago. She had a lover named Italo, whom she adored, and who loved her equally in return. They had met at the top of the mountain where they both loved to come when the flowers were in bloom and the rain and wind swept through the trees. From that time on they vowed they would be inseparable until the end of time.

He was a fervent young man who put aside his vow when he was persuaded by his Bishop to join the other knights to fight a holy war against the infidels. Before he left he Pledged his love to her and tied her scarf on his lance, then he left for the land of the non-believers.

She died a little bit each day that he was gone, and he was gone for a long time. Oh how she pined for him.

Days turned into weeks, weeks to months and then years began to pass, at first slowly and then more quickly. Still he did not return. It was too much for her and she finally became ill.

No doctor's remedy could revive her and she got sicker and sicker. She hung on to life only for her lover's return.

Her mother and father, fearing for her life, passed the word along the length and width of Switzerland and then to the land of the infidels. Finally, it reached her lover's army.

As is usual when transmitting a deed by word of mouth, the meaning will change. Longing became loathing and sick became dead. When the young knight was told she was dead, he became slightly demented and bolted from the holy army.

Italo rushed back to the mountain to mourn his loss. When he got there he went to the highest part of the mountain where they had first met. The rain came down in a torrent and the wind howled and bent the trees. Suddenly his grief overcame him and crying her name, he leaped to his death. The next morning, he was found in a crumpled heap at the foot of the mountain.

The man who brought Julietta the news looked upon her fair face and could not bear to tell her what had happened. He just told her Italo was back and she rushed to be with him. When she found him, she tore her clothes and would not leave his body. It is said she cried for three days and three nights. Finally, his family took him and prepared him for a Christian burial.

In the meantime, Julietta, now quite mad, had climbed to the top and would not come off the mountain.

That night, as the gods howled and wept their displeasure, Julietta stepped off the mountain, calling 'Italo', as she fell to wherever lovers go, for eternity."

Tomiko could see by the moonlight that Sydney's eyes were glistening and that a tear was trickling down her cheek. *It is nice to know that some of these barbarians have real feelings,* she thought.

Tomiko was right, and she was not right. Sydney was not crying only for the lovers, but also for herself. She looked down towards the lake. She dabbed her eyes and thought to herself, *They could easily change the mountain's name to Sydney. It would be so easy to jump off and stop this interminable waiting.*

"I did not mean to trouble you."

"No, Tommy, it's not just the story... it's... it's something personal. I'll tell you about it sometime."

Tomiko's face was grave and sad and she felt Sydney's pain. Then she brightened. "In the meantime, I will start our dinner. I am a vegetarian cook, I hope you will not miss the other foods."

"Whatever you cook will be fine."

By the time Tomiko served the miso soup to stimulate the appetite there was no need to miss any other food. The food was delicious.

Sydney was famished from her long ride in the mountains. She had to control herself to match her partner's delicate eating habits. They ate in silence, but clearly Sydney was impressed with the food.

"Tommy, you must share your secrets with me. The food was beyond good. I feel satisfied, yet not stuffed. How do you do it? What kind of soup was that? What did you put in it?"

Tomiko laughed. "Yes, yes, I will tell you all of it, but not all at once."

"Oh, sorry."

Tomiko delicately poured green tea, then sat down on a large pillow and crossed her legs in the Lotus position.

"The soup is called Miso. It is made of the broth of the vegetables we steamed and to which I added mushrooms and tofu."

"Tofu?"

Yes, it's a bean curd. Then I put in a soy paste called Miso, which I stir in a bit of hot water and then I add the mixture to the soup. It helps prepare the stomach for digestion and by itself is very healing."

"Like chicken soup for Jewish people."

"Chicken soup? Sorry, I do not understand."

"Jewish people think chicken soup can cure lots of things."

"I see." She did not see and Sydney could tell that the conversation was too confusing. It was time to bring up something more familiar.

"More tea?"

Sydney held her cup as Tomiko poured. "I could not help but notice that you had a tennis racket on your bag. Would you like to hit some with me tomorrow?"

"Oh, I would love to" Sydney answered excitedly.

"Yes. It is settled then. Do you like to play early? Is eight o'clock too early?"

"Eight is fine."

"I will call Eric and reserve a time for us."

Sydney stretched and luxuriated in the feeling of peace she had not felt for a long time. *I wonder what was in that food. How can you feel satisfied but not full?*

Later that night, the two women lay back on the twin futons and stared out of the large glass window that looked down on the hostel and the lake.

Tomiko thought, *We two women are so different and yet so alike.*

The moonlight shimmered off the glassy water, reflecting a larger version of itself. Occasionally a child's shout or laughter made its way up the mountain to the cabin and crickets sang their night song. Otherwise the night was still.

Tomiko sat up. "I have a very special after dinner wine I would like you to try, Syd."

"Gosh, Tommy, it would have to be really special to match the rest of your meal."

"It is, Syd. Try it, I think you will like it."

Tomiko got up and walked inside to a large cabinet and opened it. She searched for a few moments and then exclaimed, "Here it is!" and took out one of the many bottles. She placed it on the table in front of Sydney and set down two small wine glasses. Very carefully she wiped the two glasses with a cloth that appeared in her hand. She wiped both glasses with the very same motions and Sydney could swear that she took the same amount of time with each glass. Clearly Tomiko was in no hurry. She slowly and carefully put the corkscrew into the cork and opened the wine bottle. Then she wiped the mouth of the bottle with the same care as she did the glasses.

Sydney stared in fascination.

Finally Tomiko poured just a few ounces in each glass, so very carefully it was as if each drop was the Lord's blood in the mass. In fact, Sydney began to get the feeling she was at a mass and not just a simple dinner. Finally Tomiko presented the glass of wine.

Sydney carefully lifted it to her nose and sniffed it. The wine had a wonderful bouquet. Following Tomiko's lead she then sipped it. The result was a burst of flavor that lit up her mouth and warmed her. The small amount of wine seemed to evaporate in her mouth. "Tommy, this wine is wonderful! What is it?"

"It is called Tokaji. It is made in Hungary. Magda introduced me to it and I am grateful to her. It sure is better than anything I ever served, er, I mean, I ever had before."

Sydney caught the slip but ignored it. She took another sip. It was just as good the second time. "May I see the bottle?"

Tomiko handed it to her. Sydney spelled it out. "T-O-K-A-J-I,"

"Yes, but it is pronounced, Tokay, Magda tells me. But, then again, Magda tells me a lot of things."

Sydney laughed. She felt light and happy for the first time since she found out about her cancer. She realized that since she had been at the hostel she had not thought about her condition, and was not fighting the depression that had become her constant companion. *This place is good for me and these people are good for me. Maybe, like Magda, I will not be so anxious to leave.*

****

Sydney slept the deep sleep of the exhausted, but to her surprise, when she woke she was wide awake. No hangover from the food or the wine. And she was hungry.

The breakfast was more of the miso soup and homemade whole grain bread. Again to her amazement she again was not stuffed and yet she was satisfied.

Promptly at eight-thirty the two woman walked down the mountain to the well-kept courts. Both Sydney and Tomiko stretched their arms and leg muscles and then walked to opposite sides of the net. The first court was composed of Har-Tru and was manicured and brushed. The other three courts were hard courts. They were swept clean, their nets taught.

Eric knew Tomiko loved tennis and personally got up each morning at five o'clock and rolled and watered the Har-Tru court. The net and the wind screens were new and the chain link fence that surrounded the courts was painted a dull green. Since the mountain loomed above, only in the morning did the sun bathe the court as it did just now, nurturing the flowers that grew nearby. The flowers were watered every day, when Eric sprayed the court.

Sydney had also stretched in her room before she came down but it had been a few months since she had hit a tennis ball and she felt rusty. She bounced the ball a few times and then with a grunt looped her racket and sent the ball sailing towards her new friend. To her delight and amazement Tomiko moved to the ball gracefully and sent it back with more pace than it came to her. Sydney quickly moved to the ball and the rally was on.

They were both steady if nothing else. And the rallies seemed interminable. After a few minutes a sheen of sweat appeared on both their bodies and before long sweat spots appeared on their shirts under the arms and on their backs.

A small crowd had appeared and watched in awe as the small oriental and the lanky American punished the balls and then ran down each other's strokes.

"Where'd you learn to hit like that?" Sydney asked at the first break.

"Same place you did. You are very good."

"And you are too. Shall we continue?"

The crowd was appreciative of the long rallies and began to applaud when a rally came to an end.

Sydney suddenly stopped and caught a ball Tomiko hit. "Wanna play a couple a games?"

"Yes, of course. Why don't you take the first serve?"

Sydney then hit eight or ten practice serves and then held up one of the balls to signify she was ready. The small crowd quieted in anticipation of the match.

Sydney leaned back slightly while Tomiko concentrated, getting ready for the serve. Both of Sydney's arms went down and then up while Tomiko bounced in place, anticipating the ball. Sydney put the ball into the air, coiled her body then uncoiled and struck the ball with her racket. The ball curved in and landed just on the line at the 'T'. Tomiko reached out and easily sent the ball back with a one-handed return of serve. The ball was not hit deep enough and Sydney stepped in and cracked it down the line, then dashed for the net. Tomiko raced for it and got her racket on it and lifted it up for a defensive lob. Sydney stepped two steps back and then, with a scissor kick, smashed the ball and put it away. The appreciative crowd applauded. Tomiko tapped the strings of her racket with the heel of her hand and said quietly, "nice shot." The rush Sydney felt from the put-away shot warmed her. It had been a long time since she felt that good. Fifteen-love.

With both women fleet of foot and steady of hand they worked the game to fifteen-thirty. Since the points were so long, Sydney got loose very quickly. At first she had been tentative in the warm-up, but now she was confident as she stepped up again to the base line to serve. She served a flat ball that came back as fast as it went over. Sydney backed up a step, looped her racket, and sent it down the line again. This time Tomiko was over easily and snapped off a two hander that just skimmed the net and landed cross court. Sydney barely got to it and scooped it out of the Har-Tru sending it down the line. She continued past the line, put her brakes on, and scrambled to get back on the court making ruts in the Har-Tru with her effort. Tomiko barely got to it and had to send it up for a lob. Both women watched as the ball sailed up in a lazy arc and landed just an inch in back of the base line. Sydney breathed a sigh of relief. *No way I could have got to that one.* Thirty-all.

Tomiko looked composed and stepped back to the deuce court to receive serve again. Sydney was really confident now and hit another flat serve down the mid-line and went in for the volley. The ball was returned weakly about head high and Sydney crunched it to the open court with a backhand volley. Forty-thirty.

Facing the add court, Sydney served and missed the line. Second serve. Sydney lay the ball up and bent her back severely and struck the ball at seven o'clock for an American Twist. The ball struck the Har-Tru and the English took it high to Tomiko's back hand. She reached up and out and again hit a weak return. Sydney was all over it and hit an angle forehand for a winner. "Game!"

The women changed sides and Tomiko began her serve. Because she was shorter, she relied on a spin serve. It was effective and together with her solid ground strokes she worked the game to forty-fifteen. She served a spin serve to the backhand and then hit Sydney's short return with a two-fisted rocket down the line for game point. One all!

The next game was a kaleidoscope of twists, spins and flat balls that seemed to career all over the court. Neither woman would give-in and the crowd ooohed and aaahed over the long ground strokes. Finally it was Sydney's add. She spun her serve to the back hand and again got a short return. She leaped on it and nailed it down the line. Like a cat, Tomiko was there and two-fisted it cross court. With great anticipation, Sydney closed the net and spanked the backhand volley to the open court for a winner. The knot of onlookers applauded both players.

Breathing hard, Sydney sat down happily on the players bench. "Tomiko," Sydney said breathlessly as Tomiko joined her, "I have to stop. This is the first time in a long while since I played." Tomiko smiled affectionately and offered her hand. "No problem. That was very good lesson you gave me, Syd. We shall have to play again."

"Me give you a lesson? Just the opposite. Yes, let me get a few more practice sessions in and we will play a full match."

Realizing the play was over, the people watching started to leave, some of them coming over and congratulating the two woman. Soon all of them were gone.

Tomiko toweled off, smiled at Sydney and said, "I must go to the house and help Magda get lunch started. You are welcome to come with me or just enjoy the grounds. The canoes are there and the mountain is a beautiful place to be this time of the year."

Sydney patted the sweat on her brow. "I think I will just stay here for a while if you don't mind."

"Not at all." Tomiko then smiled sweetly and turned and walked towards her office.

Suddenly Sydney was alone. Slowly her joy turned flat and her elation became a sort of emptiness. She searched inside to try to find out why. Gradually it began to dawn on her. She realized she loved hitting with Tommy. Sure, it was only three games, but she loved the competition and, above all, she loved winning. But there was the rub, she wasn't winning, she was losing. She was losing where it counted, in the game of life. It had been a week since she had thought about her condition but now the thought of her problem came back with a vengeance and she was right in the middle of it again. Sydney hung her head and tears stained her cheeks. There was no way to get away from it. She longed to see Dr. Slater.

The afternoon came on, soft and sweet, but Sydney did not see or feel it. As the sun moved in the sky above her she, felt a cloak of black depression come over her and she felt the familiar wrench of her stomach. Suddenly she had to move before it engulfed her. It was as if moving would help her get away from this thing. She got up and walked quickly towards the lake to outrun the gloom.

The sun was just passing over the trees causing long shadows on the earth. The fleecy clouds were white on a darker sky. A lone bird winged its way home, cawing to her brood not to despair, she was coming.

Sydney walked along the edge of the water, her mood sinking with each step. Now she felt completely empty. *Well,* she thought, *at least the emptiness is better than the damned pain.* She sat down on the ground and stared out over the water until her tears blocked the view. She closed her eyes and the ground began to rock beneath her and she became afraid. She opened her eyes and the feeling stopped. She closed them again and the rocking started again. She willed it to stop and it did. The experience was frightening and Sydney felt small beads of sweat forming on her forehead. She felt one roll past her eye to her cheek and then drop to her mouth. She tasted its saltiness. Another continued on to her chin and disappeared onto her clothes. She was trembling. Suddenly she felt alone. No, not just alone, but more like she was the last person on Earth. An intense feeling of dread came over her and she felt the urge to get away, to find another human, to touch someone, to bury her head in her mother's breast, to run away, away from here, away from herself. *Where would I go,* she thought, *home? You can't go home again. Not original,* she thought, *but nevertheless, very true.*

A thousand thoughts cascaded down through her mind. *Who am I? What am I? Is this what I have lived for? Am I on a staircase going nowhere? Better yet, am I awake? Or is this just a dream? Is this my Heaven or the worst part of Hell? It feels like Hell. Does each step I take just lead to God or just to an empty hole in the ground?*

Sydney stared at the now murky lake. Suddenly she saw something out on the water. *My God! It's a girl, dancing on the water.* Her eyes opened wide. *It's a clown,* she thought. *Oh God, it's me, I'm the clown.*

"Okay folks, what do we have here? Yes it's Sydney Marie Bannon. Okay Sydney, this is the glorious end to your inglorious life." Sydney shook her head and the clown disappeared.

Sydney got angry and stood up. She looked up to the top of the mountain. "What the Hell is going on, God. Am I on a path from nowhere, going nowhere. But how can that be. I see you all the time, in the sunset, a perfect aria, or a mother with child at the breast. That's you, isn't it? Or is this all an illusion, a huge man-made cosmic joke?"

She waited. Nothing. "Well, Lord, don't you think you should give me a clue. This is Sydney Marie Bannon, your loyal and faithful servant. This is Sydney calling. And I want some answers."

Sydney turned to the lake. "Yes, I want some answers," she shouted over the water, "is my end an empty grave? Or do I soar into the heavens and dance with the wind, not conscious of either time or space." Tears rolled down her face. "Just like you promised when I was a little girl."

Sydney was sweating profusely when she finished. Her words echoed across the lake and she bent her head and listened for an answer, but all she heard was silence, eternal silence. She sat down, bent forward and began to rock and cry in earnest. When her tears stopped she lay down on the cool ground, her forearm under her cheek, and sobbed.

High above the lake, Tomiko stood on the deck and listened to the lament rising to her through the trees. Tears formed in her eyes and she sat down and cried, hoping that whoever the lost soul was, she would find her peace.

****

Sydney's alarm, the next morning, was the song of a bird. She stretched and sat up. What a difference, she thought, *yesterday I wanted to kill myself and this morning I feel as though I have never been more alive.* She slid into her slippers and padded to the bathroom.

Hah! I used to wake up in Manhattan and stagger around until my first cup of coffee. Here, I wake up alive and refreshed and with not a drop of anything. Tommy doesn't even keep coffee in the house. Herb teas! Yes, she has tea. I float on tea. But I have to admit I feel a lot better since she has been feeding me. Yuck! Veggies, veggies and more veggies. What I wouldn't give for a good steak.

Sydney stepped out on the deck and looked at the lake. For a moment the demons danced again. She smiled, shook her head and they instantly disappeared.

Sydney walked to the bathroom and brushed her teeth. She patted her face with water dried it and then padded to the kitchen. There seemed to be a symphony of sound outside as the birds searched for their breakfast. There was a note on the kitchen table. She smiled as she saw the small, even, scrawl.

Sydney:

Miso soup on the stove. Had an early lesson.
Come to the courts when you can.

Tomiko

Hmmm, Tomiko. I wondered where the name Tommy came from. She laughed to herself. *She sure didn't look like a Tommy.* After devouring the soup, Sydney dressed, grabbed her racket and started down the mountain. It was a glorious morning and Sydney reveled in it. The sun was filtering through the trees and a layer of dew covered the shrubs. The sky was clear and cloudless, and thousands of birds sat in the trees, preening and fluttering their wings, singing their morning song. In some places there were so many birds in the trees that the branches seemed to come alive with their movement.

From where she was, Sydney could see the courts clearly. No mistaking who it was. Tomiko was one of the two small figures gliding around, hitting the ball. The other appeared to be a young girl Sydney didn't know. *She sure hits a heavy ball,* Sydney thought. She marveled at the pace of Tomiko's ball. *As little as she is, she must have great timing. That's inborn, can't teach that.*

As the trail down the mountain turned, the court disappeared from view. Sydney saw the lake and the depression tried to start from deep within her. With a will, she pushed it down and forced her mind back to the trail and the present moment.

Off the trail, she suddenly heard a noise and involuntarily tensed. Then she heard laughter. Two people came out of the woods into view and Sydney relaxed. It was Magda and a young man she didn't know. They each had a large basket of blueberries.

"Syd! Goot morning." She turned to her companion and took his hand. Then she looked back at Sydney. "Dis is my friend, Zoltan. Zoli dis is Sydney"

"Jo reggelt," Zoltan said automatically. "Excuse, please, goot morning," he said in a thick accent, "I do not speak English wery vell." He reached out and they shook hands.

Sydney laughed. "You speak just fine. Nice to meet you."

"We were just berry picking, for breakfast. Vould you like to taste one?" Magda held out the basket she was carrying.

"No thanks, I just had miso soup and it was filling."

Magda smiled. "I see Tommy's conwerting you."

"Yes, and I like it."

Magda led the way down the narrow path as the three of them walked down the mountain, chatting amiably. When they reached the courts, Magda went on to the communal kitchen to put the berries away and Sydney and Zoltan took a seat in the makeshift stands next to the courts.

Tomiko was working with a young girl of about sixteen. The youngster was heavy set but very fast. She bent low when she hit the ball and it made for a very hard hit ball on almost every stroke. Tomiko had to stay on her toes constantly to stay in the points.

Sydney noted there was a group of people standing on the far side of the court, seemingly mesmerized. Their heads were turning right and left, eyes glued to the ball speeding back and forth across the net.

Sydney noticed something odd on the other side of the court. Eric was there, but instead of watching the ball his head was still, watching only the half court where Tomiko was. Sydney immediately saw that something in him was reaching out to her. She almost cried with the beauty of it.

Is it possible Tomiko doesn't know? Since she had been at her mountain home, Eric had never once come by. And when he called, as far as she could tell, it was always business. *Tommy had never once mentioned him, even in passing. Is it possible she doesn't know?*

Tomiko ended the playing lesson with an excellent drop shot that just cleared the net and died. The young girl scrambled for it but it was too well placed. She pulled up to the net with a big grin. "Thanks, Tommy, that was great."

Tomiko shook her head as she came to the net. "I don't know how long I will be able to teach you anything. You are getting too good."

The girl's grin got wider. "See you Wednesday."

By this time the young girl's mother had come court side and was waiting patiently. The girl packed her tennis bag and they both left, the mother waving a small goodbye to Tomiko. She waved back as she gently, almost absently, blotted her face with a towel.

Sydney left the stands and came onto the court. Tomiko nodded hello and continued to wipe her face. Sydney began to stretch her reluctant muscles while Tomiko sat down and drank some water. She then she quietly waited while Sydney finished her ritual.

Sydney looked at her blandly, her game face firmly in place. "Think we can go a set today,

Tommy?" Tomiko just hit the heel of her hand on her strings and smiled.

The set was long and hard but Tomiko prevailed, Six-three.

She had held serve throughout the set and Sydney had lost hers twice. The small crowd had applauded when they were finished and then, realizing there would be no second set, they began to disperse. Finally the two women were alone.

Sydney took a long look at Tomiko. *She's good, no doubt about it. Try as I might I have no idea how old she might be. No one is close to her. No man, no friend, no husband. Maybe Eric is just discrete. No, I would have noticed something. Why don't I just mind my own business?* She laughed to herself.

In spite of what she had just said to herself, Sydney leaned back on the bench, looked up at the mountain and said quietly, "Eric is quite handsome, don't you think?"

Tomiko stopped dabbing her face with her towel and looked at Sydney with surprise. "Why, yes, I suppose so. Are you interested in him?"

Sydney laughed longer than was necessary. "In love with me?" Sydney sat forward and looked intently at Tomiko. "I believe you really don't know," she said incredulously. "Have you ever noticed the way Eric looks at you?"

There was a pointed silence. Tomiko shook her head. "What do you mean, Syd?"

"What I mean is, he can't take his eyes off you."

"Eric,?" she said, genuinely surprised. Are you sure?" Tomiko's face turned thoughtful. "He has always been most helpful," she said more to herself then to Sydney. She shook her head as if to dismiss the matter. "Let's play a second set, Syd." Sydney's grin got wider, but she dutifully got back on the court.

After a short while a cluster of fans re-appeared and settled into the stands. The second set was tight, but Sydney finally won on an overhead smash. This time the set was seven to six with a 7-5 tie breaker.

"7-6, 7-5, that's like kissing your brother. Let's play a third set."

"Okay," Tomiko answered. They began the third set and were in a tight match, all knotted up at three-three, when Eric appeared and took his usual spot. Tomiko could not help but see him and immediately lost all concentration. She began to spray her shots all over the court, missing badly and putting the final back hand weakly in the net.

Tomiko met Sydney at the net. "Sorry, Syd."

Sydney was grinning broadly. "Nothing to be sorry about, Tommy. I'm glad for you. He's smashing. I wish he were interested in me." As soon as she said it, a picture and feelings of Paul flashed across her mind and body and she felt a cold fist in her stomach. She had not thought of him for a long while and thought his memory had faded. It had not.

She recovered. "Why don't you say something to him, Tommy?"

Tomiko gently shook her head, her black hair swirling about. "Not just yet." She looked flustered. "Why don't we climb Mount Juliette and meditate a while. Perhaps an answer of how to handle this will come to me."

On the way up, some simple answers came to Sydney. As they approached the cabin, she turned to Tomiko. "Tommy, don't set a place for me tonight. I made arrangements with Magda and Zoltan to have dinner with them," she lied.

Tomiko looked at Sydney with a puzzled look on her face, then shrugged and said, "Okay."

After Sydney showered and left, Tomiko puttered around the cabin finally sitting on the deck, trying to read, as the sun set over the lake. Restlessly, she got up and cooked a stir fry, but when it was done, couldn't eat. She walked into the woods and spread the food out for the wild animals. She did the dishes and then tried to read. She couldn't. It had turned dark and she walked to the window and stared out at the lights of the hostel. She saw the reflection of the full moon shining on the lake. It looked unreal. It was almost as if someone had painted the moon on the ripples of water. She felt anxious. She had fixed her life just the way she thought she wanted it. Why, then, was what Syd had said so disquieting. She had hit a raw nerve. Was she missing something? Or was she merely hiding from an empty life? She missed Joe, but thought she would be content with just his memory.

The quiet of the night was shattered by the phone that startled Tomiko.

It was Sydney.

"Tommy, I'm staying with the peasants tonight in the dorm. I want to spend some time with Magda and Zoltan before they leave. I'll see you tomorrow."

"Yes, of course, Syd." See you tomorrow. Goodbye."

Tomiko put the phone down and the night crept in again. She poured some sake, curled her feet under her and began to read again. After a few minutes she put the book down and stared out the window.

My wa is disturbed, she thought. I must meditate tomorrow and gain my balance again. She got up and paced. She turned on the record player and listened for the drop of the record. The glorious notes of Puccini's music filled the room. "Oh perfect," she said aloud, "Butterfly! Nothing like a Japanese woman, desperately in love with a foreigner who doesn't care a whit for her."

She again stared out the window and then stepped out on the deck. A million stars filled the sky. The moon was so big she could reach out and touch it. The fragrance of the trees was all around her and the voices of Sutherland and Corelli filled the night with music of undying, star-crossed love. Tomiko's eyes brimmed over and hot tears ran down her cheeks. *Am I crying for the lovers or for myself?*

Slowly she walked back in and picked up the phone. Reluctantly, she dialed the number.

"Front office!"

"Mary, is Eric there?"

"No, Tommy, he left a half hour ago. But I can track him down for you."

"No, no, that is alright, I will speak to him tomorrow."

Tomiko put the phone down and stared at the reflection of the moon on the lake.

...Un bel di, vedremo...
(One fine day, he'll return)

The soprano sang the feminine hope, her voice soaring.

"I know Joe will not return, but can someone take his place? Am I ready to let someone else into my heart?"

...Viene, viene. (Come, come)...

****

The morning was brisk, and a cold breeze came across the lake and cooled the land. Sydney hunched down in her jacket, glad for the protection. Magda seemed less affected by the cold and was just dressed in her usual Jeans and shirt. The two women walked slowly by the lake content not to speak but just to enjoy each other's company. Sydney listened to Magda's shirt sleeves flapping in the wind and somehow it made her lonely. The sky was filled with noisy birds going south to escape the coming winter.

Sydney looked up, watching the orderly formations heading to warmer places. "Amazing that they know when to leave and which way to go. I could learn something from them."

"Ah, Syd, you are self-destructive. I have to leave dis place to go back to school. But you, you are the most fortunate of vomen. You have vonderful friends here and you live in a beautiful house on top of a mountain. Vy would you Vant to leave?"

Sydney was thoughtful. "Magda, do you remember when I first came here, I told you I had a problem?"

Magda said "Yes," in a low, expectant voice.

Sydney stopped and faced the younger woman. She hunched down even deeper in her jacket. The words were difficult to say but she forced them out. "Magda, I have breast cancer."

Magda looked back in amazement. "But you're so young."

"Nevertheless I have it."

Magda recovered from her initial shock and prepared to listen to her friend. As young as she was, she had always been mature, an old soul, Zoltan called her. She knew Sydney wanted to talk.

"The reason I quit my job and came to Europe was because I wanted to live a little before I died."

Magda was anxious to speak but thought better of it.

"I have always wanted to see Europe and I adore opera, so I thought I would kill two birds with one stone before the stone killed me." Magda did not laugh. She was too full of pain for her friend. Slowly and quietly, she began to cry.

"Magda, vat is wrong?" It was Zoltan. He had seen the women walking and wanted to join them. He ran to Magda and held her shoulders looking deep into her eyes, his own eyes full of concern.

"I am all right, Zoltan. Syd just told me a very sad story."

"I am the sad story, Zoltan."

The young man let go of Magda and faced Sydney with a puzzled look.

Sydney turned and looked out over the lake. Suddenly, she felt flushed and a wave of warmth came over her. She unzipped her jacket and laughed to herself. *Where's a clown when you need one.*

"I have breast cancer, Zoltan. I found out about it a few months ago and came to Europe to forget myself. When I first got here, being with you and Magda and Tommy was such great medicine, that I forgot myself. But you can only hide so long. As much as I like it here, I have to get back in the saddle because my time is getting short." Sydney's eyes brimmed over.

Zoltan was shaking his head as Sydney finished speaking. "It is not alvays necessary to succumb to popular belief. Dere may be another vay for you if you have the capacity to open your mind."

Sydney's eyes narrowed. *Oh, Christ, she thought, here come the crazies.*

"Ve haf in Budapest a vonderful, natural, medical clinic. It is run by a Doctor Kodaly who is, according to my anya," (my mother), "a saint."

Magda felt Sydney's hand tighten around her arm.

"My anya developed a cancer und vent to several doctors und she got relief of der symtoms. But der cancer progressed. In desperation she vent to see dis Doctor Kodaly. He continued her regular medical treatment but unlike der others he put her on a wery strict diet und added meditation, exercise und actually insisted she go dancing on der veekends. Now der tumor she had is reduced und she feels vonderful."

"You know," Sydney said, slightly amazed, "I've only told three people in Europe about my problem and two of the three have told me about this Doctor Kodaly." Sydney was now excited. "Do you mind if I talk to your mother, Zoltan?"

"Not only do I not mind, but if you vant to consult vit Doctor Kodaly, you can stay at my home vit us und I am sure my anya vill go to der clinic vit you."

"Leave me her telephone number, Zoltan and I will think it over for a day or two and decide. Sydney's eyes brimmed over and tears began to run down her cheeks. She reached out with her arms and grabbed both her friends and drew them to her and hugged them. "I love you both," she whispered, "and I will miss you."

Zoltan gently took Magda's hand. "Come, Magda. Eric has loaded the van with our bikes and packs und he is ready to drive us to der train station. School calls und ve must go. Der train vill not vait long for us."

The two women embraced again, tears streaming down both their faces.

"Please call us ven you get to Hungary."

"I will, Magda, I promise." Without looking back at Sydney, Magda turned and ran back towards the hostel. Sydney watched her with an emptying heart.

Zoltan began to run after her but suddenly stopped and looked back at Sydney. "Ven I first got here, Tomiko made me sit and make der rock grow. Perhaps if you do dat it vill help. Ask her." Then he began to run again. "Viszont látásra! (Goodbye) he yelled over his shoulder.

"Goodbye," Sydney whispered. Their going touched her deeply and she felt an infinite sadness.

****

It was always a long walk up to the cabin and somehow, tonight, it seemed longer than usual. Sydney was glad to see that Tomiko was there when she finally got to the cabin.

Dinner was a quiet affair. While eating, Sydney tried to sort out her feelings and filter the information Zoltan had given her. She had become resigned to her fate, and now she had to get out of her comfort zone and reach for the hope she had been offered.

Always in the back of her mind was a constant question. *If there was something new on the medical horizon, wouldn't Dr. Slater know about it? Wouldn't she tell her? And most important wouldn't she try it herself?*

Sydney was startled. Tomiko had said something to her. She tried to focus.

"Something bothering you?"

She shook her head. "I'm sorry, Tommy, what did you say?"

Tomiko smiled. "Are you alright? You are very quiet this evening. Is something bothering you?"

Sydney shook her head and gave Tomiko a tight smile "You are perceptive, I do have something on my mind."

"Perhaps I can help."

"Yes, maybe you can." Sydney opened up and told her friend about her breast cancer, her chance meeting, on the plane with Maria and her urging Sydney to go to the clinic in Budapest. Then what Zoltan had said about the same clinic. "He also said something about you teaching me to make a rock grow. What's that all about?"

Tomiko laughed. "If you make the rock grow, first you have to stop being an American and become Japanese." Tomiko had to laugh again, this time at Sydney's puzzled look.

"You must find your own rock. Mine is that one." Sydney followed her finger to a boulder in the garden. "Then you must sit and become quiet and meditate on the rock. Become immersed in the rock. Become part of the rock. Let the rest of the world spin on while you and the rock become one. See it grow. Feel it grow. Become one with the rock. If you do that the infinite will answer all your questions and solve all your problems, and you will be at peace."

"Yes, it would be nice to be at peace again." Sydney suddenly felt very close to Tomiko and began to speak about how she really felt. At first her words were hesitant, like newly minted coins. Soon her feelings, that had been damned up all these months, spilled out in a torrent of words and feelings. Sydney talked and cried, her tears running down her face and dropping on her shirt. When she finished she nervously laughed but then her defenses broke down again and she cried in earnest.

Tomiko came to her and cradled her head like a mother with a hurt child.

After a long while Sydney stopped crying and began to sob. Finally she had no more tears and sat up. With a sorrowful look on her face she tried to apologize.

Tomiko smiled and told Sydney she was among friends. "Apologies are not necessary." After a few moments Tomiko nodded her head and was thoughtful. Finally she spoke once more. "You know Syd, meditation and diet will help you. For many centuries my people have known of the healing qualities of foods and how they will help you gain peacefulness. The oriental doctor uses foods like a symphony conductor, mixing them in a perfect mesh to form the music your body needs. If you go to Hungary and to the clinic, you will already have had a head start. Since you have been here with me you have taken long reflective walks around the lake. That is a form of meditation. And you have eaten nothing but a very wholesome, organic, vegetarian diet. That is, unless you're sneaking stuff on the side."

Both women laughed and then it was quiet again.

Once more Tomiko broke the silence. "Syd, if I were you, I would go. That way there is perhaps a chance. Tomiko finished by shrugging her shoulders. "If you do not go..." Tomiko shrugged.

It was quiet for a while and then Tomiko spoke again. "Syd, do you know what a Haiku is?"

"No, I don't think so," Sydney said quietly.

"A Haiku is a very structured verse in Japan that covers the situation and all the feelings by the people involved. I would like to compose a Haiku for you and your situation. May I?

"Yes of course. I would be honored."

Tomiko lowered her head and in her heart became Japanese again. In a few minutes, she lifted her head and still keeping her eyes closed spoke the Japanese poem just above a whisper.

> There is a blot on the sun
> My body will accept no fault
> The earth, water and wind will cleanse me
> I am whole again

It was deathly quiet again and both women did not speak for a long while. Finally Sydney broke the silence. "Thank you, Tomiko, that was more beautiful and healing than I could ever have hoped for.

Tomiko bowed her head slightly but remained silent. Sydney stared at the moon reflecting off the lake, sifting her thoughts and feelings while Tomiko read and meditated. Soon Sydney was peacefully asleep on the futon.

Tomiko looked at her friend with compassion. Then she whispered, "If you do not go, it might be your last chance!"

****

The clickity-clack of the train's wheels made Sydney drowsy. She wrapped the blanket around herself trying to stay warm. She was afraid she would never be warm again. She edged closer to the stove that heated the old car and soon she was fast asleep. The train screeched and bumped its way down the mountain and Sydney was jolted awake by the sudden shift of the rail car as it adjusted to the sharp grade. When she opened her eyes, she was looking straight down the mountain pass and for a moment she felt like she would fall to the floor of the valley. Her heart raced until she got her bearings and then she calmed.

It had been seven long, hard days since she left Julietta mountain and the lake, and she was exhausted. Except for the fact that she could not get warm, the whole adventure was like a dream, almost like it happened to someone else.

The day she left, the snows began to fall heavily. Soon most of the roads were closed, and Eric said to travel by bike or car was out of the question. Tomiko suggested she stay until the snow stopped, but since she had made up her mind to go to the clinic, Sydney thought it best she go see Dr. Kodaly as soon as possible. Eric volunteered to take her to the train by horse and wagon to a place that would connect to the railroad line to Hungary. Sydney agreed, and Tomiko was there to see them off.

When they were ready to go, Tomiko took Sydney's hand and looked deep into her eyes. Sydney, with a tear forming in the corner of her eye, leaned down and hugged the smaller woman and kissed her on the cheek. Eric looked on with a small smile. When Sydney sat back up she gave Eric and Tomiko a moment of privacy by looking down and adjusting the blanket on her lap. Eric was surprised to see Tomiko look at him with some depth of feeling. Her eyes seemed full of promise. He felt a rush and silently vowed to tell her how he felt when he came back.

Tomiko watched them quickly disappear into the swirling snowflakes cascading down off the mountain. She looked at the snow forming in drifts next to the road. Tomiko held her hand out palm up. The snow that landed on her hand was very cold and did not melt right away. Suddenly there was a twinge of foreboding in her heart.

Chapter 23: Switzerland

Even at the beginning, the going was difficult and several times the wagon slid sideways on the road causing man and beast no little concern. They traveled all the rest of the day, slowed by the swirling snow, and nightfall found them still high up on the mountain.

When the sun went down the trail became very dark and the temperature dropped rapidly. Eric would not share the information, but he knew there were sheets of slippery black ice under the snow.

Just after they had left Juliette mountain, the driving snow had changed to a pleasant shower of white flakes that soon covered the trail. But the wind had picked up again and they were now in a tunnel of white that blocked their view and slowed their travel to a crawl. The trail was narrow and steep and Sydney did not feel secure. When the whirling snow would stop for a moment she could see over the edge and realized it was a drop of hundreds of feet straight down with nothing to break the fall but trees and rocks. She was very glad Eric was beside her.

Gradually, the wind increased even more, and it whistled through the trees making an eerie, mournful sound. The snow, whipped by the wind, came down at almost a horizontal angle. It stung Sydney's face and she had to wrap her scarf tightly around her face to protect it. Only her eyes were bare but the cold, icy fingers of arctic air still managed to seep through her jacket and the two sweaters underneath. It chilled her to the bone.

Eric stopped and pointed to the valley below and then shouted above the wind. "Finally, we're here. That's where we have to go. See the lights?"

Sydney followed his finger with dismay. She could still see clouds below them. And it was still a very long way down. Sydney shook her head and squinted through the driving snow. At first she could see nothing, then it appeared. Two lights barely visible blinking in the dark void at the bottom of the canyon. A knot of fear began in Sydney's stomach. It looked like a desperately long way to go in what was becoming rapidly severe conditions. The cold made her mind wander. All she could think of was warmth and sleep. She tried to concentrate.

Eric was speaking again. "...should have left earlier, but how is one to know this kind of storm will come..."

She lost the next few words in the howling wind.

"...But if we are careful, we'll be fine."

Sydney knew that Eric was experienced in the mountains, but given the conditions the fear in her belly kept growing.

Eric urged the mare on and the wagon crept forward in the blinding snow. Suddenly the sound of clip-clop of the horses hooves warned Eric, but it was too late for him to act. "Ice!" he bellowed.

Without warning, the wagon began to slide sideways. Instinctively the horse locked her knees and the horse and wagon and their human cargo slid quickly towards the edge of the mountain.

Sydney saw Eric go rigid and without thinking she took a sharp intake of air, grabbed on to the side of the wagon, held her breath and braced herself as the wagon skidded towards eternity. Every muscle in Sydney's body was contracted as the wagon slid towards the edge. Her mouth tasted of gall and fear and despite the cold, she began to sweat. The thought of jumping off flashed before her.

As if to read her mind Eric shouted, "Don't move!"

Visions of her, the horse and the wagon toppling off the mountain danced in her head like a living nightmare.

The wagon groaned as it approached the edge. *Maybe it's alive,* Sydney thought, *maybe it doesn't want to die either.* Sydney shook with fear.

Almost imperceptibly, the wagon began to slow and finally skidded to a stop inches from the edge. Sydney could feel her heart pounding in her ears as she looked over the edge into the blackness below. She was still afraid to move. Slowly, but carefully, she began to breathe again.

"Syd, please, do not move. Not even a muscle." In the slowest of slow motion, Eric began to get down. First he dropped one leg off the seat, then the other. Then, using just his arm muscles he let himself down in the most gradual dismount Sydney had ever seen. His biceps and triceps trembled as they both came into play. Beads of sweat popped out on his forehead. Eric and Sydney both prayed the horse would not bolt.

The mare stood quietly, head down, catching her breath, blowing small clouds of steam out of her nostrils. Sydney could see the horse tremble with fear, her skin flinching with the cold.

Sydney became aware that the wind was making a higher pitched mournful howl as it whipped down the mountain through the trees. She trembled with fear as the cold, frigid air kept seeping its way through her clothes. She wanted to beat her arms against her body to restore the circulation, but she dared not move lest she spook the horse and drive the wagon off the cliff.

Eric now had both feet on the ground and was slowly making his way to the front of the horse patting her side as he went.

"There, there, girl. Nothing to worry about." Finally he was at her head. He patted her nose and slowly took the bridle. Gently he tugged. "Come on Gretchen, come with me." The horse took a shaky step away from the edge, then another and another.

Gradually, Sydney relaxed a little and began to tremble with relief. At last they were now safe. She took a deep breath and tears of joy rolled down her cheeks.

Eric offered her a hand and she shook it off and stepped down. Her knees buckled as she reached the ground and she caught herself by grabbing on to one of the wheels.

Eric began to take the traces off the mare.

Sydney was puzzled. She yelled over the wind, "Eric, What are you doing?"

"Too dangerous to go on. We'll stay here tonight."

"What?"

"Believe me, we were lucky. Another misstep and..." Eric drew his finger across his throat and turned back to the horse. "...We will not go on tonight."

As Sydney watched in amazement, Eric got the horse to lie down Then he scooped out a sort of a trough next to the horse. He laid a blanket on the ground and motioned for Sydney to lie down right next to the horse. Reluctantly, she did so. She snuggled as close as she could to the mare, still trembling and shaking from the cold. The horse smelled, but the mares warmth was too inviting to leave. Eric let himself down in back of Sydney, molding his body to hers. Another blanket on top of them and in a few minutes their warmth enveloped Sydney and she began to relax. For a while she would tremble and then be still for a few seconds, but finally she was warm enough and the shivering stopped.

For a moment, Sydney almost giggled and had to restrain herself from dissolving with laughter. *What would the gang at Woman's Home think if they could see me now. A horse to lean on and a good looking man pushing me from the rear? Sally would just die with envy.* Moments later cobwebs filled her head and soon, giving thanks that Eric was there, she was fast asleep.

When her eyes fluttered open, Sydney immediately knew that she was in that time between dawn and waking. Looking up she saw a few threads of light mixed in with the dark, snow-laden clouds. She felt somewhat claustrophobic with Eric close against her and the immovable horse at her front, but she tried to lay still. Finally, she just had to move. Slowly she put her hand on the horse's back.

Eric's eyes popped open. "Syd, don't move. "Eric's voice was ominous and Sydney froze. "You might spook the horse. Let me get up first, and we will see what the conditions are."

Carefully, Eric peeled himself away from Sydney and stood up. She sighed and moved away from the mare, gingerly, so not to disturb her.

Eric had the reins and tugged, and the mare clumsily got to her feet. Slowly and carefully he guided the horse to the wagon.

Brushing the snow off her coat and pants, Sydney got up, noting that at least another foot of snow had fallen during the night.

"It is all right, Syd," a smiling Eric said, "we're quite safe now."

Sydney looked around her. They were indeed on a wider part of the trail. It was still snowing but now the flakes came down gently, attaching themselves to clothes and face alike. "At least there's very little wind and it isn't bitter cold this morning."

Sydney heard a strange sound and her heart constricted in her chest.

Eric was very still, his head cocked as if he were aware of danger, too. She knew the sound but could not place it. Suddenly it hit her, "The subway," she half muttered. It reminded her of the sound the subway makes when it rumbled, far off, in the world beneath the city."

Eric put his finger on his lips to quiet her and listened even more intently. In a few moments the rumbling stopped.

Sydney noticed there was sweat on Eric's brow. "What's wrong, Eric, what is it?"

Eric smiled without mirth. "These are perfect conditions for an avalanche. That rumbling sound you heard was the snow above us shifting position.

Sydney flushed and her voice got grave. "What conditions are you talking about?"

Eric pointed up to the side of the mountain. "When the slope of a mountain is at least forty five degrees and the snow is constant, as it has been, the elevation will not hold it forever and it will come sliding down the mountain." He shook his head. "If it freezes, it will come down in slabs, bringing trees and rocks with it. If it is dry, it will be powdery, but it will still come like the devil. Sometimes at a hundred miles an hour like a white fury. If it is wet, it will take everything in front of it and simply clean off the mountain."

Sydney's voice was very small. "Everything?"

Eric nodded gravely.

"What sets it off?"

Eric shrugged. "Temperature changes, vibration from a train, or just the force of gravity from the continual snow falling."

Eric led the horse back to her and handed her the reins and her back pack. "We will have to leave the wagon. Too dangerous." He patted the horse's nose and smiled. "Gretchen will get us down." Eric went back to the wagon, got behind it and started to push the wagon off the trail.

It went over easily and Sydney heard it crashing down the slope and felt her face get warm. *That could have been us,* she thought. She shuddered, from fear, not cold.

Sydney lifted her backpack to put it on and laughed at the handle of the Dunlop racket handle sticking out. *I suppose I could find a snowman to hit against,* she thought. She laughed maniacally in her head. Suddenly she was dizzy and afraid, and fought to concentrate again. She loved the mountains, but how she longed to be on flat, solid ground again.

Eric pondered on how to get on the horse without stirrups. Finally he nodded his head, and in silence walked slowly down the trail leading the mare. He stopped at a wider place in the road and brought the horse closer to the mountain wall. With his knife, he fashioned a new halter from the traces and slipped it over the horse's face. Then he stepped on an outcropping of rock and slid onto the mare's back.

He motioned to Sydney who was watching him with interest.

Following Eric's direction Sydney stepped on the outcropping and gently slid onto the horse in back of Eric. As she wrapped her arms around his middle Sydney felt his strength through the sweater. Good, she thought, this place is not for the faint-hearted. She put her head on his back and held tightly to his waist as the horse gingerly made her way down the trail toward the valley below.

Their destination looked tantalizingly close from their vantage point, but the trail wound interminably around the mountain, and three hours later they were still very far away. The snowflakes had stopped and it was now so bright it hurt Sydney's eyes. The seeming warmth of the morning disappeared and the temperature dropped rapidly. The wind here was constant, arctic and bitter. Even close to Eric, the cold numbed her body. "How much further do you think it is?" She asked plaintively."

Eric half turned and Sydney slid on the horse's back almost falling off. She held on to Eric tightly and pulled herself back upright. "I think we have another three, maybe four hours, and then we'll be there."

Suddenly Eric went rigid. A split second later, Sydney heard an ominous rumbling. Eric stopped the horse, let Sydney down to the ground and quickly followed her down.

"What's wrong?" Sydney was frightened and puzzled.

He listened to the rumbling getting louder and looked at her gravely.

One word made her heart start pounding again. "Avalanche!"

Eric quickly went to the edge of the trail and looked down. He beckoned to Sydney without turning to her. In a second, she was by his side.

Eric's voice was serious. "Syd, in a few moments, if I am right, half the mountain will be down on us. You see those trees?"

Sydney looked over the edge at the slim trees that populated the sides of the mountain. "Yesss," she hissed softly, very afraid. The menacing sound was getting louder.

"We have to jump off here and slide down to those trees and then wrap ourselves around them. Understand?"

Sydney nodded, the fear showing on her face.

"We can do it!" he added fiercely.

The noise was getting louder and Sydney forced herself to look up. It was frightening. Eric was right, she saw snow, rocks, and everything else that was loose beginning to tumble toward them. The mountain was coming down on them in a cruel and brutal fashion.

Eric now had to yell over the noise. "On three, we'll jump. Then you slide down until you reach a tree and wrap yourself around and hold on. I will be with you." The sound was getting very loud, and Eric had to yell even louder to be heard. The horse, sensing danger, was getting frightened and was neighing loudly. One, two, tree... The mare kept neighing excitedly.

"Stop!" Sydney yelled and pointed to the horse. "What about her?"

"She'll have to fend for herself." Eric handed her one of the horses' traces. "Double tie this around yourself and the tree when you land. Come quickly, let's jump and slide."

Sydney heard the rumbling getting very loud and looked back. The sight froze her in place. Now the rushing snow was coming down at them at a fearful clip like a giant wave that would soon engulf them. Rocks and huge boulders struck the ground and then bounced into the air, crushing everything in their paths. Sydney's heart stopped. She was terrified and couldn't move.

Hurriedly, Eric jerked her to the edge and holding her hand forced her to leap with him into the unknown.

Sydney jumped over the edge and hit the snow with both feet. It was soft and she went right through the top layer and immediately lost her footing, and she began to tumble head over heels. Bushes and dead branches lay just under the snow and scratched at her face and hands as she somersaulted down the mountain. As she was turning over and over, she sensed the tree line just ahead. Right in the middle of all the chaos something funny came to her. Eric knew the trees were there. *Didn't he say, one, two, tree?* She laughed in spite of her predicament. Then she struck a tree and everything went black.

****

The blow staggered her and for a few minutes she lost consciousness. When she woke her head throbbed and her ribs ached. She was sitting with her back to the tree facing up where they had come from. She shook her head to clear the cobwebs. Something was wrong. *What was it?* Suddenly she knew. It was the noise. It sounded like an express train coming right at her. The avalanche was just above her. She made a second mistake and looked up. When she saw the enormity of the massive mountain of snow coming at her she froze like a deer in headlights and her heart stopped once more.

"My God the whole mountain is coming down on me!" Rocks and branches and tons of snow were hurtling down to cover her. Instinctively she turned her back to it, slipped around the tree, and quickly wrapped the trace about her waist and double knotted herself to the trunk. Not a millisecond too soon as just as she finished the knot the snow hit with the impact of a runaway beer truck. She made herself as small as possible, behind the tree and hung on. Soon she was enveloped in a loud, boiling, angry white vortex. The tree bent almost double under the weight of the snow and Sydney held on with all her strength. The avalanche tried mightily to take her and the tree along with it.

But, as quickly as it came, the snow was gone, tumbling itself down to the valley below.

Where Sydney had been there was nothing. No tree, no Sydney. A silent white blanket covered the area.

Her hand poked up through the snow and then her head. She shook the snow off and stood up. She smiled a rueful grin, just glad to be alive. She felt herself. No pain. She moved. Still no pain. A feeling of joy spread through her. She had not only survived, but was unhurt. She looked about her. A jolt of fear went through her. Eric was not in sight. Then she saw Gretchen. Three of the horses' legs were sticking straight out of the snow. *Poor Gretchen,* she thought, *she didn't have a chance, she was too big a target.* Sydney untied herself and struggled over to the horse with large awkward steps. She touched the horse. There was no movement. The mare had been trampled by the snow and smashed by tree and rock beyond life.

Sydney turned and began to crawl back up toward the trail. She hoped against hope that Eric was alright. And she hoped there was still a trail.

"Syd!"

She could hardly believe it but there he was. Eric was safe, and apparently sound, standing on the trail as if he never had to jump off.

With the sure footedness of a mountain goat, Eric jumped off the trail and awkwardly made his way to her.

They embraced and she cried tears of relief. His eyes were moist also. He looked her over as she laughed with nervous energy.

"You're a great date Eric. You sure know how to show a girl a good time." At that they both sat down in the snow and laughed uproariously.

After making sure Sydney was alright, Eric got Sydney back on the trail and began to lead the way down the mountain on foot.

The trail after the avalanche was still treacherous. Tree branches, rocks and stones lay across the trail strewn about as if some giant hand had thrown them in a game of dice. Some of the smaller stones lay beneath the snow making the footing unstable. Two hours later Sydney called out, "Eric, I have to stop." Gasping for precious breath, she slowly crumpled down into the snow.

Instantly, Eric was at her side.

"Have to rest," she gasped. Sydney hung her head and tried to catch her breath.

"Better not stay too long, he might think you're his lunch."

Eric was smiling and looking up above them.

Sydney squinted as she looked up at the whiteness above her. Suddenly she saw him. "God, she's beautiful," she said between gasps.

Standing majestically above them was a snow white cat. The snow leopard was about six feet long with jet black eyes and a coat so white she had to move to be seen against the snow. She stood absolutely still and watched the humans with feline intensity, her eyes like two black, burning coals.

"That's a Swiss mountain snow leopard. She's pretty alright, and deadly, too. I imagine this time of year she's plenty hungry."

With her eyes glued to the white beast, Sydney slowly stood up and made her way next to Eric. He dropped his back pack and opened it. He took the German Mauser he had stored for an emergency and stuck it in the pocket of his ski pants. "Just in case," he muttered.

Suddenly the leopard was gone. "I don't think she'll bother us, but one never knows. Keep your eyes open, Syd."

"Don't worry, I will," she said without conviction. After Sydney had recovered, they continued down the mountain with Eric leading the way. Sydney warily looked about her as they descended the trail.

The snow began again as the temperature dropped. At first just pretty white flakes floated down sticking to them and everything around them. As time went by the snow began to fall in earnest and was joined by a brisk wind. Eric had to slow down, and he too became more wary. Sydney did not notice him and was so exhausted she could only concentrate on one step at a time.

Stumbling along in her own world, Sydney did not know when the attack came. Suddenly the white flash came hurtling through the air and landed flush on Eric. Eric turned as the leopard came down on him and the back end of the cat struck Sydney in the chest and knocked her sprawling.

She lay on the ground stunned and unable to think. Then she screamed in fear and frustration.

The scream ended with the report of the Mauser going off. There was a blood curdling scream and Sydney could not tell if it were the cat or Eric. And then, all was silent again, except for the echo of the gun gently reverberating through the mountains. When the echo stopped, there was complete, deadly silence.

Sydney got up, trembling violently. She peered through the swirling snow desperately afraid for Eric. Then her heart dropped. Eric lay on the ground, his blood staining the snow next to him. Sydney reached for him and kneeled on the ground.

"I guess I got her, I'm still alive."

Sydney reached down and hugged him, blood and all. After a few moments, she got up, took a step back and surveyed Eric. His face was scratched badly and the jacket sleeve on his left arm was shredded. She looked over the rest of him but there didn't seem to be any other damage.

Eric sat up and flexed his left hand and arm. "I guess I'm okay," he said with relief.

"I think you are, all except your face." The blood was starting to coagulate and the bleeding lessened. Sydney noticed Eric's face was now showing some swelling and black and blue spots. She reached for some clean snow and applied it to Eric's wounds.

At first touch, Eric howled recoiling against the cold, but Sydney was persistent and Eric finally held still. After applying snow to Eric's face, Sydney used a towel from his backpack to clean his wounds as best she could.

When Eric got up, he went over to the snow leopard and stared at her. Sydney joined him. The cat was stretched out in her last dive and was now getting stiff with cold and rigor mortis. The snow that was still coming down heavily had partially covered the cat. "Beautiful, isn't she?" Sydney asked.

Eric touched his face. "Yes beautiful, but deadly. One thing bothers me now."

"What's that?

"Her cubs, if she has any. If she did, they'd be mighty hungry by now. Oh, well, can't do anything about that now, can we?"

With sad hearts they picked up the little gear they had left and started back down the mountain.

After four more hours of stumbling through the bitter cold wind and snow, they reached the isolated train station. "This rickety, old mountain line is the only lifeline to the main European rail lines," Eric said.

Sydney shivered and said through clenched teeth, "It may be rickety and it may be old, but it sure looks good to me."

Sydney and Eric stumbled into the ancient station house, frozen and trembling. There was an old wood stove in the corner of the room. They both looked at it with dismay. The stove was cold and looked desolate.

Eric girded himself, and sprang into action. He was out the door to the woodpile in a flash and in a few minutes walked back in with an arm full of wood.

When she saw the wood, Sydney got going, too. She opened the stove door and set the kindling she found in a bucket by the stove.

Eric dropped the wood with a clatter. He took two pieces, placed them in the stove, and lit the kindling. Soon the fire was licking up the sides of the wet wood. Eric and Sydney got close to the stove and put their hands out towards the flames. In a few minutes, the wood caught fire and began a smoky blaze. The room began to warm, and for the first time since they set out, Sydney started to feel secure.

****

Sydney still had fifty miles to go before she joined the rest of Europe. She wrapped her jacket more closely around her trying to keep in the heat. Try as it might, the old stove in the corner of the railroad car would not give out enough heat to stave off the cold coming in through the cracks around the windows. The conductor had given her a blanket, which she wrapped around her legs. When he saw her still shivering he said, "Sorry, but that's the only blanket I have."

Sydney wiped the moisture on the window with her gloved hand so she could see out. A brilliant white mantle of snow covered the land. She looked for homes but could see none. As far as the eye could see, there were undulating hills all around, ending in tall mountains that stretched to the sky.

Sydney dozed and when she woke she began to see signs of civilization. She was never so glad to see barns and houses, and all the other out buildings that made up a farm. When they reached Zurich, Sydney changed trains to a modern streamliner. She luxuriated in the warmth and the comfortable seat. She quickly fell into a troubled sleep as they sped towards Budapest, and the unknown.

****

Tomiko had been at her desk when the telegram arrived.

```
ÜBECT, SWITZERLAND
TOMMY:
CAUGHT IN AN AVALANCHE STOP
HORSE AND WAGON GONE STOP
HAD TO STAY OVERNIGHT STOP
WE ARE OK STOP
SYD ON HER WAY TO HUNGARY STOP
I WILL GET A HORSE AND BE BACK SOON STOP
THE SNOW IS BAD AND IT MAY TAKE A FEW DAYS
MISS YOU STOP
ERIC
```

****

After receiving the telegram, Tomiko went through her normal routine, but she kept one ear cocked to listen for Eric's return. For three days, she suffered through the unknown. Then on the fourth day, she heard the cry she had been waiting for.

"Eric! Hey, it's Eric! He's back."

Tomiko ran to the door of the hostel office and stared at the small crowd of people gathering around the scruffy man in the fur coat. Her hand gripped the doorknob until her fingers turned white.

Eric turned around to speak to people in back of him. He was dressed in a fur coat with the hood up to protect him from the cold. He had a unkempt beard, but Tomiko could easily tell it was him. Someone was shaking his hand in greeting, and another person was pounding him fondly on the back.

Suddenly, Tomiko felt an overwhelming rush of love and relief. She jumped the three steps of the porch and began to run to him. She had no thought of herself and had put nothing on over her shirt and jeans. Her shirt sleeves flapped in the cold wind coming down off Juliette mountain, but she felt nothing except a pounding heart.

Suddenly, he sensed her and turned to face Tomiko. When he saw her, she stopped abruptly. Eric finished thanking his well-wishers without taking his eyes off Tomiko.

She stood absolutely still, waiting. Their eyes and souls touched.

As they looked at each other, he saw her concern and his heart filled with joy. With his eyes still on Tomiko, he pushed his way out of the crowd of people and began to walk toward her. When the crowd of people realized what was happening, they quieted parted and drifted away. Eric was suddenly alone.

Tomiko began to walk towards him, and as if on cue, he started toward her. Soon they began to move toward each other more quickly until all at once they were running. When they reached within three feet of each other, they abruptly stopped again. Tomiko looked up at him, searched his bearded face and found love there. With a small sound of joy, she made the last few steps and fell into his arms, tears streaming down her face.

"Finally!" Eric muttered and took her in his arms. She almost disappeared in his muscular arms and fur coat. He pushed the hood of his parka back, and his black curls fell down to his eyes. Two tears coursed their way down his cheeks through the stubble of his beard and gently fell into her hair, cementing them to each other as no other bond could.

Eric's eyes glittered. "Tomiko..."

She put her finger on his lips and stopped him. "Do not say anything, my dearest. I know, and I love you, too."

Eric lifted her tiny hand to his face and kissed her wrist. Her other hand explored his face. She had not felt anything like this love since Joe. But this feeling was different, deeper, wider, more explosive, almost dangerous. But at the same time sensuous, sweet and adoring.

Eric looked deep into Tomiko's eyes, down to the depths of her soul. He put his hand to the back of her raven hair and pulled her to him. He brushed her eyes with his lips and then her nose. He rimmed her ear, then her cheek, and then came near her lips. Finally, he touched them. It was like electricity to Tomiko, and she pulled herself closer to him. His mouth on hers was everything Eric thought it would be. Her mouth was like velvet, and after her lips met his, it was as if they both were falling, falling...

Suddenly there was a noise. It was familiar. Eric tried to come from where he was to where the noise was. Suddenly he realized it was applause. He turned to where he had been welcomed earlier. There was a large group of people, employees, guests and friends watching them, laughing and applauding. He looked at Tomiko and smiled. She smiled back with shining eyes. Slowly they turned, and arm in arm they started walking up to their mountain home.

****

The sun touched the horizon, lit it aflame and then dropped over the lake into darkness. Tomiko absently turned the lamp on and stretched. In the background a Mozart piano concerto was laboring its way towards the final movement. When the music reached that movement the music changed from lento to capriccio. Tomiko listened in amazement and delight as she always did at the little man from Austria's ability to move her with his music.

She looked over at Eric sitting at the desk, opening the hostel's mail and smiled. *How could I have not known he loved me? All that time, wasted. I just know Joe would be happy for me.*

"What's this?" Eric said fingering the official looking letter. Something in his voice disturbed Tomiko and she put her book down, concern clouding her face.

He stared at the sealed envelope for a long while and then slid the knife under the flap and slowly sliced through it. He opened the letter and read it. His face remained stoic except for a slight narrowing of his eyes.

Tomiko watched him expectantly.

He looked up from the letter, an unusual mix of frustration and concern on his strong face.

"It's from my reserve unit. I have to report for peacekeeping duty. Apparently we are going to Korea."

Tomiko felt her heart contract. *The gods do not wait long to disturb my wa.* (harmony) "For how long?" She spoke so quietly she could barely be heard.

"I don't know. It could be a while. You know how things are over there."

"No, I do not," Tomiko said stubbornly. "Tell me why you must leave us to go there?"

Eric was surprised at the petulance and frustration in her voice. It was not like her. She was rarely emotional. He stood up and walked to the window. The moon was up by now and fleeting clouds rushed over its surface, casting shadows on the land and on his face. He stared out at the shimmering lake and heard the wind howl down from the mountain, bending the trees in its path. He thought about the avalanche and was glad to be inside. Eric absently wiped the frost from the glass. By this time Tomiko was by his side and touched his shoulder. Then she lay her head gently on his strong, muscular back and encircled her arms around his waist. She had regained her balance and asked him again, this time quietly and almost wistfully, "Please tell me why you have to go."

"Usually the origins of conflict lie in the murky past, Tomiko. Like elsewhere in the world, it could be sparked by different religions, or different cultures, even different languages. In this case, a few men at the top of each government have a differing political system. After World War II, the communists, in the north part of Korea, with Russia's help, set up a separate country with a communist dictatorship. The remaining democratic South Korea, with the help of the Americans, had a free economy and was growing and prospering. And the North didn't like it. There was a lot of killing and anger on both sides. Now they are at it again and apparently the North has invaded the South and the United Nations wants it stopped. My reserve unit has been called up to help stop the war. They have been living in a kind of a smoldering situation where anything can set it off and flame it up. The idea is for the peace-keepers to get between them and stop them from killing each other for a while, until reason takes over." His voice lowered. "I guess they are still fighting the same battle from World War II and we have to get between them, like a parent separating children. Only the stakes are higher." He smiled wistfully. "The strange thing is, when members of both sides go somewhere else to live, they seem to get along just fine."

Tomiko turned away, partially to hide the tears that appeared in her eyes. She walked to their bedroom, resigned. "I will help you pack."

In a few days Eric left, and Tomiko listened to the news every day, hoping to see a settlement to the conflict. But each day it seemed to get worse.

****

Spring was coming to the mountain and the days were noisy. Birds were flocking back and letting everyone know they were here. Tomiko was oblivious to the birds. She would hunch over the short wave and listen to the BBC. Today the correspondent was speaking into a microphone from the battlefield.

"This is Robertoor reporting live from near the 38th parallel. I am standing behind young South Korean men firing over and around barriers at an unseen enemy. Many people were injured today in mortar shelling by the attacking Northern troops. Several peacekeepers were injured..."

Tomiko stared at the radio, mesmerized, like someone that cannot take their eyes away from a terrible accident. The correspondent gave no names of the injured peacekeepers.

She knew she would not be notified by the United Nations since they were not yet married. She only hoped Eric had made arrangements with a friend to tell her if he were injured. *But what if he and the friend were hurt.* She shook her head at the thought. It was too horrible to contemplate, but she could think of nothing else.

Tomiko went to her shrine and kneeled. "Lord Buddha, if you see fit to take Eric from me, please give me the strength to follow him."

Tears streamed down her face as she reached for the knife she kept in the drawer beneath the candles. She picked it up and looked at the sharp hara-kiri blade glinting in the candlelight. Then she bent forward so low her forehead touched the floor. "Give me strength, Lord Buddha, give me strength."

Chapter 24: Korea

The sky was gray and overcast, just as it had been ever since Eric had gotten to this God-forsaken place. The cool rain had dripped constantly, making the soldier's lives miserable. They could not imagine the bitter cold that would follow.

The United Nations platoon walked warily in the rain, eyes alert, ready for action. They wore ponchos with bright bands on it so both sides could see they were peacekeepers. It was getting dark, making it hard to see, and the soldiers were concerned.

The men held their weapons at port arms, fingers on the trigger. Eric walked warily in back of the point man in the formation. The street they were on reminded him of the time he went back to Latvia after World War II. He shook his head and smiled. He was never really far from that time and he could still taste the bitter ashes of fear that thinking about it brought. He forced his mind back to the present. *This is bad enough,* he thought, *no need to dwell on the past.*

The street was filled with the rubble of the buildings from both sides shelling the town for the last five days and the men picked their way around the debris. Eric walked the infantryman's walk, his body in a semi-crouched position. He was tense to the point of trembling. The other members of the platoon were behind him spread out in a diamond shape. Each of them carried an M-1 rifle at the ready.

Eric began thinking again. *It's better not to think, just act.* But the thoughts keep coming. The United Nations had set up these patrols to keep the North and South Koreans apart. Usually the patrols were honored but sometimes the blood-lust was so high that the peace-keepers were just thought of as the enemy. That time was now and Eric's patrol knew they were between two implacable foes.

Eric's senses had never been more acute.

Ordinarily, the United Nations troops could make themselves known, get between the combatants, and both sides would be glad for the interference. Today was different. Maybe it was because someone wanted all the foreigners off Korean soil, or maybe it was all political, a chance to have a large United Nations body count. *In either event, you could be just as dead,* Eric thought. And the more the American presence, the worse it got. Thankfully, there were no Americans in his outfit. Eric silently cursed all governments. Recently he had heard that the Chinese were massing on their border. *If they come in to help the North Koreans again,* he thought, *we all just better go home.*

Eric stopped. Like the experienced soldier he was, he could almost smell the danger in the air. He held his hand up to stop the others his eyes locked on the road ahead. They were in a silent world, moving in slow motion on a lake of fear. Eric listened intently, but the only sound he heard was the rain beating a loud tattoo on his steel helmet. He peered ahead into the shadows of the burned-out buildings. The shattered windows looked back, wide eyed, like the vacant stare of the insane. He could see nothing, but he knew something was there.

Suddenly, the world erupted in fury. "Mortars!" he yelled, "Get down." The soldiers hit the ground as clods of earth rose in the air following a series of deafening explosions. The dirt and killing steel rained down on Eric as he clutched his rifle beneath him. Small rifle fire kicked up little spurts of sand all around them.

Pierre Sebastian squirmed through the mud, cursing in French as he went. His three day beard covered a handsome, angular face. His BAR was cradled in his elbows as he crawled through the mud, it was the only clean thing left. His face, hands and uniform were caked with Korean clay and dirt. He reached the radioman who was huddled down in a mortar crater and tapped him on the shoulder. He noticed the boy was trembling. "Morris!" The boy looked up at him, his eyes wide with fear. "Get on that radio and give them our coordinates and tell them to fire fifty yards ahead of us."

The boy shook his head.

"Do it, now!" The boy took courage from Pierre and began to dial headquarters. Pierre crawled away.

Pierre Sebastian was a French Canadian who had met Eric his first week in Korea. He was a profane, hard-drinking, professional soldier, as his father had been before him. He had quit school at sixteen volunteered for the Canadian Army and had fought with distinction in the European campaign. Only his barroom behavior away from the battlefield kept him from becoming a top sergeant. He was admired for his bravery by the men and officers alike.

Pierre and Eric had become fast friends ever since they arrived in Korea. They had pledged that if either had been hurt or killed they would personally see that the other's family were informed. In Eric's case, it was Tomiko. For Pierre it was his mother.

When he had made the pledge, Pierre had laughed to himself, thinking the probability remote. Now he was glad they had made that promise.

He finally reached Eric and snaked into his crater hole. He shouted at Eric over the noise. "Eric we have got to get out of here." A second round of mortar shells came in and Eric ducked his head face down in the mud.

Pierre buried his face in Eric's back. Craters appeared all around them and dirt and shrapnel rained down on them. Once more the shelling was followed by the deadly singing of small arms fire. When the firing slowed again, Sebastian carefully lifted his head. As usual he could see nothing. He put his hand on Eric's arm and shook it.

"Let's get to some cover." Pierre rose a little and let a burst go from his BAR. Pierre smiled as he heard someone howl. He loved this weapon. He would talk about it to anyone who would listen: *The Browning Automatic Rifle, .30 caliber, 48.7 inches long. weight, 19.4 pounds. Rate of fire: 500 to 600 rounds per minute. The soldier's friend.* He raised up again and gave another burst.

Eric turned over on his back and swiveling his head, looking around for a way out. "Damn! Just like an amateur, I walked right into a cursed trap."

"Could happen to anyone, mon ami," (my friend), "let's get to cover." Another burst from the BAR.

"No, it's up to me to get us out of here."

"No, Eric, headquarters will get us out. We radioed them. Just be patient and they'll spring us. Now let's get behind some cover until they come."

Suddenly a soldier in a United Nations uniform stood and began to run back the way they had come.

"No!" Eric yelled, and started to get up. Pierre pulled him back and pinned him down. A few rounds landed at the running man's feet, then they got his range. Machine gun and rifle bullets tore into him all at once and almost cut him in half. He hit the ground like a rag doll, bounced twice and then lay still. The soldier's blood seeped into the wet ground.

Eric tried to get up. Pierre held him down until he stopped struggling. There was anxiety on his face. "You see who it was?"

Pierre looked at the now twitching, dead soldier. His voice was low. "It's Alex, the corporal."

"The college boy?" Eric banged his fist in the dirt in anguish. "The bastards. We're trying to save them. Don't they understand?"

Suddenly the small arms fire began again, stitching down the road past the two men, kicking up deadly sprays of dirt.

Eric's hate-filled eyes stared down the road past the corporal. Suddenly he grabbed Pierre's shirt with his fist. "Wait, Hell! Pierre felt himself pushed away like a toy as Eric stood up with an angry roar. He grabbed his rifle and charged down the road at the unseen enemy. The air was quickly filled with killing iron.

"There are too many, Eric. Come back, come back." His shout was lost in the shelling and shooting.

Pierre made a snap decision. "Damn, I got to go get the madman." He stood up on one knee and began firing the BAR. He stopped and prepared to dash after his friend.

Pierre's heart stopped as he saw the shell land next to his friend. Eric's body flew up in the air in slow motion and landed with a crump on the road. Even from where he was Pierre could see that Eric's uniform was shredded and bloody. Pierre just knew Eric was dead before he hit the ground. He stood up, shaking with anger. "Goddamn you pigs. We're peacekeepers! What the hell are you doing?" He screamed and began to fire the BAR for cover and ran to retrieve his friends body, when a bullet struck his helmet and spun him around, knocking him down. As he was falling another struck his shoulder and a third shattered his fibula. *At last, million dollar wounds. They would finally get me the hell out of this God-forsaken place. Got to get to Eric, though, got to bring his body back...* As he faded into blackness, he thought of his friend lying bloody and dead in the road, and all the joy went out of his going home. When the darkness closed around him, he knew he would have to go to Switzerland to tell Tomiko how bravely Eric had died. As the corpsman came up to administer morphine and tell him the cavalry had arrived, he slipped into oblivion.

****

The North Korean sergeant had dark black hair and a smooth baby face. He was dressed in fatigues with the sleeves rolled up exposing two muscular forearms. With careful steps he and two privates approached the bodies. He put the muzzle of his deadly, Russian-made, burp gun on the corporal's hip and turned him over. The bottom half of the man turned but the top half stayed face down in the mud. The sergeant's expression didn't change as he quickly turned him back over again. He turned his head and spit as if there was a bad taste in his mouth, and then walked over to the second body. This time he reached down with his boot and turned the bloody body over. Eric groaned as he was turned face up. "This one's still alive," the sergeant said through clenched teeth. Then in perfect English he said, "If we save him maybe we can get some political mileage out of him, or maybe trade some prisoners for him. Let's get him back to a doctor."

Chapter 25: Switzerland

Pierre leaned on his cane as he stared up at the lovely house that looked so precariously perched on the huge mountain. His eyes drifted past the house to the mountain's crest. It was wreathed in clouds as if to crown the mountain's glory. He looked at the house again and realized it was a long climb and the cane and his leg were new to him. "It's hard enough to walk on a flat area much less a mountain," Pierre mumbled. The doctors had told him it would get easier with time. "I suppose I will find places to rest along the way. Anyway, it has to be done."

He compressed his mouth in resolve and started up the trail. With a smile, he remembered reading about General Sickles in the American Civil War, who had lost his leg at the battle of Gettysburg. Somehow he saved the leg and it was put in a museum in Washington. Sickles would go and visit his leg regularly, every week until he died. Pierre laughed as he approached the beginning of the trail up the mountain. "I would visit my leg, but what museum would have it?" He shrugged his shoulders smiled and began to walk the path up toward the cabin.

He was dressed in civilian tweeds and the climb was steep. That made it hot work. He had stopped wearing his uniform when he left the hospital. His service career was over now and he thought, *the sooner I became a civilian, the better.* He mopped his brow frequently as he negotiated the trail with the unfamiliar cane and equally unfamiliar pain in his shoulder and leg that were now his constant companions.

Thank goodness there are flat places on the climb where some thoughtful person had put benches. They are placed strategically so when one sat, they were looking out over the lake or the grounds around the hostel. It's truly a beautiful place and I promise myself to come back here on holiday the first chance I get.

By the time he reached the cabin his shoulder and leg were throbbing considerably and his limp had noticeably increased. He approached the front door and stood there for a while, trying to catch his breath.

The sun was high in the sky playing hide-and-seek with the clouds. Some birds, doing their daily tasks, flew this way and that while others sat in trees, nesting. It was so peaceful and his news so depressing, he was reluctant to knock on the door. He thought for a moment of going quickly back down the mountain and sending a telegram, or maybe just a telephone call. No, he thought, *I promised Eric I would see Tomiko, and I will.*

He reached up and quietly tapped on the door. In a few moments, the door opened and an attractive oriental woman faced him with a smile and a puzzled look on her face.

"Yes, can I help you?"

Pierre looked at her carefully. Eric's description of her did not do her justice. Her guileless face was framed by sculptured raven black hair that fell about her face. The scant make-up she wore covered cream colored skin that appeared flawless and ageless. Pierre thought, "She reminds me of the tiny Japanese dolls one could purchase in a curio shop.

Finally, he realized he had been just standing there a long while, just looking at her, remembering Eric.

"Well?" she asked, but not impatiently.

He shook his head to clear the cobwebs and the memories. "Are you Tomiko?"

The puzzled look increased. "Yes."

"I am Pierre Sebastian..."

Tomiko shook her head.

"Eric's army buddy."

The color in Tomiko's face drained. For a moment she seemed lifeless, like a piece of a dream or a nightmare. She staggered and Pierre reached out with his free hand to catch her.

She looked at him, suddenly seeming composed again. "How impolite I am," she said, mechanically, "Please come in." Tomiko held on to the furniture as she walked into the room. Somehow, she knew what was coming. She pointed absently to the futon. "Please sit down."

Pierre followed her into the room, desperately trying to think of the best way to tell her what had happened. He sat down at the edge of the futon and fidgeted with the cane not knowing quite how to begin. Suddenly, pain weld up inside him and he blurted it out. "Tomiko, Eric is dead."

All the blood left her face and Tomiko turned completely white.

Pierre thought, *She looks just like one of the Kabuki players I had seen in my R&R visits to Tokyo.*

"It happened on a patrol. He was as brave as he could be. He died charging the enemy so the rest of his men could live." Pierre hung his head in the ensuing silence, wishing desperately he were somewhere else. Tomiko's agony was palpable.

Tomiko managed a wan smile. "I cannot thank you enough for coming, Pierre." She got up and went to the window and looked out over the hostel. "While you are here, you will be our guest."

Pierre murmured a small "thank you" while thinking, *how incredibly brave she is.*

Tomiko continued to stare out the window at the icy lake. After a short while, she inquired about his wounds and Pierre told her in more detail what had happened. All during his narrative, Tomiko continued to stand at the window and look out at the lake. Finally she turned to him, still listening to him politely. He noted with relief that some of the color had returned to her face. When he had finished he stood up with some difficulty, bracing himself with the cane. "I will be leaving now."

"Please excuse me. I have been too long away from my upbringing. My manners are now non-existent. Of course, as I said, you will stay with us." Tomiko picked up the phone. "Please feel free to stay as long as you like, as my guest. I will call the office and make arrangements for you."

"That's very kind of you. This is a lovely place and it was such a long war... I would like to stay... for at least a few days, anyway."

"Good, it is settled then."

Tomiko called the office while Pierre took her place at the window and stared at the shimmering lake.

Tomiko said thank you, put the phone down and turned to Pierre. Her color had returned fully and there was no trace of pain in her face.

Pierre marveled at her composure. *Someone once told me it takes two weeks to replace a sucker. Maybe it's true. No, I am too cynical, it couldn't be, she was too shaken. She's the real deal.*

Tomiko bowed her head slightly. "If you would go back to the office they will be glad to help you get settled. I will be away for a while, but please make yourself comfortable and plan to stay as long as you like."

Pierre nodded as he and Tomiko went to the front door. As she opened it she put her hand on his. "I want to thank you for coming. I know how hard this must have been for you, both mentally and physically." Pierre, close to tears, nodded and left.

Tomiko stood at the front door and watched Pierre hobble down the trail. At the first turn, where the trail went out of sight, he turned and waved. She waved back. She stayed there a few minutes longer and then turned and went in and sat down on the futon staring into space. When Joe had died her heart turned cold. Now that it was Eric, she was on fire.

Try as she might to stay stoic, her heart wrenched, her stomach churned and the tears came freely. She was not aware when the day became night.

The first light of the next day brought a decision. She got into her ceremonial robe, took the lotus position and began to breathe deeply. Soon she was chanting, Ooohhhhhmmmmmm, deep in meditation.

At first she had a monkey mind, flitting from one thought to another, but gradually her mental and physical beings began to relax and soon she became blank, descending into a dark void. She stayed in the trance-like state until she was startled by a voice that spoke in her head. Or did she sense it? *'Shave your head. Go to the cave across the lake. Meditate'.* She blinked her eyes and came awake.

"The lord Buddha wishes me to go to the cave and meditate and that is what I will do." For the first time since she was told that Eric was dead, she approached a state that was near peace.

She shaved her head in the fashion of the monks, her raven black hair falling at her feet. She packed what she needed in a plastic bag and slung it over her shoulder. Then she began the long walk down the trail past the hostel to the lake. It was very early in the morning and almost everyone was still asleep. She passed the tennis courts and her heart wrenched. Eric took such loving care of these courts, she thought. I always believed it was because he liked doing a job well. Now I realize it was because he loved me. She could not prevent the tears from beginning to course down her cheeks. She thought of the wonderful matches she and Sydney had played. *Lord Buddha, take care of Sydney and help to get her well again.*

At the lake's edge she stopped. Small waves lapped at the edge of the sandy beach. She took off her tabi and felt the cold sand in her toes. She peeled off her robe, dropped it to the ground and stepped into the water. The cold shocked her and she stepped back out. She smiled. *"I have become a Westerner. I must again be Japanese."* With all the stoicism of her ancestors she calmly walked into the freezing water, put the plastic ties in her mouth, and ignoring the cold, began to swim to the opposite shore.

When the police arrived it was late in the day. Pierre hobbled to the edge of the sand and stood watching the small crowd. One of the regulars at the hostel was talking to the Swiss policeman. "Of course it's her. Who else would be wearing a Japanese robe like that."

"Was there any reason she would take her life? We can't just go dragging the lake on a suspicion."

Omigod, Pierre thought, *she's killed herself.* Pierre hobbled quickly through the sand to the officer.

"Excuse me officer," he said excitedly, "I may have the reason." Pierre carefully explained what had happened. all the while feeling anxious and depressed for not staying with her longer. *But, how was I to know?*

For the next two days the lake was dragged with no success. Tomiko was listed as missing, presumed dead.

Every day, Pierre would go to the lake and sit and watch. It was almost as if he expected her to rise out of the water, shake her head of excess liquid and greet him. He could not get the picture of her out of his head. *No wonder Eric adored her.* He bowed his head and made the sign of the cross.

Always when he went back to the hostel, he would stop and look up at the house on the mountain. Although he had not known Tomiko long he felt a direct connection to her. He also felt a terrible loss when he thought about her.

After two weeks, Pierre's depression began to lift and he began to think about home. *Canada, oh, Canada, you are calling me home.* He thought of his mother and the steaming food only she knew how to cook. His mouth watered at the thought.

He packed his bags and started walking towards the office to make arrangements for his leaving. The day was crisp and autumn was in the air. It was a time for football and soccer. He was glad he had decided to go home. It was time. He must put Korea behind him and look to his future.

"Hello, what's this?" There was a large crowd outside the office and they were shaking hands and clapping the back of a man in the center. *Well, someone must have won the lottery, Pierre joked to himself. I guess I should shake his hand, too.* Pierre walked towards the crowd, smiling broadly. The man in the center had his back to him but there was something familiar about him. The man began to turn and Pierre stopped dead in his tracks. His face flushed and his heart skipped a beat. "Jesus, Joseph and Mary! Eric! How did you get back from the dead?"

****

Eric was silent as they walked along the lake. "They found her robe here, Eric. The police dragged the lake for days, but couldn't find a thing." Pierre lapsed into silence. Eric had not spoken a word since he had told him about Tomiko. The silence made Pierre nervous. It wasn't natural. Shout, scream, let your feelings out. Do something! But Eric did nothing. He just plodded along the lake, head down, hour after hour.

"Let's sit a minute, Eric. I still tire easily." Both men sat on a green bench facing the lake.

Pierre tried again. "When I last saw you running down the road, I saw them get you. When that shell went off and you were blown into the air, I knew you were a dead man, I saw you land, shredded and bloodied. How did you survive?"

Eric's voice was small, cold and distant. "The shell blew me up, but it didn't hurt much until later. After a while, I was in so much pain I wished it would have killed me. I was cut badly by the shrapnel, but the Korea needed me for a political trade, so they got me to an aid station, and then a hospital and patched me up."

Pierre knew better than to ask any more questions. He slowly stood up, rested his weight on his cane with both hands and looked at Eric critically. "I am getting really tired and I need to rest. Why don't you come up to the hostel and bunk with me. Maybe we can talk some more."

Eric smiled wanly to his friend. "Pierre, you go on. I think I would like to stay here a while and think."

Pierre shrugged his shoulders and turned to leave. He shuffled a few steps and then stopped as if in thought. Then he turned and looked at Eric. He was sitting on the edge of the bench, his hands clasped, head down. "Eric..." His friend looked up at him. "...It will be okay. There may even be someone else someday." As soon as he said that, he was sorry he did.

Eric smiled a wan smile, nodded his head, compressed his lips and looked back down again.

Pierre started back towards the hostel full of foreboding. I better call mom and tell her I have to stay a while longer. When I tell her about Eric coming back, I'm sure she'll understand. Too bad! Oh, too bad Tomiko couldn't have waited.

Eric spent the rest of the afternoon staring at the watery grave. The sun had set over the mountain when he finally got up. He had fallen desperately in love with Tomiko from the first moment he set eyes on her and had suffered in silence until somehow, miraculously, she knew. When he left for Korea, he thought of nothing else but getting back to her. Now, after surviving shells and bullets and hate, he came back to, nothing.

His heart wrenched with pain and tears formed in the corners of his eyes. Slowly and deliberately he got up and started walking towards the mountain. Faster and faster he went, until he was almost running. Up, up he went, past the rock garden, past the landing, up to the front door of their home.

He opened the front door, almost expecting Tomiko to come out and rush into his arms. *Nothing. No Tomiko, no love, no life, nothing!* After getting out of the Korean concentration camp, his cup had been full again. Now it was completely empty. He felt depression creep over him like mist in a swamp.

Eric walked out on the balcony and lit a cigarette, a nice habit he picked up in Korea. The moon was up and the stars were shining brightly. Eric dragged on the cigarette and flipped it over the railing. He watched the glowing end fall until it hit a jutting rock and shower into a thousand sparks. Then it was dark again. He stared into the darkness feeling numb. Up here he felt Tommy everywhere. With just the slightest effort he could feel her hand on his. He could close his eyes and see her, touch her hair and feel her body next to his. Anguish gripped him. He felt pain and numbness at the same time. Suddenly the telephone rang, its brittle ring piercing the night. He ignored it.

What is a life, he thought, *a brief candle, lit for a while and then snuffed out. Yet I have been privileged to know and love my soul mate. But half of me is now gone.* The phone rang insistently. *Without her I am only half alive.* Finally, the phone stopped ringing. Eric walked back into the cabin and picked up the pad and pencil by the phone.

Pierre, my dear friend:...

He finished the note, put the pad down and walked back on the balcony again.

****

Pierre put the phone down. He had a worried look on his face. *I shouldn't have left him, he thought. I have to find him. Where in the Hell could he be?* Suddenly his face lit up. *I bet he just won't answer the phone. I better go up there.* Pierre went out the hostel door and started to walk as quickly as he could towards the trail up to the mountain.

Eric's heart was pounding and his head was spinning. He felt a deep ache in his chest that squeezed his heart. Suddenly his head cleared. For the first time in his life he could look beyond himself and see the infinite. Death is a part of life, he thought. Only in death is there a relief of this pain of separation. *Tommy saw that. She went to join me in death. Now, I will join her.* He stepped over the railing. "Everything fits," he said aloud, "now we will be together for all eternity..."

Eric stepped off the railing into the void. For the first time since he had come home there was joy in his heart. He felt the rush of air past his body and was more alive than ever before. He whispered into the darkness, as he fell, "Tomiko."

****

When Pierre got to the front door of the mountain house, he was exhausted and covered with sweat. He threw open the door expecting to find the worst. Quickly he went into each room. Nothing. Not a thing out of place, nothing disturbed. He sighed with relief, looked around one more time and left. He tapped his cane in front of him as he felt his way down the mountain. He peered ahead adjusting his eyes to the dark. "Hmm, better be careful, wouldn't want fall off this mountain." He looked out into the darkness. "It's a hell of a long way down."

The next day, Pierre was jolted out of sleep by a maintenance worker who had found the body. Pierre rushed to the foot of the mountain and bent down over the disfigured body to be sure. It was Eric. His heart broke. *Why? Why?* There was no answer. "Now both of them are gone," he said softly, "and the world is the worse for it." Bad leg, bad shoulder, cane and all, he gently lifted the broken body in his arms, and carried him back to the office.

Pierre was told by the police to leave Eric on the couch in the office that night. The coroner would be there in the morning to examine him and have an inquest. It would be cold enough tonight not to worry about any decomposition.

After the last policeman left, Pierre got up to go too. He walked to the door, put his hand on the door handle and looked back at his friend. An old army blanket covered him completely, hiding his face. Pierre hesitated and walked back to the body. He lifted the blanket and looked at his friend's battered and bloody face. He took a piece of paper out of his pocket and read it once again.

Pierre, my dear friend:

I searched my heart and found I cannot live without my love. I hate to leave my friends, but I must go and join her.

I will miss you.

Eric

A rush of pain and anguish hit him and he dropped the edge of the blanket and cried. In a few minutes he stopped, looked on the desk in the office and found a pen. He quickly scrawled a few words on the bottom of the note and slipped it under the blanket. He shuffled out the door, vowing never to return again.

****

The night was cold and clear and the lake was glassy. Tomiko stepped out of the lake and shook the water off her. She crossed her arms over her bare breasts, shivering in the cold. She looked around making sure she was alone and made her way towards the office where she had a spare set of clothing. She had been meditating without food and she was on the verge of being delusional. All she could think about now was warm clothes and a cup of green tea.

When she had first reached the cave, she was distraught. Try as she might to still her mind, she could not. It would not obey. Time after time, she thought of Eric and would dissolve in tears. Finally after a discipline of two days without food, she began to control her mind and could finally meditate for long periods. By the end of five days, her mind would stay in a blank state until she willed it not to. For the last few days, she was totally immersed in the gap, bordering on mindlessness.

She ran up the stairs to the office and bolted inside. A small light had been left on and she quickly made her way to the closet where the clothes were. She pulled the chain and a small bulb lit up the closet. She quickly toweled off and pulled on the jeans and shirt she knew she had left there.

Her mind still fixed on the hot tea, she started back towards the front door.

When she saw the blanket covering an odd shape, her heart stopped. Somehow she knew what it was. She also knew she was near delusional, so she had to be sure. She walked to the body, pulled down the blanket, and went into shock. After a few moments she recovered and looked into his eyes, fixed in an eternal stare. She was overcome. Slowly she sank to the floor and began to sob. *What kind of trick was this that fate was playing. Did he come back for her? Was it a sign from the Lord Buddha?* She again looked at him, past the blood and scrapes and saw his curly black hair and the blue eyes she loved so dearly. Then she saw the note.

Pierre, my dear friend:

I searched my heart and found I cannot live without my love. I hate to leave my friends but I must go and join her. I will miss you.

Eric

Then she read the scrawl left by Pierre.

I will be eternally sorry that I told you Tomiko was dead. You could have stayed alive and looked for her instead of leaping off the mountain.

I will miss you too.

Pierre

Tomiko was on her knees, tears rolling down her cheeks. She bent forward and kissed Eric on the mouth then lay her head on his chest. After a long while she stood up, and turned towards the door. Her face was fixed with resolve. Absently, she crumpled the note and dropped it on the floor as she walked out the door.

Tomiko's tears blinded her as she half walked, half ran up the trail. When she reached the cabin she began to carefully make the green tea she had longed for. When the water was ready she wiped the teacup and saucer and ritually poured the water over the loose tea and stirred it the proper amount of times. Then she carefully wiped the utensils and put them away. She dried her eyes and slowly sipped the tea, savoring each drop, until it was gone. Then she went to the shrine carefully built by Japanese hands, so long ago, and opened the exquisitely carved door. Cautiously, she pulled out a jeweled case and opened it. She kneeled and faced the shrine. She longed not to die badly. Slowly and carefully she extracted the curved blade. It was honed to razor sharpness and gleamed ominously in the dull light. Tomiko placed the tip of the long curved knife six inches to the left of her navel. She would cut across and then up, and prayed she would not cry out. She was samurai and would die with honor. Briefly she wondered why the sharp point felt so good against her skin. Suddenly she knew. The life she was ending had been a hard one in so many ways. First, the abandonment by her grandfather, then the perfection expected of her as a child in the schooling of the geishas. The entertaining of many men, always having to be at her best, when they were not. Killing the barbarian and having to run like a ronin. A western marriage to Joe and then his painful parting. And now Eric, a fiery love, and a new happiness, gone in an instant.

Tomiko loves and then is abandoned, that is my karma. Tears formed in her eyes and coursed down her cheeks. Silently, they splashed down onto her robe and disappeared into the silk.

Now she would pray to Lord Buddha for all who had preceded her into the void. She wished greatly to see her mother again, and she hoped her father would greet her in his uniform. *Oh, yes, and honored grandfather, he will greet me and I will bow to him and thank him for the life he helped choose for me. And then with great honor and politeness I will introduce all of them to my beautiful barbarians, my Eric and my Joe and also the mama-san who was my second mother. And we would all be together, always.*

She pushed the knife into her skin slowly and steeled herself for the final thrust. She had no second to take off her head and make sure she died with honor so her thrust must be true the first time.

Suddenly the shrine lit up and the room began to glow. Tomiko looked up and saw the faint outline of a young girl in a bright light. She had long flowing hair and a dress that seemed to made of gossamer. The dress flowed like waves on the sea, undulating in the soft wind. She seemed not to touch the floor but stood just above it. Tomiko smiled and nodded her head, politely. "Konichi wa, (Hello) Julietta." The vision smiled and also tipped her head. Tomiko stood up and swayed back and forth, weak from hunger. *Is this beautiful girl an illusion?* she wondered.

The girl held her left hand out. Tomiko reached for it and they touched. Now Tomiko was enveloped in her light. She heard music filling the room. *Un bel di vedremo.* (One fine day he'll return) The girl gently beckoned. Tomiko dropped the knife and it clattered unnoticed to the floor. She took a step. The apparition slowly stretched out her right arm like a ballet dancer showing the way. Tomiko looked to where she pointed and there was Eric with his arms outstretched to her. Her heart filled with love and joy. She would run to him. With a nod to the spirit, she began to run as fast as she could. Tears ran down her face and she felt the cold wind against them. She was laughing and free. In a moment she would be in his arms, together, forever. *Un bel di.*

"Eric," she whispered as she stepped off the deck into the void.

The crump of the body was heard only by the creatures of the forest that Tomiko loved so much.

Chapter 26: Budapest

Sydney was nervous. She had called Dr. Kodaly's office and after trying to get someone to understand her, she had finally spoken to an English speaking nurse. They made her appointment for ten o'clock, but asked her to be there at nine-thirty to fill out papers.

At the hotel, she was told to take the taxi to Erzsébet Körúttal, (Elizebeth Circle), and then go to number 1500, and she would be there. Sydney asked the taxi driver to stop at number 1000. She paid him and started to walk down the street trying to shed her nervousness. Suddenly she had an overwhelming desire to run. *Hah!* she said to herself, *run? Where? Maybe with this doctor I have a chance. What was it that Tommy said, A last chance!*

When she got to clinic door she stared at the paneled oak front door. It was exceptionally clean and polished. A good sign. Sydney threw her cigarette down and ground it out with the heel of her Gucci loafer. "Well, here goes." She took a deep breath and reached for the door handle. Just as she grasped it, the door opened and a young woman in her early thirties stepped out. Sydney stepped back politely holding the door open. The woman smiled weakly and said, "Jo naput, koszonom." (Good morning, thank you) As she walked off down the street, Sydney looked after her. *She didn't look too happy. I think I'll leave too,* she joked to herself. She hesitated a few seconds then with finality, she set her shoulders and walked in the front door.

The room she entered was a large, spotlessly clean room with modern Danish chairs spaced evenly against off-colored white walls. The floors were a pinkish-brown Mexican tile, with Persian rugs placed strategically around the surprisingly warm room. Two-tiered end tables were placed at every other chair with small oxygen-giving plants on the top step of each table. Magazines in Hungarian and English were placed neatly on the bottom tiers.

Just opposite the entrance was a glass enclosure with two women working industriously. One of them was older and a little heavier. The other, thin and bespectacled. Both of them stopped and looked at Sydney as she entered.

"Jo naput, I mean, good morning," the oldest one said sweetly, "are you Miss Bannon?"

Sydney smiled back. "Your English is very good."

"I lived in the U.S., in Cleveland for many years," her face soured slightly, "until my divorce." Realizing this was not the place for that discussion the receptionist smiled again and handed three papers to Sydney. "Would you please fill these out and we will get you started." Then as an afterthought, she said, "I wrote the instructions in English next to the Hungarian." The younger girl stifled a yawn and went back to her typing. Sydney said "Thank you," took the papers and turned to sit down. Her way was blocked by a dark, curly-haired five-year -old boy with the roundest face and most sparkling eyes she had ever seen. She smiled broadly in spite of herself.

"Beteg a neni?" Sydney did not understand him and turned to the receptionist.

"He is asking if you are sick," she said with a frown.

The boy's mother, understanding immediately called out, "Zoltan, ne zavard a hölgyet." (Don't bother the lady) "Gyere ide." (Come here) The nurse translated to Sydney.

Encouraged by Sydney's obvious attraction, the boy ignored his mother, smiled, and stayed right there.

Never looking away from the boy's face, Sydney told the receptionist, "Please tell his mother it's all right." Then she stuck out her right hand. The boy gave her his left and they shook hands awkwardly, but firmly. Sydney smiled and nodded to the mother, and then turned and looked at the boy again. She felt glad for this interlude that took her mind away from the fear of the unknown. "Come with me, uh, uh..." She looked at the receptionist questioningly.

The nurse nodded at the boy. "His name is Zoltan."

Sydney straightened up still holding his hand. "Come with me, Zoltan." The receptionist translated and Zoltan followed Sydney, curiously attracted to the beautiful lady. Most people in his life were dark and wore only somber clothing. This lady was different. She was bright and so were her clothes.

His mother returned to her magazine resignedly.

Sydney sat down and put the papers on the end table. Then she picked up a large ABC book, and to his delight, put Zoltan in her lap.

The boy thought she smelled and felt wonderful, and he snuggled close to her.

Sydney opened the book to the A's and pointed to a bright shiny apple. She carefully said "Aaaapple."

Zoltan looked up at her puzzled and then, excitedly, he got it. "Apple!" He smiled broadly, very proud of himself.

Sydney read and Zoltan answered patiently until they got to the H's where he was explaining what a house was, when suddenly a nurse appeared and beckoned to the boy's mother. She stood up and said, a shade harshly to the boy, "Zoltan! Gyere ide, nincs egész nap." (Come here, we haven't got all day)

The boy pouted and looked at Sydney sadly, his new adventure all but over. She pouted back and suddenly he leaped down to the floor and shrugged his shoulders, and made a face that said, oh well, in the best French tradition.

"Zoltan!" his mother threatened.

The boy bowed to Sydney and again gave her his left hand. Then he impetuously reached up and kissed her on the cheek and bounded after his mother who impatiently held the door open for him. As he passed by her, she reached down and gave him a light spank on his bottom. She smiled at

Sydney with a look that said I hope he didn't bother you too much and followed the boy inside.

Sydney looked after them, her insides in turmoil. *What am I doing? Where am I going? Why don't I have a Zoltan? Why am I missing the things that really count?* She shook her head, promising she would confront herself and answer these questions.

Sydney reached for the papers and began to write. She finished the first page quickly and turned to the second. She had a strange feeling and looked up from the papers. Standing at the door was a nurse. Instantly she felt her heart contract and she had to control herself from bolting out of the clinic.

"Miss Bannon, goot morning. My name is Maria. Vould you come wit me, please."

Aha, she thought another English speaking nurse. Sydney stood and followed the nurse into the clinic interior. The hall was gleaming white with linoleum that was so waxed Sydney could see her reflection as she walked. Dark doors labeled with their function stood at unequal distances along the hall. They passed X-ray and Laboratory doors and stopped at the door marked Office. The nurse opened the door and held it for Sydney.

Maria set down her file on the uncluttered desk and pointed to a leather chair. "Please make yourself comfortable and Dr. Kodaly vill be right wit you." Sydney nodded as the nurse left.

Sydney sat in the comfortable, claret-colored chair and leaned back. She looked about the room hoping for a clue to the man she would soon meet. The office was neat and orderly, but not the stark white of the rest of the clinic. The walls were a soft tan and the curtains had the reddish color of a leaf in the fall of the year. The desk and chairs were made of sturdy oak. They were not modern, but of a bygone year. The floor was rugged wall-to-wall with thick, rich carpet. There were fresh flowers on the desk and a fig tree in a large flower pot in the corner of the room. The only window in the room looked out onto a city street. The window was low enough that Sydney could see the passersby as they went about their business. Apparently the room was soundproof so she could see the cars but not hear them. *Thank goodness for that, she thought. Hungarian drivers were not known for their patience or politeness.*

Nervously Sydney got up and walked to the wall where a bank of diplomas hung:

Charles Kodaly, M. D.
Eötvös Loránd University

"Well, at least he's a real doctor with a real diploma," she muttered.

She reached out to the diploma and tilted it to catch the sun so she could read the small Latin print at the bottom, and did not hear the door open.

"I assure you, Miss Bannon, it is a genuine diploma from a regular medical school." The cultured European voice startled Sydney and she let the diploma fall back against the wall with a clatter.

"Excuse me," she said, flustered, "I was trying to read the Latin." She blushed and somehow wished she were smaller. The man walked towards her with his hand held out. "Charles Kodaly," he said warmly. They shook hands and the Doctor seated himself behind the large desk. He engrossed himself in her file so deeply that Sydney suddenly felt alone. *At least this man gives all his attention to the matter at hand,* she thought. Some of her anxiety left her, and somehow she felt more secure. Sydney was more than glad that she had called Dr. Slater and had her medical file sent to Dr. Kodaly.

Sydney looked about the room, but her eyes kept coming back to the man who held her fate in his hands. His features were clean cut and masculine. *He is probably in his early fifties*, she thought. He had a full head of black hair with an abundance of gray at the temples. His lab coat was open revealing a blue shirt with a conservative, burgundy tie with grey stripes. His pants were black as were his gleaming, Italian leather shoes.

Sydney's chart lay on his desk, her papers spread out like a fan. For about ten minutes, he read the results of Dr. Slater's tests and the papers she had filled out. Her whole life was in a manila folder, on an oak desk, in Budapest, in Central Europe. Isn't life strange, she thought.

Sydney's reverie came to an abrupt halt. "Well, Miss Bannon, there does not seem to be much doubt about your condition." He stopped, picked up a pencil and thoughtfully tapped the papers he had just read. He smiled at Sydney, as if he were about to share a secret with her. "No doubt an intelligent young woman like yourself wonders why we at this clinic could treat you successfully when skilled doctors at such a prestigious hospital like Dr. Slater's could not."

She nodded.

He sighed. "Sometimes I wonder myself, the answers seem so obvious. In science, occasionally, the obvious is not readily seen by those who are not ready. When Newton proposed the laws of the universe we now so readily accept, there were those in the Royal Society who called him a fraud."

Well, one question answered, Sydney thought.

The doctor rose and came around the desk holding one of the papers in his hand. He sat on the edge of the desk facing Sydney one leg on the floor, the other hanging down.

Sydney noted she was not overwhelmed as she was by the doctors in New York. This man seemed competent and assured. She felt more secure at this moment than she had since the first time she had felt the lump in her breast. She leaned forward attentively.

"We will approach your condition from several paths and arrive, hopefully, at a successful conclusion. Yours will be a four-sided program. First, we will practice regular medicine and test the tissues and your blood picture on a regular basis. We attend the latest medical seminars and participate in the latest studies, so you need not be concerned on that score."

Dr. Kodaly stood up and went back behind the desk and sat down. "Second is your diet. We are vegetarians first and macrobiotic second." He leaned back in his chair. "Demographics have shown us, that people who eat a mostly vegetarian diet, like our Japanese friends, suffer much less colon and breast cancer than we do. However, when they assimilate with us, and eat the same way we do, as exemplified by the Japanese people in your own country, they then suffer both those cancers at the same rate as Westerners do."

Sydney nodded her head thoughtfully. She had a few friends in college who were vegetarians, but she always thought it was a fad. Besides, they always wanted to get up at four or five in the morning and meditate in the woods. She remembered thinking, you can't sleep off a hangover in the woods. She forced her attention back to Dr. Kodaly.

"Macrobiotics is way of life that also started in the east where observers noticed that the people who lived in harmony with the land seemed to get along much better that those who don't. For instance what kind of body types do people in the arctic regions have?

Sydney thought for a moment, trying to picture an Eskimo.

Dr Kodaly continued without waiting for her answer. "They are smaller, rounder, more compact people. Now think of the Watusi on the equator in Africa."

"Yes, they are very tall," Sydney joined in.

"Why, do you suppose Nature would do that?"

Sydney's brow wrinkled as she thought it through for an answer. In a few moments she shrugged her shoulders and put up her hands, palms up. "I give up."

"The people in the colder climates are more compact so they can retain body warmth in the below zero temperature. The Watusi are tall and have more surface area, so they can dissipate the severe heat at the equator. The more surface area the more cooling."

Recognition came to Sydney's face and she nodded her head in understanding. Then she shrugged. "But what does that have to do with someone's health?"

Dr. Kodaly smiled. "People don't live in one place anymore. When the Eskimo goes to Florida, he swelters. Either he gets air conditioning. or he suffers in the heat. What should he eat? His staple is whale blubber, which is fat and heavy protein. In his native habitat, that is perfect for producing the heat he needs. If he eats that in Miami he might become a very sad Eskimo. As for the Watusi, if he stays at the equator and has fruits and vegetables, he stays cool. But if he goes to New York and eats fruit in the dead of winter, he retains no heat."

"I think I get it," Sydney said thoughtfully, "you eat and dress native to the area you're in."

"Yes, and if you get too far away from that, your body will rebel and even get sick, if it can't keep up."

"I see," Sydney said, her head nodding in agreement.

"Macrobiotics is not only the food you eat, but the clothing you wear and even the company you keep. Some people are in harmony with you and some raise the small hair on the back of your neck."

Sydney laughed. "I have a few of those friends."

Dr. Kodaly compressed his lips. "Yes, and for the time being, we request that you not stay around them. Also, I will request that you not wear anything but cotton and follow our routine for wake and sleep habits. Last, but not least. you must follow our diet regimen. You will eat all your meals here at the clinic. I dislike telling patients the following, but should you obtain some food from the outside that interferes with our program, the result will be dismissal from the clinic. I am sorry we must be so firm, but this is a life and death situation." Dr. Kodaly got off the desk and walked to the window and stared absently at the street. "We had a movie star at the clinic who insisted on having a junk food Sunday. We put up with it for a while, but finally I had to dismiss him and in a few months he was dead. It is sad but in that area, you must be strong, and of course we will help you along with that." He turned back to Sydney. "Any question so far?"

Sydney shook her head. She felt she was in the presence of a man who had thought out his approach and somehow she felt very secure in his hands.

"The next item after food is exercise. I see by your forms you play tennis. We have no facility here but I can make arrangements for you to play elsewhere. We encourage that. Also, you will have a coach who will guide you in the pool and the weight room. This is not to shape you up or make you strong but to give your body it's natural expression of work and movement. In your case, it won't take much work but some of the people we get here haven't moved off a couch for years."

Dr. Kodaly smiled warmly at Sydney as if he were going to tell her an anecdote. "The last, but certainly not the least, part of the program is meditation. At the same time we are cleansing your body, the Guru will be helping to cleanse your mind." Dr. Kodaly smiled broadly. "I found Guru Abinanda, or he found me, in India at a session with the teacher, Nehru. I had heard of this teacher and wished to study with him to help my patients. While I was sitting in class I noticed a young Indian man sitting near to me. In class, at lunch, even at my modest hut I stayed at, in Ramallah, wherever I went, this young man, with the brightest smile I had ever seen, followed me and sat down near me. At first it was unnerving. I tried to get away from him, but he kept showing up at my side. Finally I confronted him and asked what he wanted. He just smiled that white grin and answered 'It has been ordained that I serve you, lord.' I went to the teacher and asked him what was going on. He was even more oblique. He merely said, 'When the Lord sends a message, do not cast the messenger into the street.' Before I could ask what he meant, he left in a huff. It was almost as if he were angry with me for being upset with this intrusion in my life." Dr. Kodaly's face had an amused look as he remembered the incidents.

"Well, I thought all this very irregular, so I determined to shake him once and for all. Sure enough, I went in one place and out the other, dodged through crowds and market places until, finally, I was alone.

With great relief I went back to my hotel and began to pack, my learning in India was over and I wanted to go home, the quicker the better. I went to the desk of my hotel to check out, when I heard a lot of noise, people yelling, cars beeping all outside the hotel. Curious, I stepped outside and observed the largest traffic jam I had ever seen. Cars were backed up for miles. People were yelling as loud as they could and several policeman were making their way to the center of this storm. Something drew me to the center too, and I pushed my way there. To my complete amazement, at the middle of all this chaos was the young man with the bright smile. He was sitting in the lotus position right in the middle of the intersection. He looked up at me with the most innocent face, gave me the best smile he had and said 'Lord, I am glad you finally came, these people have to get to work.' With that he stood up, apologized to everyone and followed me into the hotel.

I gave up and just accepted that a higher power directed him to come with me. It turns out he is most invaluable in the treatment, as you will find out." Dr. Kodaly came around the desk and took her hand. "Is there anything else I can tell you."

"No, Dr. Kodaly, I'm a little bewildered, but I think I understand everything."

"Good. I hope, then, that you will come to the clinic and let us help you."

Sydney stood up. "I have already made up my mind. I would like to start right away."

Dr. Kodaly pressed a button on his desk and in a few moments the nurse appeared. "Maria, kérem mutassa meg a klinikat Miss Bannonnak." (Maria please show Miss Bannon around the clinic). The doctor turned to Sydney. "Maria speaks English well, so you will have no problem understanding her. She will show you around the clinic and then we will get started with your examination and treatment plan." Dr. Kodaly stood in front of her and offered her his hand. Sydney took it. He looked directly into her eyes, and she felt him bore into her soul. She felt as though his heart spoke to hers.

"Miss Bannon, We will do everything in our power to help you."

Maria held the door open for her and smiled. Then she said in heavily accented English, Ve vill start in the kitchen."

Dr. Kodaly sat down at his desk and began to write. Sydney stopped at the door and looked back at him. "Thank you for your help, Dr. Kodaly."

He looked up, his mind already on something else. "Thank me when you are well, Miss Bannon," and he returned to his work.

Sydney nodded, her lips compressed as she followed the nurse out the door. They both walked down the gleaming white corridor and the various doors she had seen before. Maria dutifully pointed out the X-ray and lab rooms as well as the various treatment and surgical suites. Somehow it was comforting to Sydney to see the old hospital standbys of surgery and X-ray.

"You are fortunate to have heard ov us. Dr. Kodaly does vonderful verk. Ah! Here ve are." The double swinging doors the nurse stopped at were marked 'konyha'. (kitchen) The nurse held the door open and Sydney stepped into the room. She narrowed her eyes. The entire kitchen seemed to be made of gleaming stainless steel. The walls were white and as spotless as were the employees that staffed the kitchen. Each of them wore white from head-to-toe, with hats or hair nets covering their hair and aprons covering their fronts. There was a large laundry cart in the center of the room and Sydney soon realized that should a spot appear on any article of clothing it would immediately be discarded into the cart and a fresh one exchanged. The nurse handed Sydney a hair net and she deftly put it on.

In the center of the room, overseeing all the work, was a stout man with an oval face and a large chef's cap. He was unsmiling. His eyes darted about, missing nothing. He seemed mildly annoyed at the two intruders. Maria nodded towards him and whispered to Sydney, "That is Ference, the chef. He will not speak to anyone, except the kitchen staff during work hours. Just ignore him."

Sydney laughed to herself and thought, *he looks just like a Gestapo agent, or, no, the fat man in Casablanca.*

Sydney and the nurse walked down a long stainless steel counter where a man and a woman were industriously cutting and chopping various vegetables over a sink with running water. The woman nodded vigorously and smiling nervously, stopped chopping. Sydney smiled back. With some difficulty, Sydney tried to say hello just the way she had heard it. "Jo naput." (Good morning)

It worked, the woman wiped her hands on her apron and answered excitedly, "Goot morning!" The man looked over at Sydney laconically and kept cutting.

Sydney said slowly and deliberately, "Is this your job here, cutting vegetables?"

The woman understood English and answered excitedly, "Oh no, I do many tings. All of us in the kitchen haf to know all of the jobs here, the chef insists. Today I cut vegetables, tomorrow I cook the soup, the next day I make salads. Ve all get our jobs from Ilde. She is the chef's helper and in charge of all the kitchen help." She pointed to a middle aged woman working at a baker's oven. The woman nodded and smiled back at Sydney.

Sydney smiled back. Then she turned back to the woman and her companion. "Thank you so much for all the information. I am sure I will see you both again."

Sydney touched her shoulder and the woman curtsied as Sydney left. Behind her as she walked away she heard the couple fall into rapid, animated, Hungarian.

As they walked toward the exit the nurse said softly, "The chef is macrobiotic. I am sure Dr. Kodaly told you about that. It is the preferred choice of food here. At first, eating that way seemed foreign to me, but now I like it and look forward to each meal."

Sydney nodded her head remembering Tomiko's meals.

"Is dere anyone else you vish to speak to or anything else you vould like to see here?" Sydney nodded no, and they left the kitchen. It was much cooler in the hall and Sydney realized she had moisture on her brow. She patted herself dry as she followed the nurse down the hall.

They stopped at a door marked Uszo medence/ torna. Sydney knew by the familiar smell of chlorine that it was the pool area. The nurse held the door open and Sydney stepped in. Standing between her and the pool was a dizzying array of exercise equipment. Several people, mostly older woman, were working diligently on the machines. A few of them looked up but no one stopped. Looking beyond the machines, Sydney could see that there were other people in the pool. Some were doing laps and others were doing water exercises led by a supervisor. Slowly she realized there were uniformed supervisors observing all the activities. *The place is well run, I will give them that.*

The nurse spoke over the machines and the splash of the water, her voice echoing in the large, heated room. "After you are on der program for a few days, you vill be directed here for a planned exercise program. This vill be done tree days a veek until you are finished vit der program." As an afterthought she said, almost to herself, "you vould be surprised at the shape most people are in when dey come here." She smiled and looked at Sydney's figure. "I don't tink you vill have dat problem."

As they walked towards the next destination, Sydney mused on how she felt. *This place is just naturally right for me,* she thought. Long gone hope began to well up in her breast.

Sydney became aware of the swishing sound of the nurses' nylon stockings and her starched dress. Suddenly she thought of Tomiko, and just as suddenly she was transported back to her friend and their mountain. She almost wept. *Why would I think of her now?* Slowly, the realization came upon her. The nurse, Maria, bustled everywhere, noisily. Tomiko would move silently, her cotton clothes hiding her graceful movements. For the first time since she had left, she realized how much she missed her friend and their mountain. Sydney shook her head and forced herself back to the present.

The nurse stopped and knocked at a door. She smiled nervously as they waited for an answer. In a few moments, the door opened and the nurse curtsied. "Goot morning, Guru."

The man at the door smiled and it appeared to Sydney that the whole room lit up.

"Good morning, Maria, and whom have you brought to visit me today?"

Guru, this is Miss Bannon. Miss Bannon, this is Guru Abinanda."

"Good morning, Miss Bannon," he said, beckoning them into the room. "My home is yours. Welcome.

"Thank you," Sydney said in a small voice. Somehow she felt slightly awed.

The Indian guru wore a white robe with gray slippers. He had long glistening black hair that came to his shoulders. His black beard was neatly trimmed and framed a sensuous mouth that was curled in a perpetual smile. His eyes were bright and his words engaging. He spoke with a lilting, sing-song, Indian accent.

Sydney looked around the room. It was dark with heavy curtains covering the windows. Soft indirect lighting came from a recessed area near the ceiling. Rich wall coverings of gold and claret hung on the walls displaying elephants and drivers and safari hunters. The music in the background was haunting and beautiful, played by high pitched, foreign instruments. There were chairs lined up against one wall. A raised platform was at the opposite wall with rows of pillows on the floor, facing the platform.

The guru pointed to the pillows. "Please sit and visit with me ladies."

Maria thought about her starched dress and looked uncomfortably at the pillows. "Excuse me guru, but I have a million tings to do." She turned to Sydney. I vill be back for you in a half hour and ve vill finish the orientation."

Sydney nodded. "Thank you Maria." The nurse left, the swishing sound following her down the hall.

The Guru watched her leave and then turned to Sydney. For a moment, the Guru concentrated on her so fiercely that she felt like she was the only one in his entire world. "Well, Miss Bannon, tell me something about yourself."

****

It was hard to believe that just six weeks before, Sydney was just entering Dr. Kodaly's Clinic depressed, but with but a faint glimmer of hope.

The first thing they stressed was the food. She was fortunate. The meals seemed to be a continuation of the food she had been introduced to at Tomiko's and she took to them with relish. The exercise was another thing.

The first few days were torture. She was given a personal trainer who was relentless. He gave her a fifteen minute warm-up, an arduous, thirty minute, intensive work-out and a fifteen minute cool-down period. This was done three times a day, exactly one hour after each meal. The first few days, Sydney hurt everywhere. Just to take a step was painful, and she looked forward to the hot tub soak and the massage that followed. Her body cried out to stop, but the trainer was merciless. Sydney was a city girl, and now she knew it. Gradually, she hardened to the exercise, and was delighted with her new body. She began to realize how out of shape she had become since college.

Once a week, she went to the lab where the technician took blood and tissue samples. Then she went to the examination room and was poked and prodded and looked at very carefully by two female doctors. They looked almost like twins. Each of them were about fifty years old with graying black hair that was tied tightly in a bun. They both wore large lab coats with a stethoscope in the pocket. The doctors spoke only to each other in Hungarian, and never spoke to Sydney directly. Sydney called them the Smith sisters and hoped they didn't understand English.

Sydney looked forward to her sessions with Guru Abinanda, and was soon meditating on a regular basis. After a daily meditation session, the Guru would talk to her about the order of the universe and the nature of things, and immersed her into a body of knowledge that she had only briefly touched on in college. After a few weeks with the Guru, Sydney began to see her world differently. How glad she was that she had left her job and the city and had come to this strange new land.

On the next-to-last day of her time at the clinic, the Smith brothers worked her over good. After spending an hour looking in every orifice and testing every organ and system, they finally stopped. Sydney watched, mildly amused as they had a spirited discussion in Hungarian. Finally, one of them left. The other came over to Sydney, her exam papers in her hand. "Mizz Bannon ve have finished vit you."

Sydney flushed with embarrassment. *Dammit, they understood English.*

The doctor ignored her reaction. "Ve vill inform Dr. Kodaly of our findings." She smiled for the first time. "Goot luck Mizz Bannon."

****

The next day, Sydney waited impatiently in the doctor's office. After an eternity, Dr. Kodaly walked in with the head nurse. In his hand was Sydney's file. Slowly, he laid it on the desk. As usual his face was grave and non-committal. Sydney was so nervous she was afraid she would wet her pants. She took a deep breath and tried to calm herself. The nurse began to write notes from Sydney's report.

Dr. Kodaly began, "Well, Miss Sydney Bannon, I have some news for you. I think you better sit down. Sydney felt her knees shake as she sat on the edge of the chair. The doctor's face was still grave, but Sydney thought she noticed a small smile playing around his lips. Even then her heart seemed stuck in her throat. Then Dr. Kodaly smiled fully. "All the tests show that the cancer is under control. And if you continue with the regimen we have established, there is no reason to expect it to return."

For a split second, Sydney was jubilant, then the past caught up with her and she completely broke down and began to cry uncontrollably. Dr. Kodaly patted her shoulder, but looked very uncomfortable with this burst of emotion. His nurse was not, and cried right along with Sydney.

After a time, Sydney stopped crying and dabbed her eyes. The nurse took her hand and said "Jaj

Istanem." (Oh my God) "I am so happy for you."
Tears were still running down her cheeks as she left
the room.

Sydney stood up and took Dr. Kodaly's hand.
"Thank you, Dr. Kodaly, I... I... But..."

The doctor looked puzzled. "What is it, Miss
Bannon?"

"Oh, nothing..." Sydney smiled and turned to
leave. Near the door, she turned back again.

"If there is something. Please feel free to speak,
Miss Bannon."

Sydney took a step back towards the doctor and
squared her shoulders. "Yes, there is something that
really troubles me."

"Yes, Miss Bannon. What is it?"

Sydney started speaking slowly, the ideas forming
as she spoke, soon she was speaking rapidly a
torrent of words pouring out. "As you know, when I
was in New York, I went to the most prestigious
cancer clinic in the city. The doctor who attended me
had a University degree, a Medical School degree,
lord knows how many years of residency, plus many
years of research."

A small smile began to play on the doctor's face.
Sydney ignored it and plunged on.

"I would say her credentials were the equal of
yours if not more so. And yet, I feel if I had stayed
under her care I might not be alive today."

Sydney felt her emotions getting the best of her
and she stopped.

Dr. Kodaly, reading the situation correctly, waited patiently for her to recover.

"Why, why, why didn't she use these methods that worked so well on me. Surely she knew. Or if she didn't, why don't you tell her." Sydney voice was raising and she knew it. She stopped, slightly embarrassed, and waited for an answer.

Dr. Kodaly was thoughtful. His face quickly changed expressions a few times as if he were having some inner conflict. Finally his face relaxed and he gave Sydney a rare smile. "Please sit down Miss Bannon."

Sidney reluctantly sat down.

"My dear Miss Bannon, the question you ask has also troubled me greatly. Actually, I think of it every day." He stopped, stood up and began to pace. After a few moments he stopped and faced Sydney. "Have you ever heard of the Philosopher's stone?"

Sydney leaned forward, her face full of interest. "No, I don't think so."

"Perhaps you have heard of alchemy. Alchemists spent a lifetime trying to change simple elements into gold."

Sydney looked incredulous. "Yes, but they were charlatans, weren't they?"

"Yes, and no." The doctor paced a few steps and then turned back to Sydney. "Do you know the names Agrippa? Kleopatra?" He smiled again. "Kleopatra, not with a C but a K."

Again she nodded, "No."

"How about Sir Isaac Newton?"

"Of course."

"Well believe it or not, Sir Isaac was not only responsible for enlightening the world but was an alchemist of the first order. In fact, so was Boyle, Bacon, Christopher Wren, Halley, of comets fame, and so many men of letters one could hardly count them all."

Sydney was totally immersed in what the doctor was saying. She leaned forward in her chair and listened with rapt attention.

"You see the men of alchemy had certain beliefs. And that was their common denominator. The first one was that only the pure of heart could practice the art. So all the charlatans you mentioned could not really be alchemists. Second, and most important, the alchemist had to devise chemical and mechanical means to make the philosopher's stone. The philosopher's stone was the alchemist's holy grail that would turn the base metals into gold."

Sydney leaned back and shook her head. "But Dr. Kodaly, what does that have to do with educating other doctors?"

"Be patient my dear girl, be patient." Dr. Kodaly walked to the bookcase next to the window. Carefully he took a book from the shelf. The cover said advanced chemistry. He tapped the book. "Because they needed to make certain substances they believed would convert the gold, we are indebted to them for the following: distillation, autoclaves, Bunsen burners, beakers, slides, almost all the modern lab equipment and also atomic and quantum physics theory. Most important of all, they gave us the scientific method, a system of proving, through experimentation, theories and hypotheses."

He almost laughed. "And all this was in the name of turning base elements into gold."

The doctor sat down on the edge of the desk. "The only difference between the Alchemist and the scientist is that the scientist does tests that are consistent and reproducible. The alchemist did lots of testing but shrouded his work in mystery and secrecy and did the testing only to make the products that would react with the metals. Instead of double blind studies, he used faith and observation, hoping to find the ultimate philosopher's stone to make the gold for himself."

Sydney's face was wreathed in puzzlement. "I understand their motive, but I fail to see the connection."

"The alternative community, like this clinic, is the very same as Alchemy. They see results, form a theory and then test it clinically, with liberal amounts of faith. If it seems to work they use it. Like the alchemist they use the clinical result and reason it out." Dr. Kodaly paused and took a deep breath. "Along with others in orthodox medicine, Dr. Slater could not accept that. I do. Together with regular medicine, I have found the philosopher's stone and I share it with my patients."

Sydney stood up and took his hand. "Dr. Kodaly, you are a very brave man. And I for one am very grateful for your courage."

****

The rest of her time at the clinic was a blur. She was so excited, she hardly heard Dr. Kodaly's warnings about slipping back to old habits. *As if I would ever jeopardize my health in any way again!*

There were tearful goodbyes at the front desk, with a promise to have her luggage sent to her hotel, then she was free. She stepped into the sunshine, took a deep breath and laughed out loud. Passersby looked at her as if they were in the presence of a simple minded relative but she didn't care. *I am free, free, free at last.* For some strange reason, Sydney wanted to get to the Danube. She began to walk quickly towards it and then she broke to trot. Finally she reached the water's edge. She stopped as she came to the bank. She looked out over the wide expanse of water, then turned and walked along the edge of the water, exulting in the view. The swans were out and she joined them with her mind, as she had done with the rock on the mountain. She felt them and their freedom. She heard children's voices and turned towards them. They were playing soccer and she stopped to watch. Suddenly, a badly kicked ball came bouncing towards her. She deftly picked it up as the kicker came toward her to retrieve it. He slowed down then stopped and looked her over.

"Kerem vissza dobni a labdat?" (Lady, can I have the ball?)

Suddenly the joy left Sydney. This boy could have been Paul at this age. Same black wavy hair. Same strong jaw. And the deepest brown eyes you would ever see.

"...A labdat, kerem." (Give the ball, lady, please)

"How about I play on your side?"

The boy shrugged and looked at his mates, not understanding one word of what Sydney said.

She smiled and kicked the ball back towards the group. They laughed at her bad kick and she shrugged and laughed with them. The black-haired boy made a face of exasperation and ran back to his friends.

Maria, Magda and especially Zoltan. I must tell them. I must thank them, I must thank them all. Sydney started running. She would find a phone and call all her friends.

When Sydney finally found a telephone, she was so excited she could hardly get the coin in the slot. While the phone rang she repeated to herself over and over again, "Please be home, Magda, please be home." She waited expectantly.

"Hallo."

"Magda, is that you? I have the most wonderful news... Yes, I am alright. Yes, he gave me a totally clean bill of health. Yes, yes, I am ecstatic, we must celebrate. What is the best restaurant in all of Budapest? The Margitkert Étterem restaurant, yes, perfect. On Margit utca 15. Great! At seven o'clock. Yes, yes, my life will begin again at seven o'clock. I will call Mari and you, please call Zoltan. I will be well again, and with my three best friends at Christmas dinner. What could be better. See you at seven."

Sydney put the phone down and twirled about in the street, singing about gypsies and food and about how lucky she was. The people passing by gave the madwoman a wide berth.

Sydney took a long, happy walk to the Astoria hotel. It started to snow and the temperature dropped, but Sydney didn't even notice. The old hotel never looked better to her. She was calmer now, but not much. Joy filled her heart and her step. She was glowing as she passed the doorman, who opened the door.

"Jo Naput, (Good day) Madam."

Sydney did an exaggerated bow. "Jo naput, Béla." She laughed, put a five dollar bill in his hand and dashed through the door.

Béla looked at the five dollar bill and shrugged his shoulders. "Hulye Amerikai," (Crazy Americans) he muttered.

Sydney was still smiling as she unlocked the door to her room. She had rented a suite with a living room and bedroom. The Christmas tree stood blinking in the corner of the living room and she bowed to it as she had to Béla. "Jo Naput, Christmas tree. I hope you have had as good a day as I have."

She laughed at nothing and started to strip as she went towards the bathroom. Her clothes, like flotsam in the wake of a ship, lay strewn about in a trail to the bathroom. By the time she reached the tub she was naked. She turned on the water and while the tub filled she looked at her figure in the full length mirror. She turned to the side and instinctively pulled in her tummy. Then she looked at her breasts with a rush of relief. She tested the water and happily stepped into the tub and gratefully sunk into the warmth of the heated water. Suddenly she bolted up, cascading the water on the tile floor. "My God, I have to call Theresa." She reached for the phone next to the tub and then thought better of it. "I'll wait for tomorrow. I might have to make some decisions, and I better not be in orbit when I talk to her. Look at me talking to myself out loud. Maybe I'm already an old maid." Laughing uproariously she dialed the front desk. "Please send up a masseuse in exactly one hour." She slid back in the steaming water and luxuriated again. When the hour was nearly up, Sydney reluctantly got out of the tub.

Sleepily she dried herself, slipped on a robe and got into bed. She started to read while she waited for the masseuse. As she read, a smile crept across her face. She realized for the first time in a long time she had a strong sexual urge. She laughed to herself. "Good thing the bellhop's not here," she said to herself, and then she laughed aloud. Then her face got cunning and she leered into the mirror. "But the masseuse will be." She laughed again but louder. "No, I better leave the girls to Theresa." Then she laughed until tears rolled down her cheeks.

In a few minutes there was a knock on the door and Sydney opened it to a large woman with a German accent who said her name was Helga. The woman gave her a towel and she slipped off her robe and lay on her portable table and relaxed as best she could.

Helga spread the fragrant oil on Sydney and began to knead her muscles. Sydney sighed and let her body sag. Helga's fingers were like steel probes and soon she was finding the trigger points that Sydney had stored up. Deeper and deeper she worked down to the bottom layers of muscle, reaching for and stretching the ligaments and tendons. The pain was exquisite, yet it was healing, and slowly but surely Sydney's tension began to let go and her muscles started to relax. With the relaxation came a letting go of the all the worry, frustration and fear of the past year.

First a tear rolled down Sydney's cheek from the corner of one eye. Then she began to sob. Soon she was crying uncontrollably. Helga kept on kneading and whispered in her native tongue, Schrei kleines, schreien Ihre schrerz weg. (Cry, little one, cry your pain away)

Sydney fell into a dreamless sleep. When she awoke Helga was gone. She sat up and stretched and realized how sore she was. She looked at the time and was startled. "Six o'clock!" she exclaimed and jumped out of bed. She rummaged through her clothes. "All these clothes and nothing to wear." *What do I have that is light, gay and alive?* she thought. *Yes alive. It's good to be alive.* She fingered her red Chanel dress with the gold buttons. "This is good," she murmured. "Ah, yes, with my black boots, all to celebrate Christmas." She put on the dress and then slipped on the jacket. She went to the mirror and turned right and then left. "Yes, yes, perfect. Now my fur jacket and hat, and I'm off to Margitkert and the Gypsies."

****

Alex wiped the imaginary dust off the fender of the sleekest car ever built. The Eurocar's engineers built it to give competition to the Cadillac, yet retain its hint of sports car elegance. "I tell you Paul this is the greatest car ever made!"

Alex Tremain was the perfect salesman. Always bouncing around, trying to please, and talkative to a fault. Sometimes Paul wasn't sure he picked the right man for Hungary, but one look at Alex's sales numbers calmed his fears.

"Paul, would you look at that!"

"What Alex," he said without looking, a trace of annoyance in his voice.

"That broad there. What a body! Dressed like Mrs. Christmas. Gorgeous red dress, platinum hair. Man, the way that dress clings... She's covered, but she just can't hide the goodies."

"Alex," Paul said with feigned exasperation, "I wish I had time for that nonsense, but we have to get this car ready for the buyer. You promised it to him by eight o'clock, not me."

"Yeah, yeah."

Paul squatted down. "Claude, you about done?"

"Yes sir, just putting the last bolt in now."

"O.K. Let me know when you're clear."

"Clear!" Claude slid from under the auto and Paul got in behind the wheel.

He turned the key and the massive engine roared to life and then quickly settled down and purred like a quiet kitten. "Great, Claude. Now, you go home. I don't want your wife calling me Scrooge, among other names." Paul peeled a hundred dollar bill from his money clip and handed it to the mechanic. "Buy a present for the kiddies on the way home."

"Thank you, Mr. Grant.

Alex was craning his neck trying to look over the Christmas crowd moving past the window. "Damn, she's gone. You should've looked. She was worth seeing. She has this gorgeous red dress on that..."

Paul smiled and interrupted. "Alex, if you paid as much attention to selling cars as you do to women, we'd both be rich." Both men laughed. "Now, let's you and I go get some dinner. But don't forget you have to be back by eight."

The men put on their overcoats and stepped out into the night. It was a clear cold evening and Paul hunched his shoulders inside the coat to hold in the warmth. A group of children and two adults stood on the sidewalk singing Come All Ye Faithful. The children's noses were red from the cold and the adults stamped their feet as they sang, but they stayed at their posts and brought Christmas cheer to the passersby. Paul thought that they looked as if they could be from out of an old woodcut from Christmas, 1850.

Suddenly, out of the group came a young boy's tenor voice, clear and high.

...Come all ye faithful, joyful and triumphant,
oh come let us adore him, oh come let us adore him,
oh come let us adore him, Christ, the Lord...

Paul was thrilled. He asked Alex how to say thank you. Alex told him and he walked up to the group of singers and nodding his head said "Curcinem. (thank you) Merry Christmas."

One of the adults bowed slightly. "Sivasem, You are werry velcome."

Paul came back to Alex. "Wasn't that beautiful?"

"Very. Where shall we go for dinner?"

Paul smiled and shook his head. "You have no soul, Alex. When they open you up at judgment day, all they will find are hundred dollar bills. I'm sure we'll find something along this street."

Alex was excited about his new sales position and talked and bubbled as they walked down the gaily lit street.

Paul glanced at Alex. *I hope I picked the right man for sales manager in Budapest.* But he knew he had. Alex, despite his scattered nature, was quite focused when it came to selling cars. Paul had run all of Eurocars' salesmen from North America through the IBM computer, asking just two questions. First, is he or she in the top ten percentile in sales. Second, does he or she have a working knowledge of the Hungarian language. Alex more than fit the bill in both cases. His folks had come to the States in forty-six, and had taught Alex Hungarian as a second language. He had dropped out of college at twenty and began as a salesman at Eurocars in Toronto, Canada. He soon led all other salesman in that city and the local management was about to promote him to sales manager when the inquiry came down from Paul.

"Man, this is my lucky day. There she is again."

"Who?"

"The girl in the red dress. Hey! She is going into that restaurant. How about us going there for dinner?"

Paul indulged him. "Sure, why not."

As they stepped into the restaurant, they were hit with a rush of warm air and wild gypsy music. Paul finally relaxed his shoulders and rubbed his cold hands. He luxuriated in the warmth. The restaurant was brightly lit, with a babble of sound in a dozen languages from wine-loosened tongues. The ornamented tree next to the door blinked its Christmas message, and every window had candles in it, burning brightly beckoning the cold and the hungry. It was very crowded, with a large group of people waiting to be seated.

The gypsy music stopped suddenly, and the players left the stage and mixed with the crowd. In a few minutes the owner turned on the record player. It would have to do until the gypsies came back. It was a Christmas album and the golden voice of Mario Lanza started drifting clearly above the drone of the customers.

...Oh, Holy Night...

Alex gave his name to a young woman with a clipboard and she wrote it importantly, promising to call him soon. Then he began to look around to find the girl in red. Suddenly, he grabbed Paul's elbow. "There she is!"

Paul followed his excited nod, slightly amused. Then he saw her. She certainly was beautiful from the back. Paul kept looking. There was something familiar about her... Something stirred deep inside him. Somehow she looked both strange and familiar. He shrugged his shoulders. *She couldn't be someone I know. I don't know a soul in Budapest.*

She was standing and talking to an older woman, and a younger couple who were seated. *Probably her family,* he thought. He started to turn away when she tossed her head and laughed. The motion caught Paul and his heart stopped. He was having difficulty catching his breath when she half-turned and then he was stunned. Everyone else in the restaurant disappeared, and he began to walk towards her.

"Hey, I saw her first, big guy." Alex was speaking, but Paul couldn't hear him.

...It is the night of the dear Savior's birth...

A small intense pain began in the pit of Paul's stomach and increased as he went towards the woman. As he approached, she laughed and tossed her head again as she took off her black hat. Paul's heart wrenched as her platinum hair cascaded down her neck and shoulders.

As he stopped just in back of her, the three companions looked past her and stared up at him.

Zoltan began to rise, but Magda wisely stopped him with her hand on his arm.

"Sydney?"

Sydney stopped in mid-laugh and her knees buckled. She caught herself and began to turn in slow motion. They looked at each other in disbelief.

All at once, the talking and laughing and clinking of the utensils stopped, and there was dead silence in the room. Every eye was locked on them.

...fall on your knees, oh hear the angel voices...

Slowly, very slowly, Paul reached out and touched her cheek to see if she were real. As if in a dream, Sydney put the palm of her hand gently, oh so gently, on the back of his hand. There was no sound but the beating of their hearts. Paul and Sydney were alone in the world.

Suddenly sound came back to Paul in a rush, and even the voice of Lanza hurt his ears. He closed his eyes and shook his head like a puppy shaking off the rain. He looked at her again. "Sydney, is it really you?"

"Yes, Paul, I... I..."

A tear formed in the corner of her eye and began to roll gently down her cheek. Paul smiled and put a finger in its path. The tear trickled down to his finger and slowly moved to his palm. Overcome with feeling he put his other hand at her back and slowly, carefully, he drew her to him until the perfume of her overwhelmed him. He bent over and placed his lips on her soft velvet mouth and the rapture of it made him know how an addict feels when sated. The essence of her coursed through his blood, urged on by the pounding of his heart.

"Oh Paul, Paul, I love you." There was nothing in the universe that Sydney could have said at that moment that would have been more right.

They embraced to the applause of the entire restaurant.

"Well, I'll be damned," Alex muttered to himself.

...Oh, night divine, oh night divine...

Chapter 27: Switzerland

It was Spring. The trees stretched to the sky, glad to wake from their winter sleep, and the brook ran noisily at Sydney's feet. Hesitantly, she stepped on the small bridge spanning the spring and stopped. She looked up at the magnificent mountain and her eyes moistened at the sight of the cabin jutting out into space. For a brief instant, in a flashback, she saw Tomiko step out on the deck and gaily wave to her. It was so real she almost started to wave back. Memories crowded in on her and made her hesitant to move off the bridge.

A gentle hand on her shoulder brought her back.

"Something wrong, Syd?"

She shook her head. "Too many ghosts, Paul."

She took his hand and firmly resolved to go on. She forced herself to make the first step, and they were soon both trudging up the hill. The climb was bittersweet for Sydney. Each rock and tree had its own memory.

Sydney stopped. Paul stopped with her and waited respectfully. "That's my rock, Paul. I grew it from a pebble."

Paul smiled and nodded. "Syd, are you sure you want to do this?"

Sydney looked at him with love and pain in her eyes. "Yes, Paul, I have to."

The rest of the walk was quiet, Paul letting Sydney set the pace. Finally they approached the door of the cabin. Her heart was racing, but she could not tell if it was the climb or the painful memories. She hesitated and then opened the door and stepped in. For a moment, she felt like she had never left. The cabin was just as she last saw it. The futons looked out over the hostel to the lake. The newly budded trees swayed in the wind coursing over the mountain.

Tomiko's books lay on the table, her reading glasses lay on the open page as if she had just gone to make tea and would be right back. Sydney sat down on the edge of the futon and stared out the window. Her eyes brimmed and tears began to roll down her cheeks and fell on her cotton shirt, staining it. In an instant, Paul was at her side. He touched her shoulder. She patted his hand, but kept staring into space, remembering.

After a few minutes, she got up and walked to her bedroom door. Her mind and heart became overwhelmed with the past. She felt her heart pounding in her ears. She opened the door and looked in. The bed was made and the room was warm and inviting. She turned and looked at Tomiko's bedroom door. She almost expected to her to walk in and say 'Hello Syd, let us have some tea.' It was too much. Tears rolled down her face and she began to sob. Paul came to her. He felt helpless, but at least he was there. He held her close, but she patted his arm and gently broke free. She needed to be alone with her memories. She smiled a wan smile at him and walked back out on the deck. Paul read the situation correctly and stayed behind.

Sydney looked down at the lake. The water was shimmering on the lake and a cool breeze was moving through the trees. Even in the daytime, it made a mournful sound. Sydney could feel the presence of Eric and Tomiko.

Her mind raced as she thought of a snatch of memory. Some little thing she could not quite put her finger on. Then it came to her in a rush. One night, Tomiko had been talking to her about Joe. She never mentioned Joe after she committed to Eric so it must have been when Sydney first came to the hostel.

What was it she said... It was the haiku, yes the haiku. What was it again?

> The world is light and dark
> The sun is up and down
> Life is a brief candle and gone
> But the living must go on

Sydney bent her head and tears came freely down her cheeks. She raised her fist toward heaven. *Those two candles burned bright, and they are gone. But I will live and I will go on.* "Tomiko," she said aloud, "I promise you I will live, and I will honor you both for the rest of my life."

Chapter 28: West Virginia (1943)

The sun that came up over the West Virginia mountains did not warm the earth.

Suzy Lee lay shivering under the thin blanket. She was so cold that tears ran from dark eyes, down her sunken cheeks. She shook constantly, her body trying to get her tiny muscles warm her.

Suzy Lee Catlow was the middle child of three who lived in the depression starved mountains of West Virginia. Her mother and older brother tried to work the farm, but falling prices were the result of a glut on the market. The family had sold off all the valuable stock, and only one horse and cow remained. Fortunately, the government man came by once a month and left enough food to keep them alive.

In better times, Suzy would have been a happy child. Even now she sang and danced to the music from the Crosley radio she cherished, and sometimes the government man would leave a book for her. She dearly loved the books and read them over and over until the pages were dog-eared.

She was at that place, between childhood and maturity, but her freckles and pigtails showed her more girl than woman.

Hunger often tugged at her belly, and when she did not think about the cold, visions of food danced in her head. She couldn't wait until morning when Mamma spooned out the grits the government man had left earlier. She only hoped that Teal didn't get to it first. *He'd sell the grits for cigarettes in a blink, if Mamma'd let him.* She wished fervently that he would leave and that her daddy would come home again.

Suzy looked around the darkened room. Everything seemed empty and cold. She thought of her father. Poor daddy. I wonder if he's here with me right now. She peered about the room hoping to catch a glimpse of him. She stared at the front door, hoping against all hope that the door would open and he would be standing there, like he used to, and she would run to him and jump in his arms and he would nuzzle her neck, and scrape his beard on her cheek and everything in her world would be in order again. But the door didn't open and her father didn't come.

Suddenly Suzy froze. A hand appeared on the flimsy curtain that separated her corner from the rest of the room. She prayed fervently it wasn't, but as the curtain slid back, she knew it was. Teal had finally come to call.

The tall, angular man stepped behind the curtain and sat down on the bed. He smelled of sweat and cigarettes and whisky. He didn't make a sudden move, but Suzy was afraid of him and scooted back away from him until she was stopped by the cabin wall. She drew the thin blanket up to her chest and pushed her back against the wall. She shook, but this time from fear not cold. The wind whistled through the chinks in the wall and the icy air moved around her body. But Suzy's adrenaline was pumping through her body and she couldn't feel anything but fear.

Suzy stared at Teal, her fear-filled eyes open wide. Teal looked back at her, his eyes half closed, a malevolent look above his twisted smile. Absently, he touched his beard then scratched his cheek. He was a thin man with a scar on his right cheek and a tattoo on his left. His hair was always pulled back in a dirty pony tail and he always dressed in black, even when he slept. Suzy had never seen him clean. Many times she had begged her Momma to throw him out, but her momma said, 'Times iz hard an' he helps ter pay the rent. 'Sides, it's good to have a man 'round the house, gives ya a feelin' of security.'

He scratched his chest. "I been layin' in the other room, wit yore mamma, thinkin' 'bout you, girl. Yore gettin' to be a big girl now and I believe you need some proper schoolin'."

"I already go to school, Teal. You better get outta here." Suzy moved forward. "I'm goin' to get my Mamma." She pulled back the cover and tried to slide past him.

As quick as a coiled snake Teal was upon her. With one hand he threw her back on the bed, quickly put his hand over her mouth, and held her firmly to the bed. She tried to scream but all that she could manage was a muffled sob. With his free hand he pulled away her patched sleeping gown and clumsily fingered her privacy.

Terrified beyond belief, Suzy tried to push him away but as lean as he was, the manual labor Teal did made him very strong. She was no match for him and he held her in a vise-like grip.

In a few moments, Suzy realized she could not get away and she lay still, husbanding her strength for another try if he let his guard down. If only she could get her mouth free she could yell and her mother and older brother could come and help her. As she lay still, she heard Teal's labored breathing. He was speaking softly into her ear.

"If'n you tells yore mamma or yore brother, what ahm adoin' wit you, ahm goin ter kill them both an' Tommy too. An' then ah'll wring yore neck lak a chicken." His hand clamped tighter on her mouth. "You unnerstans me?" Suzy fearfully nodded her head, her eyes still wide with fear, and Teal relaxed his grip on her mouth. She could not stop shaking.

Teal reached down with his free hand and fumbled below his waist for a moment and then tightened his grip on Suzy's mouth again. With a quick move, the man was on top of her. The girl froze in fear. Suddenly Suzy felt a sharp pain in her groin and tried to scream again. Teal quickly pressed her mouth again. She flailed her arms about and then dug her nails into his back and drew blood. He did not even seem to notice. Suzy realized, even through her fear, that he was in a great state of agitation. She had never seen anyone act like this before and it frightened her. Then suddenly, he coiled in spasms, uttered a short cry, and then his body seemed to relax. Still, he held his hand over her mouth, and still, her eyes were wide with terror.

Suzy lay quietly, praying that the man would not do whatever he did again. She was deathly still, barely breathing, hoping this nightmare would end. There was pain and throbbing in her private area and she wanted to cry but didn't dare.

Slowly, Teal got off her and lay next to her. Gingerly, he lifted his hand away from her mouth. Suzy continued to lay still, sobbing, not daring to move.

Teal leaned over and Suzy tensed again. He put his mouth close to her ear. She could again smell the stale whisky and cigarettes and it made her sick.

"'Member now, no tattlin' or ah'll kill yore mamma and wring yore neck." Then, as if he had an afterthought, he cocked his head and said, with a crooked smile, "If'n you liked that, maybe we could do it again, tomorrer."

Suddenly he was gone. Suzy lay deathly still in the disheveled bed, too hurt to cry. She felt the painful area and it felt sticky. All at once, relief and pain overcame her and she began to sob silently. She put her thumb in her mouth, curled into a fetal ball and stared at the cabin wall, her mind a thousand miles from this wretched place.

At daylight, Suzy sat up and looked around her bed. To her amazement there was blood everywhere. Quickly she got up, stripped her bunk and took off her gown. She quietly dressed and picked up the bloody bundle and left the cabin. It was freezing outside but she didn't seem to notice. She went to a copse of trees, where the pig pen was, and put the garments behind the lean-to for the pigs. Then she went to her favorite place, a boulder where she had sat and read the few books she got from the government man, and stared into space. Usually she whiled away the time here, reading and dreaming of kings and queens and faraway places, but just now, shame and pain and fear were all mixed up inside her and she just sat, hands on her knees, staring and rocking back and forth.

When the cold finally forced Suzy back to the cabin, she was glad to see her mother was at the stove cooking the customary grits for breakfast. Tommy, the youngest was still asleep. Her older brother Jimmy Lee was sitting at the table chewing on a cold piece of ham and ignoring her, as usual. Suzy looked around the kitchen. No Teal, good. Suzy breathed easier, Teal has probably gone to work.

Amy Catlow slowed her stirring and stared at her daughter. "Where you been, you shiftless thing." She saw Suzy cringe and immediately felt sorry she had said that. *The poor girl has been through enough lately. Barely gettin' enough to eat. Why do I always do that to my daughter? Why? maybe because my mother did it so thoroughly to me.* She smiled ruefully as she remembered leaving the farm and the dust, the interminable wind, and the family packing the old Ford. The twin pestilence of depression and drought had reached Oklahoma at the same time.

****

Amy was born in Oklahoma. She remembered growing up on the farm and all the good things that happen to a young girl in the country.

When she was twelve the rain stopped. She remembered vividly bringing her father his lunch in a basket. He would stop his plowing, take off his woven farmer hat, wipe his moist brow with the back of his arm and squint at the sun. "Got to rain sometime," he would mutter and then he would grab Amy and hug her to him. She could still smell the mixture of sweat and the Prince Albert pipe tobacco he smoked.

But it didn't rain, and the farm suffered. First the land turned brown, and the crops failed. Then the animals started to die. That was the hardest for Amy to bear. Finally, it was too much for Mr. Catlow and he simply gave up. Eventually the bank man came out and the long fight was over. They had to leave.

She remembered the pain in her stomach to this day as the family packed the old Ford and left for California where they might find work. She could still see the cows laying on their sides, their ribs sticking out and breathing hard as they met their fate. Old Bessie, her beautiful roan horse, now looking sickly, watched plaintively, his head sticking out over the broken down corral fence, as the family packed to leave.

Momma wouldn't let Amy give her horse even a small apple. "That's fer the folks, Amy. 'Sides, thet little bit uv food won't help her no-how."

Before they left, Amy sat on the fence stroking the horses neck and crying fiercely. That particular pain would stay with Amy until she died.

For a while, the family lived out of their car. At first it was hard going. The Californians didn't want any part of the Oakies, as they were known, and didn't mind letting them know it. Finally, the family got a break. Mother Catlow saw a sign on the road:

| *ORANGE PICKERS NEEDED* |

She went to the foreman and was hired. Fifty cents a day. She got her husband and Amy hired too. The family now made one dollar and fifty cents a day and even got a shack to live in. It was enough, they were saved.

Amy met her husband-to-be, Sam Catlow, in the orange groves. She was sixteen, and slim and fair. She was soon pregnant with Jimmy Lee, and was a very frightened young girl. Her father made Sam marry his daughter and gave them a bed in the family shack. They both continued to work in the groves.

On one of the few days that Amy could not get up to work, she lay in the bed, her stomach swollen with child. Sam sat down on the bed next to her. He had a soiled letter in his hand. He was a cold, but not a callous man, who even in his ignorance, treated his wife with respect and dignity. People thought of him as stupid, but it was just his reserve that stopped him from speaking out. He was thin and wiry with an agile body and an equally quick mind. In better times, he would have been a college student. Hard times had made him a field hand.

"Amy, girl..." He had a faint smile on his face. It looked strange to Amy because Sam never smiled. "This here letter says my daddy's done died."

Amy nodded her head.

"Says here he left me his farm. But to keep it, I gotta homestead it. Else it goes back to the tax collector. I gotta go back to West Virginny an' you gotta go with me."

Amy nodded stoically, afraid to tell him how full of pain and fear she was.

When they got to West Virginia, the region was in turmoil. The mines were being struck by John L. Lewis and the mine workers union. The depression of the thirties had never really left this area and now that the National Recovery Act was history, times were hard. To top it off, Amy Catlow got pregnant two years in a row, and then Sam died.

During the strike Sam was just trying to go to work when he was confronted by two union goons. One word led to another and finally there was a fight. Sam was thin and wiry, but as strong as an ox, and in a few minutes the two union men were on the ground. Sam dusted himself off and started walking to the mine. One of the men sat up, wiped his bloody mouth and reached into his coat. He pulled out a snub-nosed thirty eight and shot Sam in the back. The bullet severed his aorta and Sam was dead before he hit the ground.

Sam's sister, Sarah lived on the next farm and she was an angel to Amy and the two babies. They practically lived at her house while Amy struggled to get back on her feet.

Try as she might, even after twelve years the rocky soil would not give a fallow crop, and then the cow's milk got sub-standard. The farm was a failure. To make some of the ends meet, Amy took in a young border. Before long, because of poverty and loneliness, she was sharing her bed with him.

****

Amy watched Suzy Lee gingerly sit down at the kitchen table. "Where you been? I seed yer bed stuff was gone. Where is yer bed stuff? You peed in it?"

Suzy looked away from her mother. "I, I..." She sat down at the table and looked down, ashamed to look at her mother.

Her mother stopped stirring and sat down next to her. There was a strange look of concern and anger on her face. "Show me what you did with them bed clothes."

Suzy's eyes filled with tears. *Teal will kill my mother and wring my neck. What should I do?*

Suddenly her mother spoke in a way she had never heard before. The voice was raised and angry and forceful. Where are yer clothes and the bedding? Amy had feared something might happen. She prayed it had not.

Suddenly Jimmy Lee looked up, curious, his face was hard.

Impelled by the force of Amy's voice, Suzy got up and walked out the front door. Her mother was right behind her and Jimmy followed close behind.

When they reached the pig pen Suzy pointed out the stained garments and was ashamed. Her mother took them apart, looked at them separately and closed her eyes and leaned against the pen. It groaned under her slight weight.

"What's goin' on Ma."

"I've been a fool," she said mostly to herself. "You go on to work, boy, I'll talk to you later."

Jimmy shrugged and began to leave. After a few steps he half turned. "Ah'll have some grits and shet the stove off."

Amy nodded her head and turned to Suzy. The girl was facing towards her mother, head down, rocking gently side to side. "Suzy Lee!..." The abrupt sound of her name stopped the rocking. I want you to tell me the truth, now. Did Teal bother you last night? She was still hoping and praying that Suzy had just begun an early period.

"No, no, Mamma, I, I..."

Her mother grabbed Suzy's arm. Suzy recoiled in fear and started crying. "Don't lie to me child. Did Teal do this?" She pointed to the stained garments.

Suzy panicked. Teal would kill them both, but the rage in her mother's face compelled her to speak. In a voice so small and child-like, her mother had to lean forward to hear it, Suzy told her mother every detail of what had happened. When she finished, her mother's face was like granite, but despite all that had happened, somehow Suzy felt better.

"You go and wash yerself in yer private place, real good, and don't tell no one 'bout what happened. Not even yer brother." Then she said, almost to herself, "'Specially not to yer brother."

The rest of the day dragged by for Suzy. Her mother insisted she stay home from school, for which Suzy was grateful. She would be mortified if any of her classmates ever found out about her secret.

For some reason, her mother seemed to find more chores for her than usual, but she was glad to be kept busy, it took her mind off painful memories. Even then, some little thing would remind her of Teal and her stomach would flip and she would feel shame. Depression would settle over her like a sticky cloak.

Suzy dreaded the evening when Teal would come back. The clock ticked by too fast and too slow.

Teal came home towards evening and Suzy's mother greeted him like nothing had ever happened. Suzy was distraught. *If Mama don't care, he'll do it again. The young girl made a firm resolution. If it happens again, I will leave, forever.*

That night Suzy got into bed with fear. She could not go to sleep and sat up with her back to the wall, drawing up her blanket all the way to her neck. She bent forward and wrapped her arms around her knees, and stared at the curtain constantly, waiting for that dreaded hand to appear.

Despite the adrenaline that made her heart pump wildly at first, and the foreboding that filled her, she began to nod. Soon her eyes closed and before she could stop it, she was fast asleep.

The sound that woke her was strange to her ears. She sat bolt upright in bed and strained her ears to hear it again. Nothing. Was it a scream? No, she would have heard that more clearly as small as this place is. *But maybe they had a pillow over the person's mouth. Oh, you're just an old scaredy cat, Suzy,* she said to herself. When the pounding of her heart slowed, she lay back down again, saying to herself that the noise was nothing. She closed her eyes and tried to sleep.

There it was again. At the sound, Suzy sat bolt upright, wide awake. This time she knew what it was. A heavy object had just hit the floor. It sounded like it was coming from her mother's room. "Oh, God, maybe he's hurt Momma," she cringed.

Forgetting herself, Suzy leaped from the cold bed and started towards her mother's room. Suddenly the door opened and instinctively she ducked down behind the tattered couch. Slowly, she raised her head until she could again see the door to her mother's room. Framed in the doorway, in the dim light, was Jimmy Lee. He had a wild and angry look on his face that frightened Suzy. Jimmy was dragging something wrapped in his mother's blanket. Then she saw her mother. She was bent over helping to push the object with her son. She had a face of stone. Suzy could only make out snatches of their conversation.

"Deep in the woods..."

"...Never find him, Ma..."

"Good, a Christian...... fer the likes of him..."

They had stepped outside with the blanket and loaded it into the wheel barrow. Her mother stood up and put her hand in the small of her back and stretched backward to ease the pain in her back from lifting. Then she turned and started back to the front door. Suzy scrambled back to her bed and quickly put the cover up to her neck, pretending to be asleep.

Her mother carefully opened the curtain and looked at her daughter. "Good," she muttered, "we didn't wake them." Soundlessly she turned and again left the cabin.

As soon as she heard the front door close, Suzy was up and at the window again. She couldn't imagine what it was her mother and Jimmy Lee didn't want her to see.

She watched them wheel the barrow towards the creek. "I wonder," she said to herself. She stepped out the front door and watched them go to the edge of the creek. Then she saw Jimmy Lee take the shovel out of the barrow and start to dig. "They're goin' to bury somethin'," Suzy murmured, quietly.

Something was wrong. *Where was Teal. He's stronger than Jimmy Lee.* "Why isn't he digging?" Suzy kept wondering.

Suddenly a knowing, mixed with fear and anxiety, gripped the girl and she fairly leaped back into the cabin and quickly went to her mother's room. There was already a lamp burning in the bedroom and it threw a flickering shaft of light about the room. Suzy stopped at the partly-opened door and fear overtook her like a mantle, her skin began to feel clammy. She thought about opening the door and facing Teal again and almost ran back to her bed. Steeling herself and trying to quiet her pounding heart, she reached for the doorknob and opened the door just a little wider and peeked in.

It was a small room taken up mostly by the large feather bed that had been bought in more prosperous times. There was a small dresser with a wash basin on it, and a rack to hang clothes against the wall. The last piece of furniture in the room was a cedar chest that held the blankets in the summer.

Her heart still pounding, she stepped into the room. It was deathly quiet. No one here. Gaining courage, she walked over to the bed and looked at the disheveled sheets. Somehow they looked strange and discolored. At least there was no Teal. *God I hate him.* Suddenly she stopped and cocked her head. "Teal," she muttered, "where is he? I know he came ho..." She went tense and her fist went to her mouth. Now she knew. "It's Teal... It's Teal in the wheelbarrow, I know it," she muttered. Everything now came into focus. She looked more closely at the sheets. They were discolored alright, they were colored in blood. In the flickering lamp-light, she could now see the blood spatters on the bedpost and the pillows. It was everywhere. *God,* she thought, grimacing, *it's like they killed a pig in here.* She looked at the floor and there was a large smear of blood leading out of the room. She followed it all the way to the front door where it stopped.

Suzy sat down on the cold floor and stared into space. She searched her feelings but there were none. She was glad he was dead. She wished for it fervently ever since he had attacked her and it was just as if God had answered her prayer.

"Suzy, Suzy Lee!"

She heard her name coming from far off. She tried to concentrate. Suddenly everything came back to the here and now with a rush. Someone was shaking her and yelling.

"Suzy Lee, What did you see? How much did you see?

She looked up and saw her mother bending over her. Her black-gray hair hung down in strands almost covering her eyes. The familiar wrinkles on her careworn face looked deep in the bright moonlight.

"I saw you an' Jimmy Lee buryin' somethin.'" Then she blurted out the rest. "It were Teal, weren't it?"

Amy got down on one knee and smoothed the young girl's hair. "They's some things better left unsaid, girl. You go on back to bed an' fergit what you seed."

Just then Jimmy Lee came back and walked through the front door. "What's goin on, Ma?" Then saw Suzy. "What the hell you doin' up, Suzy Lee?" he thundered.

Mother put her hand on Suzy's shoulder. "Shush! You'll wake the dead with yer yellin', we don't want Tommy Lee up too." She turned back to Suzy. Now, Suzy, I want you to fergit what you saw and go on back to bed." She looked out the window at the sky just beginning to lighten. "That Teal won't bother you no more." Suzy did not move. Amy hesitated a moment and then looked up at her son. "Jimmy Lee, kneel on down here." Jimmy quickly got on one knee. Amy put one hand on each of their shoulders.

"Chillun, you got to fergit what happened here tonight." Her face hardened. "He deserved what he got." Her hand tightened on the girls shoulder and her voice got raspy. "No one attacks one a mine without payin' the price." She looked rapidly back and forth to each child. "Now, I want you to put your hands on mine." She put her hand on the floor. Quickly Jimmy Lee put his hand on his mother's.

Suzy was slower, but after a moment she put her hand on Jimmy's. Her heart was pounding and she wanted to run, but something kept her rooted to the spot. She waited, with her breath coming in short spurts, her body twitching with unknown fear.

Her mother began to speak in a grave voice. "I want you chillun to fergit completely about tonight and to swear that you'll never tell another soul 'bout what happened here." She stopped and looked hard at Suzy.

Jimmy Lee answered first. "You bet, Ma, ah'll never tell no one."

"Suzy Lee?"

Suzy looked at her mother, tears beginning to roll down her cheeks. "Yes'm Mamma, I swear, too."

"Good, now let's clean up 'round here." She had just noticed they were kneeling in Teal's blood.

****

It was three weeks before the sheriff came. His old Plymouth pulled up in the driveway while Suzy was in the kitchen putting the breakfast dishes away. When she looked out the window, through the cracked glass, she saw his car drive up with the star on the door. Her heart froze. Her first instinct was to run, but Jimmy was in the kitchen too, and he was watching her carefully.

Amy watched the sheriff park the car, her wrinkled face calm and stoic.

Jimmy Lee got up. "Suzy, you go to yer place an' stay put in yer bed. Jes read a while 'til the sheriff leaves. Go on now." With that he sauntered slowly out to his mother. He and the sheriff got there about the same time.

Suzy stayed out of sight and stared at the sheriff's back through the window. She could see her mother clearly and the side of Jimmy Lee's face. She was amazed at how innocent they both looked.

"Mawnin' Miz Catlow." The sheriff drawled and took off his hat as he approached the woman. He was a balding man of forty five with a beer belly and an easy manner. He had been sheriff for years and most people liked and trusted him. He wiped his moist brow with a large, red handkerchief.

"Mawnin, Sheriff," Mrs. Catlow said and casually leaned on her hoe. Suzy marveled. *If she's nervous, she sure didn't show it.*

The Sheriff half turned and pointed to the car. "Thet feller there says his brother, Teal, wuz livin' here with y'all and that he's done disappeared. Used ter go home an' play poker every Friday night but he hasn't been home fer three weeks now. Says he went to his work and the boss says Teal hasn't been there fer three weeks either. You know anythin' 'bout it?"

Amy squinted at the car as if she were trying to look inside. Then she stood up straight and looked the sheriff in the eye. "No, Sheriff, he wuz rentin' a room from us an' jes didn't show up one night. Thet's the last we seed of him, right, Jimmy Lee."

"Right, Mom, he jes disappeared..."

Just as Jimmy Lee finished what he was saying the car door opened and a man bolted out. He made a few steps towards the three people and then stopped staying close to the sanctuary of the sheriff's car.

As soon as she saw him get out of the car, Suzy got very frightened. He looked just like Teal, except he wasn't Teal.

As soon as he stopped he began yelling. "You kilt him, you people done kilt him. He would never go off without tellin' us first. And he wasn't no renter. He was sleepin' with the old lady. He done tol me he was." His face got a nasty look. "Said she was a bad lay, too."

Jimmy's fist curled and uncurled and he made a step towards the stranger.

The sheriff put his hand out on Jimmy's arm and stopped him. "Hol' it, right there, boy. Ah'll take care of this." He turned towards the stranger. "Listen here, don't go accusin' these good folks, 'til we have some hard evidence." The sheriff's voice turned cold. "Now, get back in the car." He turned back to Mrs. Catlow. "Sorry ma'am, but we will have to search the place. You got any objections?"

"No, Sir." Amy suddenly was tense and the lines in her face suddenly seemed to grow deeper.

"Good, we'll come back tomorrer and give the place a good goin' over with some dogs. See you then." As soon as he said tomorrow, Amy's face relaxed and she began to breathe again.

Amy and Jimmy Lee watched the sheriff's car leave with Teal's angry brother. As the car passed them they heard the man say with some heat, "Why can't we search the place now?" They could not hear the Sheriff's reply but his hat was bobbing up and down and his face was red as he spoke back to Teal's brother in anger.

As soon as the car was out of sight, Amy and Jimmy put their heads together. He was nodding his head, yes, as he walked back towards the kitchen. He stared at Suzy for a moment, when he walked in. "I thought I tol you to go back to yer room."

"You can't tell me what to do," she said sarcastically. "Yer only my brother, not my boss." He tried to swat her, but she was too quick and she dodged the blow.

Amy stepped into the kitchen. "You two, stop it! We got enough ter worry 'bout without you two gettin' inter it. Now finish yer chores."

The winter night came early and Amy insisted Suzy be in bed soon after dark. She obeyed her mother but sleep did not come easily. In fact, ever since that fatal night, Suzy had not slept well. This night she had a double reason not to sleep. She was still feeling the mental effects of the rape and she knew something else was going to happen.

Just after midnight her premonition came true. It started with a noise from the kitchen followed by guarded whispers. Suzy quietly got out of the bed and crept silently towards the kitchen. She heard her mother clearly. "Get the lye from the barn, and be quick about it, we have a lot to do."

After a few minutes Jimmy and Amy had loaded the wheel barrow and were headed towards the place they had buried Teal. Suzy watched with fear and loathing, but she could not take her eyes off the clandestine pair.

Jimmy went far past the original grave, all the way to the creek. He took the shovel out of the barrow and started to dig. Suzy was puzzled. This was nowhere near where they had been the night before. *I wonder what's going on?* She shook her head, but continued to watch. After a few minutes, Jimmy stopped and wiped his brow. In an instant, his mother went right up to him and agitatedly told him something Suzy could not hear. Jimmy shrugged and started digging again. In fifteen more minutes, he stopped and gestured to his mother. She came over and looked at the hole he had dug and nodded her head. Jimmy then lifted a bag he had brought and poured part of the contents into the hole. Suzy was confused. *Why do that in the middle of the night?*

Jimmy put the shovel and the bag back in the barrow and started back towards the house. Suzy was just about to give up watching when Jimmy stopped at the place they had dug the night before. Quickly she became vigilant again. He began to dig and soon the moonlight showed him lifting the striped blanket out of its pestilential hole. Staggering a little, under the weight, he dumped it into the barrow and started wheeling it to the creek. His mother helped him lift the blanket a second time and place it on the ground. They both grabbed the end of the blanket and pulled on it. They had planned well and the body rolled right next to its new crypt. With a push of Jimmy's foot, Teal's body rolled into its new home. Jimmy then sprinkled the rest of the bag over the body, emptied a second bag over that and rapidly filled the hole with dirt. After he finished they both tamped down the dirt and put lots of branches and leaves over the grave.

When they got back to the house Suzy had jumped back in bed, laid back down again, but she couldn't close her eyes. She heard the pump in the kitchen working and supposed they were washing up. After they finished, she heard her mother's door squeak shut and the house became quiet again.

Suzy closed her eyes and prepared to face her demons as she tried to fall asleep once more. For a long while she stared at the ceiling, then her eyes fluttered close and she fell into a troubled sleep. In less than an hour, a hand touched her shoulder and she fairly leaped from the bed with a small cry.

"God, child, I didn't mean ter scare ya so."

"Oh Ma, Ma," Suzy hugged her mother's bony frame, "I'm so glad it's you."

"I can't sleep so I thought I better speak to ya now while things are fresh in mah mind." Amy hesitated, trying to decide how much to tell her young daughter. "You know me'n yer brother wuz out tonight?"

"Yes'm."

"You know what we wuz doin'," she said, gravely.

Suzy hung her head. "Yes'm."

"We got rid of him good, this time." She took her daughter's hand and squeezed it so hard Suzy almost cried out.

"There is one thing you must never do, Suzy Lee, and that's to tell anyone, and I mean anyone, what you seed tonight. You understand? This is a family secret that you must take to your grave."

Suzy's eyes were open wide as she nodded yes to her mother, her pigtails bobbing furiously.

Chapter 29: New York

"Grave... grave... take it to your grave..."

"Momma, Momma?"

Susan sat up bolt right in the bed. She was sweating profusely and breathing hard. Her heart was pounding in her ears and the room was spinning.

"Oh, God, will I ever be able to sleep again?"

"Huh, wassa matter?"

"Go back to sleep, Betty. I was just having a bad dream."

Betty sat up and turned on the lamp. She reached to the night stand and lit a cigarette. She offered one to Susan. She shook her head, no.

"Same dream?"

"Yeah, it's always the same."

"Why don't you tell me about it. It might help."

"For the thousandth time, no! It's personal."

"Well, see a shrink then." Irritation crept into Betty's voice." Anything would be better than being wakened every night."

Now it was Susan's turn to be irritated. She felt the familiar flash of anger and turned on Betty. "If you don't like it you can just get the hell outta here!" Susan abruptly got out of the bed and slipped her feet easily into her slippers. She stormed into the bathroom.

"Okay, I will. I'm getting tired of your sleepwalking. I'll look for something tomorrow."

Susan popped her head out of the bathroom. Her eyes were flashing. "No, today. Yeah, you can go back to your boyfriend, where I found you. I think you like boys better than real women anyway. And you find something today. I don't want you here when I get back."

"How would you know about guys. You won't let a guy even come near you."

"Well at least I'm a real lesbo, not a fake that swings back and forth."

"Go to Hell."

Susan tried to calm down but couldn't. She dressed in the spare room and went back into the bedroom.

Betty was angrily dragging on the cigarette when Susan returned to the room. She was dressed completely in black, showing her strawberry blonde hair at its best. Instantly, Betty felt a sexual urge and her mind changed from anger to getting Susan back to bed.

No chance. Susan's skin color was pale and her face was set like a granite wall. Her voice was ominous. "Be packed and out of here when I get back from work."

By the time Susan made coffee and left the building, the streets were already crowded. She loved being an anonymous face in the crowd. This was nothing like West Virginia. There, everyone knew your name, how much you were worth and how many times a day you went to the bathroom. Suddenly she was thoughtful. *No, I guess they don't know everything.* As always, as soon as the thought of the family secret hit her she began to feel queasy. Quickly pushing it down she turned her mind to other things as she walked down to the subway.

After a short ride, she reached Times Square. She got out of the train and was swept along by the early morning crowd heading for work. When she got above ground again she exited just across from the Woman's Home building. It was still early so she sat on a bench in the small park across the street from the entrance. She opened her purse, took out a cigarette and flicked the lighter. As the flame flared, Susan's eyes locked on it and in an instant she was sixteen again and back in West Virginia. Her face hardened as she thought of the fire in the cabin.

****

True to his word, the next day, the sheriff and his deputies came back with their dogs, and searched the rocky pastures on the farm. Amy and her two children watched the proceedings with interest. Aside from chasing a few squirrels, the dogs found nothing. The lye had worked well.

After three hours of searching and digging, the sheriff called his men in and walked over to the family They were gathered in a knot, still watching with interest.

Ma'am, Ah'm sure sorry to have bothered y'all. Y'all have a good day now an' we'll be gettin' on outta here.

The door to the sheriff's car burst open and Teal's brother spilled out. His face was enraged. "They's gettin' away with murder, Sheriff."

The sheriff slowly turned to Teal's brother and shrugged. The man then angrily confronted the family and shouted, "Sure, Sheriff, they had lots of time to get rid of the body." He then shook his fist at the family. "I'll get you people for murderin' mah brother if'n it takes the rest of mah life."

Jimmy Lee took a step towards Teal's brother but the sheriff put his large bulk between them. Suzy cringed behind her mother, not because she feared being hurt, but because the brother looked so much like the man who had raped her.

As usual, it took a long time for Suzy to fall asleep that night. She finally dozed off into her nightmarish world. As usual, she woke with a start. She was bathed in sweat as her nocturnal demons pursued her. She sat up and put her feet on the floor and rested on the side of the bed trying to quiet her beating heart. Suddenly, her head cocked as she smelled something strange but familiar. She sniffed once, twice and then quickly stood up. There was a strange light coming from behind her curtain. Quickly she pulled the curtain back and her heart fell. "Fire!" she yelled, "in Momma's room."

Suzy ran towards the flames. The door was closed as it usually was and she reached for the doorknob to open it. "Ooooooowwww," she screamed as the heat of the doorknob burned her hand. Grabbing the bottom of her gown she put it around the knob and tried again. This time she could stand the heat and turned the knob.

Heat and energy had been building up behind the door and as Suzy turned the knob the door blew open as if a giant hand had snatched it. The force of the hot air and flames threw Suzy to the ground like a rag doll. The heat singed her face and hair but she ignored the pain and got up and went back towards the open door.

The entire room was aflame and burning furiously. Through the smoke and flames she got a glimpse of her mother that would stay with her the rest of her life and fuel her already devilish nightmares. Amy was wrapped in the fire that would burn in her daughter's brain forever. She staggered towards the girl, her fiery arms outstretched like a demon beckoning to the nether regions.

"Momma, Momma," Suzy screamed. She put her forearm over her eyes and tried to enter the holocaust. Her mother gave a demonic yell and crumpled to the ground.

Suddenly a hand grabbed her shoulder and pulled her back. Her heart was pounding wildly and she fought to go back for her mother. "Stay back, Suzy, let me go in." Jimmy Lee pointed to the pump at the sink. They both ran over to it. Clumsily he primed the pump and then began to raise and lower the handle furiously.

When the water finally came, Suzy knew what she had to do. She took the filled bucket from the sink and dumped it all on her brother. Soaking, he turned to go back into the flaming room. He took a step and then stopped and yelled over the noise. "Get Tommy out, now!" With that he dashed into the burning room.

For a split second, Suzy hesitated and then she went to Tommy's bed. Thankfully he was still sleeping and offered no resistance when she lifted him up then set him down on his feet. He was groggy and followed her, half asleep, toward the front door. Suzy took him by the hand and led him outside into the cool air.

After the heat of the fire, the cold air hit her with the force of a slap. "Now Tommy, you stay right here an' I'll be right back. I'm gonna get Ma." Tommy shook his head yes. He was shaking and clearly frightened, but Suzy just had to go and help her mother.

She turned and dashed back towards the burning building. Just as she reached the steps to the front door, it opened and a blackened Jimmy Lee stepped out. One look at his face and his head shaking side to side and Suzy knew it was too late. "Momma," she shrieked, and tried to rush past him. He easily stopped her, mostly because at a deeper level she knew her gesture was futile.

Suzy fell to the ground and sobbed her grief, saying over and over, "What will happen to us, what will happen to us." From her place on the ground, she could not see the hardening of Jimmy Lee's face nor the resolve that came over him. But she did hear one thing that made her go even colder.

"Teal's brother! It were him." The coldness in Jimmy's voice made Suzy stopped crying and look up at her brother. He looked back down at her. "There was a rock with some burnt straw tied ter it at the foot of a broken winder. Ah'm goin' ter go git him, now."

Suzy was horrified as Jimmy Lee went to the shed to get the shotgun. She ran to him. "Don't go Jimmy Lee, he'll be waitin' fer you."

"Get outta my way, little sister. He's a dog what needs killin'. You take care a Tommy an' I'll be right back."

Jimmy saddled the horse and with a nod and a grunt pulled the bridle and left at a slow pace, his eyes fixed straight ahead.

Suzy watched him, her eyes wide and full of fear, as Tommy clung to her ragged gown and wept like the frightened little boy he was.

The cabin burned furiously all night and by morning it was just a pile of smoking embers. Tommy slept on the ground and Suzy sat by him, bent over, her arms wrapped around her knees, rocking back and forth. Her eyes, fixed on her mother's tomb, were red with the weeping she had done through the night, and her heart ached for her Momma.

Jimmy Lee never came home and Suzy was at a complete loss as to what to do next. Finally, she made up her mind. Her Aunt Sarah lived just a few miles off and she got set to walk over there. She knew she could leave Tommy there and then she would go find out about Jimmy Lee.

She gently woke Tommy Lee, and with a glance back at the burnt cabin, began the three mile walk to Aunt Sarah's house.

Usually, it was a pleasant walk to Aunt Sarah's with the reward of cold milk and a piece of chocolate cake when you got there, but today Suzy could not think of such things. She did not see the robins or the cawing blue jays or the crows that lived in the numerous trees that lined the road. Today she would not see the frogs that lined the creek or the occasional snake that slithered across the road to drink at the creek. All she could think of was the misfortune that had befallen her. First being attacked by Teal and then losing her mother. It was almost too much.

At first Suzy was not aware that the car coming towards her was the sheriff's. When he stopped, she could see that his usually smiling face was grim. Briefly she wondered why until she looked in back of him and saw that Jimmy Lee was in the back seat. And he was hand-cuffed.

"Suzy Girl, Jimmy Lee here got to go to town with me. You goin' to yer Aunt Sary's? Good." He glanced back at the boy. "Jimmy Lee done blew Teal's brother's head off. You jes cain't do that in mah county. I got to take him up to the county lock-up. You an' the boy gonna be okay?"

Suzy nodded dumbly and then ran to the car window. Jimmy put both his palms up on the glass and his sister did the same. She could see his handcuffs and tears began to roll down both her cheeks. "Why did you do it Jimmy? I begged you not to."

The window stayed closed and Jimmy had to raise his voice. "What's done is done, lil' sister. You go on to Aunt Sary's place. She'll take care of you both. I'll be back, bye and bye." His voice faded. "Ah'm the man of the house now, you do what ah says."

The sheriff looked back at Jimmy. "Don't count on it, boy, this state don't cotton to murder, even if'n he had it comin'" He turned back to Suzy. "Ah'll come back and let you know what's goin' to happen to Jimmy Lee."

As the car rolled down the road, Suzy ran after it. "Don't leave us Jimmy Lee. We need you. How will we get along?" As the car picked up speed, Suzy stopped running and stood in the middle of the road, feeling abandoned. "How will we get along?"

The sheriff never came back and neither did Jimmy Lee. He was later sentenced, by a judge who was impervious to his families pleas, to second degree murder and given a sentence of eight to ten years.

Before the first year was out, a man from the state prison came to the house and told her that Jimmy Lee Catlow had been knifed to death by person or persons unknown. He handed the boy's pitiful belongings to the desolate girl. What he didn't tell her was that Jimmy had been knifed by a black man in a scuffle that was never quite satisfactorily explained. The next day he was avenged by a friend. The black prisoner was found face down with a screwdriver in his back. The warden then considered the matter closed.

****

Aunt Sarah was a kind woman. A plumper, happier version of her late brother. She bustled about the house making her brother's children feel welcome.

Suzy was too depressed to feel the warmth from her aunt and went through the days listless and distressed. She spent the daytime helping Aunt Sarah and the nights wandering through the woods trying to make sense of the world she had been thrust into.

Suzy made up her mind she would no longer go to school. At Aunt Sarah's urging, Suzy applied for several jobs in town. Upon her application to the telephone company, it was noticed that her accent was less pronounced than most of the other girls that applied, And she was hired that day. After diction lessons and learning the operator's job, life became somewhat routine. One day her supervisor ordered her to secretarial school where she learned new and valuable skills. When she finished secretarial school she was told to go to the supervisor's office. The other girls had talked about the supervisor whose name was Roberta Perkins.

They said she was a spinster and very hard on the girls. Suzy prepared for the worst.

The room was empty when Suzy entered. She sat down and crossed her legs and dutifully waited. In a few minutes the door opened abruptly and a woman briskly entered the room and quickly went to a desk. For a few minutes, she ignored Suzy and studied a document on her desk, holding a pencil in her hand. Suzy sat nervously, waiting for the woman to finish reading.

She was cold, austere looking woman of about thirty five, with coal black hair that was tied in a tight bun at the back of her head. Her face was all angles and her white skin seemed stretched tightly over her facial bones. She wore bright red lipstick that emphasized a thin mouth that seemed to be pursed as if she were going to kiss a small child. She wore a black pin-stripe business suit and black leather heels. The granny glasses she wore on the end of her nose made her look somewhat older.

When she finished reading the document, she raised her eyes up over the half glasses and looked critically at Suzy. Finally, she said officiously, "You are Suzy Lee Catlow?"

Suzy lowered her eyes. "Yes ma'am."

"My name is Miss Perkins," she said in a clipped voice. "I am presently the supervisor of operators in this area."

Suzy raised her eyes, leaned forward in her chair and said with some eagerness, "Yes, ma'am, I know."

Miss Perkins leaned back stiffly in her chair and tapped her pencil on the desk. She looked at Suzy carefully. In the past two years Suzy's body had filled out to womanly proportions. Her breasts and hips trimmed down to a narrow waist and her long blonde hair hung about her shoulders framing a light colored face with dark brown eyes and full red lips. Miss Perkins had noticed. She had seen Suzy before and in fact, had asked for her.

Miss Perkins leaned back in her chair. "I have been given a supervisor's position in New York City," she said, her pride showing through, "and I need a secretary." Miss Perkins got up and paced. "The company did not want to hire a local person because of the union problems that they might bring in with them." She stopped and looked directly at Suzy. "You know, all those communists and Jews in New York, they're all troublemakers."

Suzy nodded her head eagerly, not knowing what Miss Perkins was talking about.

Miss Perkins sat down and looked directly at Suzy. Her pencil now beating a staccato on the desk. "The company wants me to bring a local girl with me and I, er, they, have chosen you..., that is if you want to go, Miss, ah, Miss Catlow." Miss Perkins' voice dropped with anticipation.

Suzy was stunned. She sat staring at Miss Perkins, her eyes unblinking. "Leave here...? Go to New York?"

Miss Perkins heart dropped with Suzy's hesitation. "There would be a slight raise in salary..."

"Yes, ma'am, I'll go," Suzy interrupted.

Miss Perkins stopped in the middle of her run-on sentence and cleared her throat, vastly relieved. She had been praying that Suzy would say yes. "Yes, well, yes, uh you may take the rest of the day off and settle your affairs. I know that you have few ties here, so I am planning to leave Friday on the noon train to Beckley, and then on to New York." She turned away. "The company has us sharing a sleeper on the train and then you will have a week off, with pay, to find an apartment in New York and get yourself settled." She waited for a moment and then turned back, her thin mouth spreading into a small smile. "Have you any questions?"

Suzy's mind was in a whirl. She felt like the luckiest girl in the world. She never even looked at Miss Perkins, but stared into her glorious future. "Nno, nnno ma'am," she stuttered.

Miss Perkin's smile got a little larger. " Well then, go on and get ready and be at the train station at half past eleven on Friday."

Suzy got up early Friday morning and finished packing her clothing. She went down to breakfast, where she found a teary Aunt Sarah.

Suzy patiently explained to her for the hundredth time, that she was not going neither to Sodom nor Gomorrah, and that they didn't really shoot you down in the street in New York. When her aunt finally stopped crying and calmed down, Suzy told her that she would be sending her money every week for Tommy. She then went to Tommy's room to urge him to get to school and to say goodbye. After he left, she went for a last walk in the pasture behind the big farm house. For a long time, she stared at the mountains trying to convince herself that she really wanted to live in a big city.

Finally it was time to go. Suzy said another tearful goodbye to Aunt Sarah, and her uncle drove her to the station.

She was sitting on her trunk when Miss Perkins showed up. She gave Suzy her ticket and then got ready to board. Suzy was pleased that Miss Perkins seemed very friendly and almost warm to her today. She marveled at the inconsistency of people.

Then, with her heart pounding, she boarded the train for her first trip away from the West Virginia mountains.

After a slow start, the train picked up speed and was now careening through the countryside at a fearful clip. Suzy marveled at the room they had been given. They actually had their own room in a train going across the country to New York. She could hardly believe it. Suzy wondered where they would sleep but she was too nervous and excited to ask. She sat on a seat and watched the earth speed by her window. She was fascinated by the speed with which the train covered the distances between the towns that dotted the landscape. Before dinner, they were at Beckley. There they transferred to a large express that would whisk them on to New York.

After they changed trains, they went to their new room on the much larger train. The room they now occupied had its own bathroom. The porter showed them how to make the beds and backed out of the room as the train started up for New York.

Suzy was really excited now as she watched the train build up speed. The towns were larger and the cities immense. Smoke billowed past the window and a screeching sound of metal on metal filled the afternoon. Into this cacophony of sound the engineer injected the familiar train whistle. Suzy was overjoyed. It was a mad world and she was Alice going to Wonderland.

Miss Perkins suggested they wash up and go to dinner. In a few minutes they were seated at a table in the dining room having the first of several drinks. Suzy marveled that Miss Perkins was so different than when she first met her. She looked so much younger and prettier now.

Both of them ate very little. Suzy was so excited and Miss Perkins favored the whisky more than the food. Suzy had never had alcohol before, and Miss Perkins suggested she start with some wine. It was delicious and Suzy had two glasses of it. Soon, she was dizzy and laughing at everything Miss Perkins said.

The rocking of the train and the wine Miss Perkins insisted she drink at dinner made Suzy light headed and she stumbled several times as she made her way towards their sleeper.

When they got to their compartment Miss Perkins reached around her and opened the door. Suzy could feel the warmth of her body and giggled. They entered the room and Miss Perkins quickly disappeared into the bathroom. The porter had made up both of the beds. Suzy sat on the edge of one and smiled. The room was going round and round, but it was a pleasant feeling and she just felt like smiling.

Slowly and languorously Suzy got out of her skirt and began to fumble with the buttons on her blouse. Miss Perkins stepped out of the bathroom and Suzy noted dimly that her hair was down and that she was dressed in silk pajamas. Suzy gave her a silly smile.

"Let me help you with that." In an instant, Miss Perkins was beside Suzy helping her with the buttons.

"Thank you Miss Perkins," Suzy said sing-song, like a little girl.

Miss Perkins gave her a knowing smile. "Why don't you call me Roberta for the rest of the trip." Suzy nodded with a smile and Roberta slipped the unbuttoned blouse off her shoulders.

Suzy reached for her pajamas and started to get up to go to the bathroom to take her panties and bra off and put on her bed clothes. Carolyn's touch stopped her.

"You seem tense Susan. Let me relax you." It was the first time anyone had ever called her Susan and she liked it. It was more dignified. *Miss Perkins, er, Roberta certainly was a cut above her usual friends and if she said it was alright, it was alright.* Susan giggled.

Roberta began to massage her shoulders. No one had ever done that for her before, and it felt really good. Roberta's fingers probed Susan's muscles expertly and she squirmed pleasantly under the pressure. Soon her body began to relax and the tension of the first day away from home seemed to melt away. "Let me get you more comfortable." Roberta quickly undid her bra and it fell carelessly to the floor. Gently, she let Susan down on the bed. Slowly but surely her fingers began to wander from the shoulders to the arms, then lightly across the tops of her breasts. Susan felt her body respond in a way it had never done before. Her muscles began to move of their own accord and suddenly she felt her fingertips on Roberta's silk pajamas. She reached under the sleeves and began stroking her arms, enjoying the feel of her skin. Roberta was now moving her fingers across her breasts and stroking the nipples. Suzy felt them get hard and at the same time felt her panties getting moist. By now she didn't much care. This was too much fun.

Susan's hips began to move in a strange but familiar motion when Roberta surprised her by leaning over and gently kissing her on the mouth. Roberta's mouth was soft and warm, and Susan responded with enthusiasm. A few boys had tried to kiss her when she was younger, but somehow it was unsatisfactory and she stopped letting them touch her. This was different. She felt Roberta's tongue in her mouth and it set her aflame. Roberta now moved over her and was kissing her breasts. Through her half closed eyes she saw Roberta's melon shaped breasts just above her. She reached up and took one of her nipples in her mouth and began to bite and suck gently. Roberta gasped audibly and began to groan. She responded by kissing Susan's rock hard nipples and stomach. Carefully she reached down and hooked Susan's panties with her thumbs and slid them down. The slick moistness that greeted her fingers told her that Susan was ready.

****

The affair with Roberta ended badly, and Susan was soon walking the streets looking for a new job. She had moved out of their apartment and had gotten her own flat in Greenwich Village. She had saved some money while they were together, and she had gotten a month's severance pay. It would have to last until she found something else.

One good thing about the three months with Roberta. It told Susan where her sexual preference was. She soon learned where other lesbians went to meet people and, with her black clothes and blond hair, she was an instant favorite with the others.

She had short affairs with several of the women until she met Betty. They shared a lot of the same interests and Susan was overjoyed when she found out Betty was also from West Virginia. After a short while, Betty moved in and gave the relationship some stability. That is, it seemed stable until Susan found out that Betty also dated men. When she confronted her about it, she was told not to be so uptight and to try it herself, she might like it.

Outraged, Susan thought about throwing her out of her apartment, but the thought of her being alone again stopped her. But, now she was beyond that and just wanted her out.

Susan drummed her fingers on the table in the lesbian bar. A couple of women came over and asked Susan to dance but she curtly turned them down. Betty was thirty minutes late and she wanted her front door key back. As she waited, the warmth of her anger began to creep up her neck and flush her face. Suddenly she was startled by a familiar voice.

"Well, hello Susan."

Susan looked up, still seeing red, not comprehending who it was talking to her. All at once she recognized Roberta.

"I have been looking for you."

"Well you found me, have a seat." Susan was barely civil.

"Thanks."

Susan looked critically at her former lover. New York had been good to her. She looked relaxed and tan and fit. She had gained a few pounds but it had spread over her frame and enhanced her looks. She now wore her hair down all the time. Her former thin smile was now full and sexual. Despite her anger, Susan felt a rush.

Time had also been good to Susan and Roberta's heart skipped a beat as she looked across at the blonde beauty. She was always amazed that this girl could go without make-up and still look gorgeous. She also looked poised and self-confident. The country girl had learned her lessons well and quickly.

Susan took a long drag on her cigarette. Roberta's feelings stirred, but she quickly pushed them down.

"What you got on your mind?"

Roberta looked down as if to think for a minute and then looked at Susan. "I treated you badly, setting you adrift in the city alone, no friends, no job. I felt bad when it happened, and I feel worse now."

Susan smiled a half smile that made Roberta's heart beat faster. She pushed it down again. "I have a friend named Roz who is good friends with the editor of Woman's Home magazine. Her name is Theresa Bannon and she is looking for a secretary. I called Roz and told her about you. As a favor to me, she will speak to her and try to get you an interview."

"No thanks, I don't want a job where I have to fuck the boss."

"No, she won't even know anything about that. It's a straight secretary's job."

Susan pondered for a few minutes. "Might be fun at that. Yeah, have her call me." Susan took out a pen and paper and jotted her number for Roberta. Just then, Betty walked in the front door. Susan stood up, her face red. "There you are, you bitch, where you been?"

****

Susan ground out the cigarette with her heel and looked at her watch. Five minutes until nine o'clock, time to go to work.

Susan loved her job at Woman's Home. She got there, usually at nine and would stay until her boss, Theresa Bannon, would leave. She knew she could get Theresa interested in her but it was simply too dangerous. Some people didn't mix business and pleasure well. Besides, Theresa was partnered with Roz. It just wouldn't be ethical, she thought. Roz got me the job. How would it be if I stabbed her in the back after that. And, she didn't know if Theresa would even like her. Better not take a chance. Good jobs like this one were hard to find.

At first she found it difficult because of the men in the building. One by one, they tried to hit on her. Married, single, it didn't seem to make much difference. Finally, she hit on a solution. She bought a cheap engagement ring and put it on her left hand. That seemed to stop most of the ardent males in their tracks. They didn't want to compete with an engagement.

Although Susan was out a lot after work, she spent many a night alone thinking about Theresa and about how she could have her cake and eat it too.

Chapter 30: New York

Theresa:

Well ,it's finally here and I can't believe it. Paul and I will be married by the Bishop, on St. Mathews Island, at one o'clock on Christmas day. Please be there. Of course you will be my Matron of Honor. If you do not come I will not marry and will be a cranky old maid the rest of my life and probably live with you for punishment.

I love you.

Syd

P.S. There will be a room reserved for you at the Hotel De La Mer.

Theresa put the invitation back down on her desk and sat down. *No, dear sister,* Theresa thought, *it's not you who will be the old maid, but me. I wonder if that bastard father of mine will be there? No, I won't go, I can't. I don't want to be in the same room as him. I won't, I can't. As much as it may hurt my sister, I can't.*

Theresa walked to the large window looking out over New York. The rain pelted the window and made her sad. She always felt sad when it rained.

There was a soft knock on the large oak door and Susan stepped in. "Miss Bannon," she said softly, "is there anything else before I leave?"

Theresa looked at her in surprise. "Is it five already?" Theresa put back on her official face and walked back to her desk and sat down.

Susan smiled and looked at her watch. "Yes, Ma'am it's 5:20."

"Yes, yes, Susan, of course. Go on and enjoy the evening." Susan suddenly realized she knew nothing about her secretary. *Was she married? Did she have children? Who did she go home to?* Theresa made a mental note to ask tomorrow. She smiled benevolently. "I'll see you tomorrow."

Susan turned to go, started to close the door then stopped and turned back to Theresa. Suddenly there was a different look in her eyes and somehow it looked familiar to Theresa. Susan stepped back into the room and closed the door behind her. "Are you sure you're alright? Is there anything else I can do for you?"

Theresa now fully recognized the look and flushed. *This is too close to home,* she thought. She sure could use the company, but it could turn complicated. *Still, Susan is very attractive and really built well. It's tempting. Maybe another time. Roz will have to do tonight.* "No Susan, I'm fine. I just got a note from my sister, Sydney and I have to make a decision." She put her hand on the desk with finality as if to end the conversation. Susan didn't move.

Susan looked genuinely concerned. "Sydney's alright, isn't she?"

Theresa smiled. "She is doing just fine. In fact, she's getting married." Theresa could not help but stare at Susan and wonder what it would be like to touch that young body.

Susan beamed. "Oh, please wish her the best for me."

Susan took a step forward and Theresa shrank back. "Theresa," she said familiarly, "you look like you have the weight of the world on your shoulders. I have a cure for you." She quickly walked around the desk and got in back of Theresa.

Theresa was taken aback by the informal use of her first name, but pushed the feeling down and said nothing.

"Come on, just relax."

Red flags popped up in her head, but as if she were a robot, Theresa let Susan tip her forward and slip off her jacket. Slowly and expertly, Susan began to knead the muscles in Theresa's shoulders. At the same time Theresa began to smell the girl's perfume and feel her youth and she became aroused. Gently, but forcefully, Susan massaged her neck and arms, occasionally letting her fingers wander to the top of the swell of Theresa's breasts. Theresa began to melt with the treatment, but at the same time she became wet with desire. Slowly but surely, with each stroke, Susan's delicate hands slipped further under her bra until she brushed her nipples that stood out firmly. Susan tipped Theresa's head back and began to massage her flaming red hair with her fingers. Theresa felt the hair pull against her scalp and it began to tingle.

Susan gently slipped her hands from Theresa's hair and cupped her face. Slowly and carefully she began to massage her temples with her thumbs. Theresa had had facials before, but this was a brand new sensation. Susan's warm hands massaged her cheeks and brow and Theresa felt all her wrinkles disappear.

Theresa was glad the room was dark because she knew she was flushed red. Her brow was moist as was her loins. Suddenly she felt Susan's lips on hers. She had a soft, velvet mouth designed to tempt the hardest heart. Susan's tongue lit a fire in her mouth and her neck muscles went taught, and she shuddered with pleasure. For a moment Theresa tried to resist, but stopped when she felt the younger woman's hand on the inside of her thigh, fingering her moistness.

With renewed vigor, she pulled Susan towards her and kissed her back forcefully. In the dark, Susan smiled victoriously and let herself be taken.

****

Father:

I plan to marry Paul at 1 pm on the twenty-fifth of December on Saint Mathews Island, off the coast of France. BUT, I will not marry if you are not there. So, as you can clearly see ,my future happiness rests in your hands. If you do not want your youngest daughter, unmarried and cranky the rest of her life, (and living with you), be there. Of course, you will give the lovely bride away. (Won't you be glad?)

I cannot wait to see you!

All my love,

Sydney

P.S. There will be a room reserved for you at the Hotel De La Mer. (You can't miss, it's the only hotel there.)

Thomas read and re-read the perfumed note. The words began to swim as his eyes glistened over. Gently he put the note down and stared out the window of the study. Rain pelted the window panes and filled the day with melancholy.

With a sigh, he lifted himself out of the leather arm chair and walked to the window. He leaned against the window frame and looked out at the wet lawn. The boughs of the trees seemed to bend like a man hunched over with age. The summer flowers shimmered and glittered in the rain.

I should feel joyful, Thomas thought, *but I don't.* He thought of Sydney as he always did, a bright, bubbly little girl of five, with shining platinum hair, the very picture of her mother. He could actually feel his hand going through her hair as he soothed some hurt she got on one of their outings. He longed to comfort her, to capture that part of their youth again. Tears welled up in his eyes and flowed down his cheeks. *And her mother, her sainted mother. How I miss her.* Abruptly, he wiped his eyes and quickly went back to the desk to reply.

Chapter 31: Saint Mathews Island

The sea birds looked black against the fluffy cumulus clouds as they drifted above the calm water. Silently, their wings outstretched, they glided in a lazy circle on the sea breeze, staring at the water in fixed concentration. Suddenly one of them would collapse their wings and dive straight down, plummeting maniacally into the water. In a millisecond, he would surface with an unfortunate fish in his beak. The bird would toss its head to shake the water off and caw loudly. The poor fish would struggle for a few moments and then lie still, its fate assured. Thomas watched the age old cycle of life with resignation through the window of the old hotel.

The sun was just coming over the horizon as Thomas left his room and walked out of the hotel lobby. He looked fondly at the beach and the water beyond. *What God had wrought,* he thought and smiled.

Gingerly, he walked out of his deck shoes and stepped into the sand. It was cool to his feet and for a moment chilled him. With a large grin on his face, he made his way towards the water. When he got to the edge, he put his foot in. The icy shock surprised him and he quickly pulled his foot back. *No wonder those people on the Titanic didn't last.* He thought about their misfortune for a moment, shook his head and headed down the beach.

Thomas smiled, contentment filling his heart. Finally, one of his daughters will marry. He wondered briefly why she had so suddenly left this young man, and when they had gotten back together again. Sydney would not tell him and he would never pry. In any event, they were back together and he was content.

He thought of Sydney first as a little girl, and then as a young lady. Now she was a woman. So much like her mother. Same eyes, same hair, a perfect disposition. And smart. *How do these young people get so smart?*

Sandpipers absently moved up and back with the surf, their legs moving almost faster than the eye. Thomas watched with fascination. He felt at peace with the world now that this daughter would marry. Perhaps now he could have some progeny to carry on, if not a son with his name, then a daughter with his business.

He had been summoned to this place by a single elegant card.

Mr. and Mrs. Paul Grant, Sr.
are pleased to announce
the marriage of their son,
Paul Jr.
to
Sydney Marie Bannon,
daughter of Mr. Thomas Bannon
The ceremony will be performed on the
Twenty-fifth day of December
in the Year of our Lord
Nineteen Hundred and Fifty-three
The Bishop of Normandy will preside

There was a cryptic note enclosed.

Daddy:
I have beaten the enemy at my breast.
Of course you will give the bride away.
Love,
Syd

"Owwwwww..." Suddenly, Thomas's reverie turned to a painful yowl. Lost deep in thought, he had stepped on a bed of shells. Half laughing and half cursing his stupidity, Thomas hopped out of the shell bed and sat on a dune, his back to the sea. He looked up at the barren beach, first one way and then another, and then turned and watched the sun touch the horizon.

It was getting late and he wanted to get back before dark. He reached down and felt his painful foot. He turned the bottom of his foot towards himself and muttered, "damn." Blood was seeping out of a cut on his foot, spreading out over the sand. He wiped the blood with his hand. Suddenly it was 1944 again. His stomach churned and he saw the corporal's blood on his hands and he was back on Omaha Beach. The fear was overwhelming!

Chapter 32: Normandy (1944)

The LST wallowed through the surf. Bullets were pinging against the steel hull and whining overhead. Thomas looked over the gunwale and saw the sun just breaking the horizon. He shook uncontrollably. Dear God, he prayed, don't let me be a coward. Thomas was in the middle of the LST and men were pushing him from all sides. He felt claustrophobic. It was D-day, June sixth, 1944 and the invasion was on. The men of the First and Fifth Companies, First Battalion, Fifth Army were packed like sardines in an LST on their way to history. They were about to land on Hitler's Festung Europa! (Fortress Europe) That is, if they landed. Bombs were now raining all around them, threatening total annihilation. A shell landed next to the LST and sprayed its evil load of shrapnel against the metal hull. Thomas crouched down toward a fetal ball and began to retch. Men about him were doing the same thing. Sick with fear, Thomas leaned against the man next to him. The man leaned back. They took comfort in each other.

The boat stopped, startling Thomas. For a moment he stopped shaking. "Okay, you guys, get out. I got to go get another load," the coxswain yelled.

The captain was standing near Thomas and he could see the captains face turn red. The officer stood up, ignoring the bullets whizzing over his head and Thomas took courage from his bravery and relaxed, but just a little.

"Hey, Navy," the captain yelled back, "Wot the Hell you talkin' 'bout. We're still a hunred yahds from shore. Go on in closuh."

"Can't do it, sir, I have orders to get back, right away."

The noise was now becoming deafening. Exploding bombs rocked the LST and the big guns from the allied ships were answering back. They wallowed in the surf making an inviting target. The coxswain was shaking with fear.

Thomas strained to hear the captain. For a moment neither man spoke then he saw the captain's face turned red as he started pushing his way through the men towards the driver. He slogged through the water and vomit with a determined look on his face and the men squeezed apart to make way for him. The captain finally got to the back of the boat and stood straddle legged, hands on his hips, in front of the coxswain. Bullets whipped about his head pinging on the sides of the craft. The men ducked down as low as they could but kept their eyes on the two men.

"Navy, if'n we gets in the watuh heah, we won't make it to shore nohow. I want you to get onto the beach, like you're supposed to."

Thomas could see the coxswain was shaking. "Damn, he's just afraid," Thomas muttered. "If the captain was shaking, it was from anger, his face is livid."

"Can't do it, sir," the coxswain said, staring into space, still shaking with fear, "got to get back."

The men gawked at the captain, forgetting their own misery for a moment. Slowly the captain reached to his side and unsnapped his holster. Even with the terrible noise of war, every man on board heard the menacing snap. The captain pulled out his forty five and deliberately pointed it at the coxswain's head. The sailors eyes went wide as saucers. They were fixed on the muzzle of the gun. "Navy, get this scow on the beach. NOW!"

For a full minute the sailor didn't move. Neither did the captain. The gun stayed pointed right between his eyes. Time stood still for everyone on board and Thomas got the feeling that this drama was the more important than the invasion. "Forget the damn war," he muttered.

Without moving a muscle other than his thumb, the captain cocked the weapon. That sound was even more ominous. Thomas held his breath. "You got ten seconds, Navy... Nine... eight... seven..." The captain stared, unblinking, at the sailor, his gun steady. No one doubted he would pull the trigger. Thomas prayed silently.

"Five, four, three, two..."

At "one," the sailor sprung to life. "Yes, sir." In a split second, the LST's engines growled and the boat began to speed towards shore again.

For a few minutes the LST sped forward. Finally it stopped and the door at the front of the craft dropped down. For the first time Thomas saw the raw beach. It was a scene from Hell. For a second, Thomas wanted to get in a fetal ball and fall to the floor of the craft. Instead, he made the sign of the cross and squeezed his rifle.

"Okay, troopers, hit the beach." The captain was waving his pistol urging them out. The first two men stepped off the LST and were welcomed to France by German bullets. Both men fell into the water, dead.

Bullets were whizzing about the heads of the other men as they disembarked. The intensity increased as they slogged towards the shore. The men in back of the first group hesitated and pushed back. "Don't stay heah, you idiots, get off this tub and get inland, go, GO!" He pushed the backs of soldiers at his front and reluctantly the men began to move.

Thomas dropped off the LST into the water. Holding his rifle above his head he waddled towards the shore. Even though they had gotten much closer to the beach the water was still deep. Thomas shuddered to think of what would have happened if the captain hadn't gotten them in further. With the weight of his pack and the M-1 rifle he carried, he would have sunk like a stone.

Thomas slogged through the surf to the shore crouching as low as he could. Allied artillery shells whizzed overhead and landed with a tremendous noise. German 88s answered with devastating accuracy. Machine gun bullets and small arms fire stitched the ground and the water.

Thomas ducked behind the steel prongs of one of Rommel's Belgian Gates, a steel pile, an explosive mine, and wooden stakes, slanting seaward. His heart was pounding, making whooshing noises in his ears. The famed German general had his engineers not only put the Belgian Gates up, but also steel, and wood, and concrete obstacles all along the shore to foul up the LSTs.

The protection Thomas got from the gate was slight and not much comfort but still it was something. Thomas realized that to survive, he had to get inland. Here he was a sitting duck from the machine guns. He stepped towards the shore and almost went under. He had stepped into a depression in the sand and sunk down like a stone as it filled with water. He held his rifle up to prevent water from fouling it. Just then a bullet struck the stock almost knocking it out of his hand. Instantly his fear increased. *Damn, that was close,* Thomas thought, *if I hadn't stepped in that hole, the bullet would have got me.*

Thomas struggled out of the hole and made it to drier sand. He hit the beach prone and buried his face in the sand. Bullets kicked up all around him making a plopping sound as they buried themselves in the sand. Thomas raised his head and peered over the sand. The brim of his steel pot framed the scene from Hell that would be indelibly imprinted on his brain, forever. He had arrived at Omaha Beach.

"Form on me, form on me." The captain was just ahead of Thomas, lying on his stomach, just behind a small sand dune and waving at the men to come on towards the high ground.

Thomas prepared to go to him. He looked up at the route he would have to run. Dead men littered the beach so close together he could walk on them, without touching the ground. Bullets kept hitting the dead soldiers again and again, making a thudding sound when they struck. Each time they were hit, the dead men made a jerking movement. To Thomas, it was like a macabre dance of death.

Thomas surveyed the beach at his front. Just ahead was a shingle, a sheet of stones and boulders put there by the Germans to slow the soldiers and stop any auto traffic on the beach. Ahead of the Shingle was the seawall. If a soldier could get to the seawall he would be safe from the machine gun bullets. Bannon put his hand on the ground and got ready to get up and run for the seawall.

Suddenly the captain paid the price for his bravery. A mortar shell burst right next to him and silenced him forever. Thomas dropped his head back into the sand and cried.

After a few minutes, the firing slackened and Thomas again lifted his head. He wiped at the tears in his eyes with the back of his hand and got sand in them for his trouble. He blinked fiercely to ease the annoyance. He looked over at the captain. He was lying on his back apparently intact. *Maybe he wasn't dead*, Thomas thought. With hope in his heart, he pushed off and crawled to the officer on his belly, cradling his M-1 in his elbows. Bullets pinged and thudded all around him, and he was glad the army made him do this in practice.

Along with the other men, Bannon bitched and moaned when the captain got them up at 4:30 and made them crawl through the wet mud at Fort Dix, with live machine gun rounds firing over their heads. Now the Germans didn't try to fire high, they were firing right at them.

When Thomas got to the captain, his heart sunk. There was blood on his chest and his eyes were open, and he was staring into space, sightless. Thomas touched the rosary beads in his pocket, said a small prayer then closed the Southerner's eyes.

The fire slackened again and Thomas' heart stopped pounding in his chest. He looked at the captain again and his heart wrenched. His dog tag was laying exposed on his chest and Thomas quickly read it:

```
LEE, ALAN
RA12537160
CAPTAIN
PROTESTANT
```

In his mind Thomas added what he knew: Born December 20th 1919, Tuscaloosa, Alabama, Married, two children, Graduate, engineering degree, University of Alabama.

Prospects before, unlimited. Now, zero.

And dead, oh so dead.

Thomas froze. Small arms and machine gun fire picked up again and he heard feet pounding in the sand. He swiveled his head and saw other American soldiers running towards him. One soldier dove and landed behind the relative safety of the dune.

"Damn," the new soldier gasped, his breath coming in short bursts, "no wonder you stayed here, this is pretty good, just like a country club." Thomas breathed a sigh of relief. It was the BAR man, Donavan. Lots of fire power now.

"Damn, is that the Cap?"

"Yeah."

"Damn."

All at once, the world erupted in the ghastly sound of exploding metal. Both men tried to burrow into the sand as mortar shells landed all around them. Suddenly, Thomas heard an unearthly sound, one that the sisters of Sacred Heart High School would have said came from Demons in the bowels of the earth. It froze Thomas' heart. He lifted his head. *Good God, it was Donavan.*

Donavan lay on his back, screaming in pain. Thomas stared at him wide eyed. There was only a tangled, bloody mess where both of his legs had been.

Thomas started shaking and his first impulse was to run. "God, why did you put me in Hell?" he muttered. Gaining a little control, he reached out and touched Donavan on the shoulder. The wounded man reached back and grabbed Thomas' shirt with surprising strength.

"Don't leave me, Bannon." Donavan's face was red and contorted beyond recognition. He was writhing in pain.

Thomas was calmer now. "I won't leave you, Patty." Thomas looked behind him. "Medic, Medic," he yelled. No one came. "I'll get you back to a doctor, Patty." Still on his stomach, Thomas broke open the vial of morphine all the soldiers carried and stuck it in Donavan's arm through his sleeve.

Still on his belly, machine gun bullets flying just above his head, Thomas then grabbed Donavan's collar and began to turn him towards the shore. The resultant howl stopped him cold. Sweat poured down Donavan's face. His eyes were wild. He gritted his teeth and again reached over and grabbed Thomas' shirt.

"It's no use, Bannon. I'm no good for anything anymore. Shoot me, man, shoot me." Again Donavan howled with pain and misery. Thomas closed his eyes and scrunched up his face, trying to block the sound. The mortar shells started to come in again and the fearful sound made Thomas drop his head down and burrow in the sand again. In a few minutes the mortars slackened but the machine gun fire kept up its staccato song, raking the beach with death.

Donavan's pain was past endurance and between howls of anguish he pleaded with Thomas. "They shoot horses, don't they? Shoot me, Bannon, please, shoot me. Aaaaaiiiiiiieeeeeeee."

Hating himself, Thomas reached over for the gun on the hip of the dead captain. Suddenly he realized why the machine gunners had such accurate aim on their position. The dead captain's arm was oddly stuck above the small dune and the German gunners could take aim on it. He pushed the arm down and unbuttoned his holster.

Donavan's shrieking and howling was louder, Suddenly he stopped and babbled about his mother and sister. He drooled from the corner of his mouth and his eyes glazed over.

Thomas fingered the trigger. He pointed the muzzle at the boy's head and pushed off the safety. Even in all the noise and confusion the click of the safety sounded too loud. Thomas pointed the gun and tried to squeeze the trigger but he couldn't. His hand began to shake and sweat poured down his face. With his finger still on the trigger, he shakily put the weapon down in the sand.

Suddenly, Donavan let out a sound that only the Devil could have made. AAAEEEEIIIIIYAAA! Instinctively, Thomas joined the scream with one of his own and in one motion, lifted his arm, put the muzzle to Donavan's head and squeezed the trigger. Blood spattered over his gun hand but the screaming stopped. For the second time in a few minutes, Thomas put his head down and cried.

Thomas distanced himself as far as he could from the still twitching body but still stayed behind the dune. From a distance, he heard a voice yell an order. "Get to the high ground, we can't stay here."

He's right, Thomas thought, *but how do I get out of here. They would get me in a second.* Thomas took a chance and peered over the dune. Men were getting up and moving out. He would too. He put his rifle in his right hand and pushed up with his left. As soon as his helmet got above the dune it brought a new round of machine gun fire at his front. They had him zeroed in. Thomas dropped back on the sand again. The firing slowed and finally stopped.

I guess I'll have to wait until someone flanks them and wipes them out. Thomas then heard a strange sound. It was laughter, mocking him. *Where in the Hell was it coming from?* Then he realized it was coming from the Germans in front of him. They were laughing because they had him pinned down and they were playing with him.

Slowly color began to rise in his face as he felt the slow burn of anger. *Laughing? Laughing are they? Laughing at Thomas Bannon?* "No one laughs at me," he yelled out loud. With a quick glance at the two dead men, Thomas grabbed Donovan's BAR and shaking with anger jumped up and began to run at the German position bracketing them with fire. Quickly they started answering him back, but just as quickly he fell behind several large boulders at the shingle and their bullets just bounced off the rocks and on to the beach, throwing a shower of sand on him.

Now it was a cat and mouse game, but the Germans had the upper hand. They aimed the machine gun at the dune and waited, taunting him to try again.

Thomas was thinking quickly. He rolled on his back and pulled a grenade from his belt. He pulled the fuse and counted to ten and let it fly. The lead

German tried to catch it but it blew up in his hands severing them at the wrists. At the sound of the concussion, Thomas jumped up again and started firing from the hip running as fast as he could to the German position.

The grenade had done its work and two of the three man team lay dead behind their small redoubt. The third staggered up to a standing position, smoke blackening his face. He had his hands up high and was repeating over and over, "Kamerad, kamerad, nicht schiessen, nicht scheissen" (Friend, friend, don't shoot, don't shoot).

Thomas came up in front of the surrendering German, his bloodshot eyes full of hate. The German was just a boy, tall and blonde. His uniform was slightly too small for him and his arms and legs stuck out a little, like a farm boy come to town. Thomas would have found it funny any other time.

"Fuck Hitler, fuck Rommel," the boy said, spitting, "I surrender."

Then the boy smiled and that was too much for Thomas. With a picture of the captain and the mutilated head of Donavan in his mind, Thomas pointed the BAR at the German's middle. "You lying, dirty, German bastard," Thomas yelled and shaking with anger he pulled the trigger of the BAR. The German boy flew backward as if pulled by a marionette's strings, and fell in a bloody heap in the sand.

Thomas stared at the dead boy for a few seconds that seemed to him like minutes. He couldn't quite comprehend what had happened or what he had done but he knew his life was changed forever. He felt weak in the knees and had to sit down. He sat on the dune and stared back the way he had come and marveled that he was still alive. Suddenly, he had the realization that something was different but he didn't quite know what it was. Then it hit him. It was quiet. The war had moved inland and had left him behind.

Slowly Thomas got to his feet and he realized how exhausted he was. *Best to go back and get with a new outfit,* he thought, than to barge off and get captured. He picked up his rifle and shouldered the BAR and began to trudge back towards the littered shore. Halfway there, the clouds opened up and the rains came. Lightning and thunder lit up the sky followed by the rumbling of the dissatisfied gods in their heavens. The rain came down in sheets and Thomas had to lower his head and scrunch down his neck to prevent the rain from getting down his shirt. *I guess God wants to cleanse his earth of our foolishness,* he thought.

When Thomas went back to the dune, where the bodies were still silent in death, he stopped and got the captain's and Donavan's dog tags. He stared at the mute testimony of war for a moment, sighed and continued on his way.

It was a sickening trail. The brief rain stopped and the fog lifted to reveal a macabre sight. Bodies littered the ground as far as the eye could see. Thomas was sad to see that most of them were Americans.

As he approached the shore, Thomas saw a tent with a red cross on it. Doctors and nurses were scurrying around inside trying to save the wounded. He walked towards the front opening to try to find someone he could give the dog tags.

Thomas noticed a soldier seated in a camp stool near the front flap of the tent. As Thomas came up to him he noticed a very strange look on the man's face. Thomas greeted him with a nod, but the soldier just looked past him with a fixed, vacant stare. His eyes were black, hollow and empty. His skin was sallow and his jaw was slack. His mouth corners were turned down and saliva dribbled from both corners.

The boy's mind had just crumbled in battle. Too much shelling and too much killing. Thomas knew just how he felt. He shifted the BAR to the right shoulder and squeezed the man's arm with his left. The soldier looked up at him but nothing registered. No matter, Thomas was simply saluting another veteran. He understood.

Chapter 33: St. Mathews Island

Thomas looked at the deep green sea and saw the sun clear the horizon. He turned and started back towards the hotel fingering his neck where the general had hung the distinguished Service Cross after the battle. *I wonder,* Thomas thought, *if they would have given it to me if they knew I shot an unarmed man who was young, blonde and had ill-fitting clothing.* Slowly he walked along the water, his mind filled with thoughts made worse by the spectacular beauty around him.

****

As Thomas approached the hotel he realized how well his daughter had chosen. The island was a lovely stretch of sand and trees surrounded by a threatening sea.

The old hotel stood squat and solid, like a Moorish fort, its large windows, like vacant eyes, stared into an adventurous past. Its doors had opened to gentlemen and belles and pirates and seafaring men. The smell of salt was in its soul. The wide, old, oaken French doors were like its mouth, opening wide, devouring and disgorging people who had business or pleasure inside. From a distance the structure looked agreeable. It was only when one got close that one could see the damage that time had done. *Just as it has to me,* Thomas thought.

He stepped into the lobby and was greeted by a loud exchange inside. His mood deepened when he saw it was Theresa at the desk.

"But we have a reservation..." Theresa said, angrily. Thomas looked in back of her. As he expected, her companion was another woman. *This one's younger and prettier,* he thought, *I wonder what happened to Roz?*

"Don't you honor reservations?"

The desk clerk was young and handsome, a genetic mix of African and French so prevalent in the islands. He smiled and looked apologetic at the same time. Thomas noted his teeth were as white as snow.

"I understand your anger, Madame, however in the mix-up, the other Theresa Bannon got the room."

"But it's my room. Just ask her to leave. And anyway, who is the other Theresa Bannon?" For just a moment Theresa's curiosity overcame her anger.

"Impossible, Madame, we cannot do that. We will make other arrangements for you and your, uh, friend." The clerk picked up a registration card and looked at it. "The other Mrs. Bannon is an older woman and is from..." The clerk looked up from the card with a white smile, "...Pennsylvania."

Thomas stepped in, his voice quiet and reserved. "It's your aunt Theresa. Your mother's sister, from Pittsburg. Actually, we named you after her. She is pushing eighty and I don't think she would do well turned out in the street."

"Oh, Aunt Terry!" Theresa turned towards Thomas and her face flushed and hardened. "Hello, Father." She turned back to the desk. "I can't seem to get this man to understand that he should honor my reservation. Maybe you could speak his language." The clerk turned to Thomas, glad to have to deal with another man. This angry woman was vexing to him.

"Monsieur, I have told the madam, there has been a mix-up..."

"Yes, yes, I know. Why don't you put my daughter in my suite. There is plenty of room. Perhaps her friend could stay with one of the bridesmaids."

Theresa's face remained cold, but she somehow seemed relieved. She turned to look at her friend sitting on one of her suitcases. "Susan?" She asked, a question on her face.

Susan looked bored. She looked at her nails and spoke without looking at any of them, her nasal mountain twang grating to Thomas. "Sure, Theresa, I'd rather do that than have to go back and forth from another place."

Thomas turned to the clerk. "Why don't you bring all the bags up to the room and we can find another place for the young woman later."

"No need," Theresa said, "she will stay with me." She knew that would make Thomas uncomfortable and she struck home.

"Very well," Thomas said pleasantly, inwardly annoyed, "why don't you go on up and make yourselves comfortable. I will be up later."

The younger woman got up and walked towards the desk. "Oh, yes. Susan, this is my father, Thomas Bannon. Father, this is Susan." Thomas and Susan exchanged nods while Theresa signed the register. By then the bellhop had gathered the bags and was waiting patiently.

"After you ladies freshen up a bit, why don't you come back down to the restaurant and join me at breakfast?"

"No thank you, father," she said frostily, "you've done quite enough."

Thomas knew what she referred to happened a long time ago.

Thomas heard Susan's voice faintly as they walked to the elevator. "But I want to have breakfast with him." He could not hear Theresa's answer.

Thomas examined his inner feelings as he walked towards the restaurant. Every time he spoke to Theresa, he got the same feeling of anger and incompleteness. It was if there were something more that could be said or done, but the gulf between them wouldn't allow it. He sighed and vowed silently to try to bond with her again. At least they would be in close proximity until after the wedding. For a moment the bad feelings came back and almost overwhelmed him. Now he wasn't so sure if the close contact was so good after all.

After breakfasting by himself, Thomas started back to his suite. The women should be settled by now, he thought. With each step his stomach tightened and when he finally approached the door he was very tense.

The arguing behind the closed bedroom door was intense and loud. Thomas' first instinct was to leave, but for some reason he seemed rooted to the spot. He stood there, one hand on the doorknob and one foot inside the door.

"You bitch!"

"Me a bitch? You're the one who wants to control me. Don't tell me who I can talk to, or see. I'll do what I want, and when I want to!"

Theresa's voice went ballistic. "You're just a secretary and you'll do what I tell you." As soon as it was out of her mouth, Theresa regretted what she had said.

For a few moments, there was complete silence behind the bedroom door. Thomas felt embarrassed for the women and turned to leave. Before he could step out the door Susan stormed out of the bedroom and barged past him leaving a trail of perfume and anger.

Thomas stood half in and half out of the doorway as Theresa came out and stood in the door frame. She glowered at Thomas.

"Go ahead, gloat. You're right, just a couple of dykes venting at each other, that's all you see. Well, it isn't always like that." Tears came to Theresa's eyes and she slammed the door shut.

Thomas started to leave, but some instinct held him in the room. Slowly he opened the door and went to the bedroom. He knocked softly and stood there not quite knowing what to say.

"Go way."

Thomas knocked again and this time opened the door. His heart was pounding. Theresa was lying on the bed. She turned her head to look at him and his heart constricted when he saw the pain in her tear stained face. He remembered better times.

"Go way," she repeated and put her face back down on the bed. Thomas took a deep breath, raised his courage and walked to the edge of the bed and sat down. Slowly and carefully he put his hand, feather soft, on her shoulder. She did not tighten up and he was encouraged. Not wanting to press his luck, he just sat still and waited for Theresa to stop crying. After a few minutes she stopped, moved from under his touch to the edge of the bed and sat up. She glared at him for a moment and then went to the bathroom. Thomas heard the water start and stop and waited patiently for her to return. Theresa opened the door and stood there patting her face. Her eyes were red and accusing.

"Well, go ahead and say something," she said angrily, "everybody says it behind my back, say it to my face. Tell me what a disgrace I am. Lecture me about having a relationship with a man and having children of my own. Go ahead, tell me." Her voice was shrill.

Thomas tried to speak but he croaked. His throat was dry. He cleared his throat and began in a soft voice. "I don't know what to say. I can't say that I don't want those things for you, but you're an adult and you have to decide those things for your..."

Theresa exploded. "Decide? Decide? I can decide, I can decide on the spread sheet of an accountant's report. I can decide whether it's sound financially to purchase another magazine. I can even decide if an ad campaign is sound fiscally. But am I able to make a decision on a dress, or what to have at a dinner party? No! Am I able to want a husband? Children? A home? No! It's safer with another woman. I feel safe. Why? You!" she spat out angrily, "you fixed me with men forever!" She pointed a quivering finger at him. "It was you that told me how bad I was and that I smelled. I didn't smell, I never smelled. But, God help me, I still have to bathe three times a day, just to get the stink off, and there is no stink. It isn't even there." Theresa put her head in her hands. "God help me."

Thomas felt crushed. He sat on the bed, head down, every fiber of his being wanting to run and leave this painful place. Fighting his desire to go he forced himself to sit there and endure the pain. Finally, he lifted his head and spoke. "Theresa, when you were young I loved you with all my heart. As you got older you changed into a young woman..." Thomas lowered his head again. "I... I began to get terrible feelings when you sat on my lap... He looked up. ...like you loved to do..." He stopped as Theresa caught his eye with her stare.

"What... what kind of feelings." Theresa asked, curious but somehow dreading the answer.

"I... I can't answer that now. P-p-perhaps an-n-nother time...," he stuttered.

Theresa sensed an answer for her pain. "No, Father, now. Tell me now!"

Thomas got up and walked to the window and looked out over the beach to the water. How he wished he were on his boat on the water sailing away from this relentless girl probing his shame.

Theresa came up right behind him and said once again, "Now Father, now."

Thomas turned to his daughter. "When it first happened I went to the priest immediately." Thomas lowered his voice. "He was no help. In fact he threw me out of the church. I have not been back since."

Theresa brought her father back. What is 'IT', Father, what kind of feelings did you have? What happened?" Her voice was insistent, begging him to answer.

Thomas dropped his head. "When you sat in my lap I got..." Thomas dropped his voice so low Theresa had to bend forward to hear him. He looked up at her, courageously. ... I got ...aroused."

There was a stunned silence in the room. Slowly Theresa sat down by her father and joined him in staring at the sea. For thirty minutes, neither of them moved or spoke. Finally, Theresa spoke, her heart opening as the newly minted words came out.

"Thomas." When he heard her use his name so kindly, he almost cried. "I have read extensively on sexual behavior of men and women, particularly when I began to have so much trouble with men.

What you experienced with me is normal and quite common with men who have daughters. Most men recognize it, have a laugh or two, and deal with it, subtly.

Thomas looked at his daughter, his eyes wide with amazement. Instead of her blowing up, as he had expected, she was actually consoling him. He stared at Theresa intently. "You mean you can find it in your heart to forgive me?"

Suddenly, Theresa looked older and careworn. Inside her a great weight had been lifted and she was exhausted from the years of battle. It was over now and she just wanted to lick her wounds.

She looked down at her hands in her lap. "I don't know if I can forgive more than thirty years of pain in a few minutes." She looked in her father's eyes and saw the misery there. "But we certainly can begin here and now to be father and daughter."

Now there were tears in both their eyes.

Chapter 34: St. Tropéz

Sydney propped herself up on her elbows. She felt the warmth of the sun bathe her face. She smiled the smile of the secure and loved. She stretched and sat up looking for Paul. He was just coming out of the surf. The morning sun glinted off his wet, bronze body and she smiled again as she thought of last night and felt a rush. They had spent the first night of their honeymoon having a leisurely dinner and then they spent a good part of the night making sensuous, energetic love. She could still feel his hard body moving over hers and she shivered with the memory.

She looked at her left hand. The diamond sparkled in the bright sun. "Mrs. Paul Grant, she murmured." She savored the sound. She smiled a third time when she thought of Theresa. Both she and their father had both shown up at the wedding. Somehow, after so many years, they had made peace with each other. The fear Sydney had when she first saw them at the wedding faded into the real love she had for both of them.

Sydney bent over and reached for her drink and her breasts moved against the lunch tray. She smiled and silently counted them. One, two, just as

God intended. She thought of Dr. Kodaly and quietly blessed him. And Maria and Zoltan and Magda, too. She dwelled for a few moments on Tomiko and a rush of tears stained her cheeks. Brusquely, she wiped at them with the back of her hand. *Tomiko would not want me to cry for her,* she thought. *I know she is in the universe just exactly where she wants to be. I owe her so much. I just wish she could be here for just a few moments with me so I could thank her and tell her goodbye. I do hope she is with the people she loved so much.*

What was that Haiku she taught me... Oh, yes.

There is a blot on the sun
My body will accept no fault
The earth, water and wind will cleanse me
I am whole again

There was a blot on me and she and my friends refuse to accept it. Dr. Kodaly used the natural things around us to get me well, and now dear Tomiko, I am whole again.

"Sydney... hey, Sydney, come on, the surf is great."

Sydney got up and waved back. She started running. The joy in her heart gave her wings and she raced to Paul. Eagerly he embraced her and they kissed. Slowly they went to their knees in the sand and then, still in an embrace, to the watery floor.

They rolled over on the surf, first she on top, then he, all the while their lips still locked in the kiss.

The surf pounded the shore and covered them with a foam blanket. They were both whole again.

The end